Master Data
Management
in Practice

Master Data Management in Practice

Achieving True Customer MDM

DALTON CERVO
MARK ALLEN

WILEY

John Wiley & Sons, Inc.

Published by John Wiley & Sons, Inc., Hoboken, New Jersey.
Published simultaneously in Canada.

For general information on our other products and services or for technical support, please contact our Customer Care Department within the United States at (800) 762-2974, outside the United States at (317) 572-3993, or via fax at (317) 572-4002.

Wiley also publishes its books in a variety of electronic formats. Some content that appears in print may not be available in electronic books. For more information about Wiley products, visit our web site at www.wiley.com.

Library of Congress Cataloging-in-Publication Data:

Cervo, Dalton, 1967–
  Master data management in practice: achieving true customer MDM/Dalton Cervo, Mark Allen.
      p. cm. – (Wiley corporate f&a; 559)
    Includes index.
    ISBN 978-0-470-91055-9 (hardback); ISBN 978-1-118-08566-0 (ebk);
    ISBN 978-1-118-08567-7 (ebk); ISBN 978-1-118-08568-4
  1. Customer relations–Data processing.   2. Data warehousing.
  3. Data integration (Computer science)   I. Allen, Mark, 1953- II. Title.
    HF5415.5.C43 2011
    658.4'038–dc22   2011007523

Printed in the United States of America

10 9 8 7 6 5 4 3 2 1

In memory of my father,
who set many good examples in my life,
but none more important than
the constant search for knowledge.
—Dalton

To my wonderful family: my wife, Bobbie;
my daughter, Kim; and my son, Matt;
for all their love and support
throughout this project.
—Mark

Contents

Foreword

Everything should be made as simple as possible,
but not simpler.

—*Albert Einstein*

W HEN EVAN LEVY AND I wrote *Customer Data Integration: Reaching a Single Version of the Truth* (John Wiley & Sons, 2006), we were confident we'd chosen a topic of high business import, one with innumerable use cases and a clear value proposition. Our book was the first book published on the topic of CDI—now commonly known as customer master data management (MDM)—and it was a direct result of our having seen what had happened at companies that didn't have MDM.

Earlier in the decade, my second book, *The CRM Handbook* (Addison Wesley, 2000), was published just as customer relationship management was getting white-hot. Companies were investing tens of millions buying CRM systems, redesigning customer-facing business processes, and training customer-facing staff members in cross-selling conversations.

After all the vendor hype, millions in investment, and inordinate executive mindshare, it turned out that CRM systems were generating data that was no more useful than it was before CRM. CRM had been a downright failure—industry analysts were throwing around the 80 percent figure—at these early-adopter companies, most of which had naively believed the vendors and taken a *ready, shoot, aim!* approach to CRM delivery.

The ongoing phenomenon of duplicate or incomplete customer records continued to be the culprit behind compliance fines, fraught financial reporting, eroding sales revenues, and embarrassing marketing gaffes. Even with CRM in place, billing, support, inventory, order management, and other systems weren't sharing customer data, and when they were it was often the result of years spent building and maintaining custom code. "We're data rich, but information poor," became the refrain of millions of executives whose budgets were attached to multimillion dollar system failures and perpetual programming. Why wouldn't companies adopt MDM?

As the buzz about our CDI book reverberated in both IT and business circles, the most common question wasn't definitional. Executives on both sides of the fence "got" MDM. They'd been waiting for a way to tie customer data together across systems and business processes. They were sold. What they wanted to know again and again was:

"Where do we start?"

The question was deceptive in its simplicity. Many secretly wished we'd whip out a template or hand them a checklist. A few brazenly asked to see our methodologies. And some duly retained us to develop detailed roadmaps for MDM delivery. One thing we confirmed—and proved again and again—was that while MDM might solve similar business problems from one company to the next, no two MDM roadmaps were ever the same. There was no template for MDM delivery. Replicate another company's MDM plan at your peril.

After all, there are too many wildcards for there to be a single, standardized plan for MDM. These include:

- **The need for a business case.** Some managers have the organizational authority to explain a broad problem and its implications, and get the budget to go fix it. Some companies can't start anything new unless someone's calculated hard return on investment numbers. The way MDM is pitched in the organization can affect its delivery.

- **A company's incumbent skill sets.** Some companies launch MDM efforts having existing data stewards, policies for data usage, and an understanding of operational systems development issues. Others still struggle with how to manage and store data, hoping that MDM will automate data integration using staff who can only be dedicated part-time to the effort (and that it will be cheap).

- **The need for sponsorship.** The mandate of executive sponsorship means different things at different companies. Top-down MDM may mean C-level involvement. Bottom-up MDM might mean a visionary middle manager and a bright team of intrepid data stewards working late for a month or two to deliver meaningful data in the context of a real project, then showing off their good work.

- **Existing data management capabilities.** Some companies have data people. These people understand the data in the context in which it's used, and they and their colleagues have crafted deliberate strategies for managing that data. Other companies still see data as a by-product of their packaged applications. The behaviors across this continuum can inform where to begin.

■ **The weight of data governance.** As Evan and I said in our book (and many times since), data governance—the policy making and oversight of corporate information—is critical to sustainable MDM. A company's grasp of data governance and its role in MDM is directly proportional to its chances for MDM success.

Mark and Dalton have written about these topics and other topics from a bird's eye view. They turn out the core components of MDM—data governance, ROI analysis, implementation processes, data stewardship, and data quality being among them—in a way that's as easy for beginners to grasp as it is for experienced practitioners to execute. As seasoned MDM delivery experts themselves, they've seen the pitfalls from on high and warn you away from them even as they help navigate a better path for delivery.

MDM has come a long way since we wrote what we like to think of as the seminal book on the topic. People have stopped equating MDM with analytic databases or metadata or middleware. They understand that in many cases it's the missing link between their companies' technology infrastructures and relevant, timely interactions with customers. Yes, our CDI book was the first book on MDM, but not the last. And for Mark and Dalton's readers, that's fabulous news indeed!

Jill Dyché
February 2011

Preface

A STEADY MOVEMENT TOWARD Master Data Management (MDM) practices is underway. While managing data has always been a key component to a company's success, the emergence of MDM practices has provided a much more stable foundation for business intelligence (BI) and process improvement to build on. MDM also creates perhaps the most pervasive business and IT challenge that any data management initiative can present. MDM is a forcing function that, if implemented right, can uncover and enable correction of long-standing dirty laundry and systemic business problems related to a company's data and the associated processes.

In parallel, there are many excellent *what and why* focused books that are establishing the overall recognition, definition, and value proposition, which is driving companies to consider and position MDM initiatives in their business planning.

At the forefront of this movement, and typically the starting point for a company's MDM discipline, is the focus on the customer data domain, or what is commonly referred to as Customer MDM. Customer MDM is primarily aimed at achieving better cross-functional discipline, quality control, and standardization of a company's customer identity data in order to achieve an accurate and shared *source of truth* about an existing or prospective customer.

However, the dilemma with executing MDM is that it is an emerging discipline and there has been a general lack of any substantive and practical instruction for MDM planning and implementation as a business practice. In recognizing this gap, we have chosen to focus this book largely on the *how* and *where* aspects of planning, implementing, and supporting the business practice of Customer MDM from a program manager and data steward point of view. This book assumes you have already considered the overall merits for a Customer MDM initiative and are now looking for more tangible planning and implementation guidance. Or perhaps you haven't quite made that investment decision and are looking a bit deeper into the experiential and practical considerations of implementing MDM as part of your decision process. For either case, we believe this book will prove to be extremely valuable due to our "how and where" focus.

The key objectives of this book are:

- Convey practical guidance, foundation, and planning approaches geared toward the implementation of Customer MDM.
- Show readers how the comprehensive insights and techniques learned from the challenges, questions, advice, and instruction presented in this book apply to their internal scenarios.
- Provide context and content generic enough to apply to various architectures and customer master deployment strategies that commonly exist.
- Beyond just covering the fundamentals for planning and implementing Customer MDM, cover advanced practices key to achieving the extended value proposition from a Customer MDM initiative.

We have drawn this book's context largely from our own business and IT experiences and personal perspectives reflecting many years of work in the data management trenches. The insight and guidance we share reflects a wide spectrum of experience ranging from highly disparate system infrastructures where simply trying to get any edge with improving data quality and standardization was considered a victory, to the highly integrated infrastructure and challenges associated with data migration, process integration, and ongoing management of an enterprise-wide customer master and data hub model.

The target audiences for this book are the directors, managers, consultants, analysts, data stewards, and enterprise data and solution architects who are looking for practical guidance, options, and potential gotchas related to the planning, implementation, and maintenance practices associated with Customer MDM.

We have segmented this book into four parts that provide a logical order for this audience.

 ## PART I: PLANNING YOUR CUSTOMER MDM INITIATIVE

This segment addresses the aspects of defining the underlying scope, approach, architecture, and objectives necessary for planning a Customer MDM initiative. We review the various types of MDM initiatives and how each has a somewhat different objective and carries distinct levels of complexity, risk, and impact.

Implementing a successful Customer MDM initiative starts with choosing the right approach that will drive the proper fitting of the MDM practices to an enterprise architecture and business model. This section closely examines the planning and decisions needed regarding the MDM objectives in general, the concept and dynamic of data ownership, why cultural change may be needed for your MDM initiative to succeed, and what type of products, tools, and vendor services need to be considered for priming your MDM engine.

 ## PART II: THE IMPLEMENTATION FUNDAMENTALS

This segment provides practical insight, guidance, options, and examples related to the implementation of what we consider the four foundational disciplines of Customer MDM: (1) Data Governance, (2) Data Stewardship, (3) Data Quality Management, and (4) Data Access Management. These disciplines need to be clearly understood, put into context regarding a company's Customer MDM focus, and properly implemented in order for the MDM initiative to be successful. This section starts with the focus on data governance then progresses through the other three disciplines in a logical manner. Failed or only partially implemented MDM projects typically boil down to systemic issues and strategic flaws in the implementation of one or more of these disciplines. This section provides insight and direction needed to successfully implement the fundamentals of these disciplines.

 ## PART III: ACHIEVING A STEADY STATE

Customer MDM is a set of ongoing processes and disciplines, not just the implementation of a plan and its key parts. Like other business or domestic practices in our lives, what we plan, gather, and build does not typically or automatically clean and maintain itself. That requires ongoing practices and discipline. Data and data management is no different. In this section, we focus on these practices, the fine-tuning, and the competencies that will not only drive a steady state of MDM but also will drive recognition that a well-implemented MDM model can stand on its own merits as a highly valued business practice. Part III focuses on the concepts and practices of data maintenance and monitoring to ensure quality and control are managed well. We will show how the achievement of successful maintenance and monitoring practices will lead to many self-governing and self-maintaining closed loop practices. In addition, we cover the characteristics and concepts associated with a mature MDM model such as transitioning your data management participants to become well-engaged MDM practitioners and how to communicate the success and benefits that have emerged from implementing solid MDM practices.

 ## PART IV: ADVANCED PRACTICES

At the forefront of every MDM initiative are the expectations of achieving the end state objectives and advanced data management practices that are critical to the future success of the company. In the Customer MDM area, one of the primary objectives, and often considered the Holy Grail, is to enable the *customer 360° view*. Enabling this requires many additional data elements and data management practices to come together that are not often well understood or fully considered in the MDM plan. Not achieving a clear 360° view of the customer can be viewed as a major failure of the Customer MDM initiative; therefore, in Part IV we take a deep dive into this subject and then close out this segment and the overall context of the book by discussing future concepts and implications associated with Customer MDM. This includes how Customer MDM can be a leading practice for the design and implementation of an overarching Enterprise Data Governance framework, and how Customer MDM can survive, and even assist with, organizational changes that invariably will occur within a company.

Acknowledgments

WANT TO THANK my wonderful wife, Milene, and our extraordinary children Ettore and Gian Lucca for their love and support. Thanks to my caring mother, Aracy, and my two older brothers, Dan and Dartagnan, who were always excellent role models to me.

A very special thanks to my co-author, Mark Allen, for his outstanding contribution, dedication, and friendship. But it is not only about our partnership in this book. In our professional career together, Mark's vision, leadership, and mentoring provided me with opportunities to expand my knowledge and experiences. On many levels, this book would not have been possible without him.

A huge thanks to Phil Simon, friend, co-author, and fellow Rush fan, who gave me an opportunity to contribute to his second book, which eventually led to this one.

Thanks to Jill Dyché, a friend and colleague, and one of the smartest people I've ever met. It is truly an honor that Jill wrote the foreword to our book. Another big thanks to recognized experts I admire immensely, and kindly have agreed to endorse our book: David Loshin, Phil Simon, Jim Harris, Dylan Jones, Peter Jaumann, Ron Powell, and Tony Fisher.

Thanks to past colleagues at Sun Microsystems and Raytheon: Duer Reeves, Rene Grippo, Russ Albert, Brent Zionic, Milt McPeek, Steve Karakitsios, Phil Priest, and Mike Ruggles.

Thanks to fellow colleagues at DataFlux, who are too many to list, but especially Katie Fabiszak for her insightful review of parts of the book, and Scott Gidley, Daniel Teachey, Gail Baker, and Tony Fisher for their constant support. Another thanks goes to the social media community, where I have met incredibly smart people, such as: Henrik Liliendahl Sørensen, Dan Power, Ken O'Connor, Rich Murnane, Charles Blyth, Arkady Maydanchik, and so many others.

Thanks to my hockey and motorcycle buddy, Ralph Hartwig, a proud friend who would tell everybody we met that I was writing a book.

Last, but not least, thanks to Tim Burgard, Stacey Rivera, Laura Cherkas, and Kimberly Marini at John Wiley & Sons for all their assistance throughout the development and production of this book.

—Dalton Cervo

First, I want to thank my co-author Dalton Cervo for not only his tremendous contribution and dedication to this book, but also for his friendship and collaborative nature that greatly contributed to a very smooth, complimentary experience we enjoyed throughout writing this book. Throughout our professional experiences together, it has always been a great pleasure working with Dalton. I look forward to more opportunity to collaborate with Dalton in the future.

I am very grateful to Duer Reeves, Michele Parry, Pete Pazmany, Meg Heller, and Bernie Knost. This book would not have been possible for me if over the years they had not given me the job opportunities, leadership roles, mentoring, and support throughout many programs and projects that have contributed to the knowledge and experiences that I have been fortunate to be able to share in this book.

A special thanks to my past staff members and colleagues at Sun Microsystems and Oracle who I enjoyed many journeys with and who were instrumental in the concepts, plans, and solutions in which I have been involved. I would like to particularly recognize Sandra Keifer-Roberts, Jeannie Cole, Barb Wilson, Christa Isenhart, Leah Jenkins, Paul Welding, Jayme Otto, Peter Jaumann, Jason Bristow, Andy Grodahl, and Brent Zionic. I would also like to express my appreciation to the many talented and supportive folks at DataFlux, D&B, and Deloitte with whom I had the pleasure of sharing ideas and working.

Thanks to Phil Simon for his guidance and support that helped us get this book in motion.

Thanks to Jill Dyché for all her generous time, encouragement, and support. We are very honored to have Jill as the foreword author.

Thanks to David Loshin, Phil Simon, Jim Harris, Dylan Jones, Peter Jaumann, Ron Powell, and Tony Fisher whose endorsements we are very proud to have received. Thanks to Aaron Zornes for his review and feedback. And thanks in general to the many friends and acquaintances in the MDM and Data Governance communities who have expressed their encouragement and interest about this book.

I am deeply grateful to my lovely wife, Bobbie, and our wonderful children, Kim and Matt, for all their patience and encouragement.

Last, but not least, I'd like to express my thanks to Tim Burgard, Stacey Rivera, Laura Cherkas, and Kimberly Marini at John Wiley & Sons for all their guidance and support throughout the development and production of this book.

—Mark Allen

Introduction

TODAY'S BUSINESS ENVIRONMENT REQUIRES companies to find a way to differentiate themselves from their competition and thrive amid increased pressure to succeed. While a company's data is obviously extremely important to drive and gauge success, the data is often poorly organized and underutilized due to quality and consistency issues. This can be particularly true with master data.

Master data provides a foundation and a connecting function for business intelligence (BI) by the way in which it interacts and connects with transactional data from multiple business areas such as sales, service, order management, purchasing, manufacturing, billing, accounts receivable, and accounts payable (AP). Master data consists of information critical to a company's operations and BI, and is usually categorized into master data entity areas (also often referred to as *data domains*) such as customers, products, suppliers, partners, employees, materials, and so on. While often nontransactional in nature, master data is utilized in most transactional processes and operations, and serves BI by providing data for analytics and reporting. Although defined as master data, this data often exists in duplicate, fragmented, and inconsistent forms in disparate systems across the organization and typically lacks a common data management approach.

Master Data Management (MDM) practices have arisen primarily to address these data quality and fragmentation issues. For years, there has been a huge proliferation of data due to cheap storage and increased digitization. Furthermore, compartmentalized solutions have added to the fragmentation of information considerably, magnifying data duplication and lack of a common entity identification. Organizations came to the realization that the most effective way to address this growing problem is by creating a single source approach for management of master data based on high standards of quality and governance serving the entire business.

Unfortunately, this is easier said than done. At the root of these data quality issues is the well-acknowledged *garbage in, garbage out* (GIGO) problem from which most legacy environments still suffer. This persistent problem creates the underlying enterprise data management challenge that MDM is focused on addressing. Historically, data management focuses centered in Data Warehouse, Customer Relationship Management (CRM), and Customer Data Integration (CDI) practices have not actually tried to broadly solve the GIGO problem. Instead, those practices have focused primarily on the reconciliation, organization, and improvement of the data after the point of entry or just within specific process areas. Thus, the GIGO factor persists and continues to pollute the transactional data, the master data, and BI.

Although there is certainly good rationale and benefit to a back-end reconciliation and scrubbing approach, there is also a consequence whereby these practices themselves can create yet more process or context-specific fragmentation moving enterprise data further from a system of record and source of truth. CDI practices are geared more toward a source of truth outcome but CDI is still often implemented just with specific data environments. In spite of the limitations or data specific application, these types of data management practices have set the stage for what is now being recognized with MDM as a more holistic set of techniques and approaches that can span business practices and aim at developing enterprise-wide data quality management and governance practices.

It is fair to point out that MDM practices are not likely, nor should they be expected, to fully eliminate the GIGO problem. Instead, through focus on improving the control and consistency of the master data shared by both the operational and business intelligence processes, and through data governance-driven policies and standards aimed at improving the data management practices associated with a data entity area, the degree and impact of the GIGO problems can be greatly minimized. This focus around gaining control and management of the shared data is a key concept also described in various data governance maturity models that illustrate how data management practices have been evolving from undisciplined or independently oriented application practices toward MDM disciplines focused on enterprise-wide data integration and governance models supported by ubiquitous oriented technologies and best practices.

Many excellent books have been published that address the *what* and *why* aspects of MDM, and dive into key topic areas that distinguish MDM in the data management space. These publications have established the overall recognition, definition, and the value proposition that is driving companies to consider and position MDM initiatives in their business and IT strategies. There are a number of books we highly recommend. Please refer to the Recommended Reading section of this book for specific recommendations.

When navigating through a topic such as MDM, it is not unexpected to find variation in the specific context and definition. We feel that the following Gartner definition and context best articulates MDM:

> Master data management is a technology-enabled business discipline that helps organizations achieve a "single version of the truth" in such important areas as customers, products and accounts.
>
> In MDM, the business and the IT organization work together to ensure the uniformity, accuracy, semantic persistence, stewardship and accountability of the enterprise's official, shared master data. Organizations apply MDM to eliminate endless, time-consuming debates about "whose data is right," which can lead to poor decision making and business performance.[1]

Although the MDM movement is well underway, how to develop the business discipline and how business and IT work together to enable this is still very much a topic for debate and often a work in progress dynamic as an MDM initiative takes shape. A closer look across the MDM market reveals a lack of much practical instruction for MDM planning and implementation from a business practice perspective. How the business needs to be engaged to create the business discipline has not been well articulated.

The lack of this type of instruction is actually not a new or unique problem in the data management arena. Consider that just as data management has traditionally been centered in more application and IT-oriented practices, the planning and instructional aspects of data management have also been tailored to specific application or vendor product scenarios and usually stem from vendor literature, consultant material and white papers, or simply from self-discovery. Unfortunately, though, growth and execution of MDM as a business practice will continue to be subject to a slow and unpaved road if the business planning and implementation teams continue to be faced with too much self-discovery where the vendor or consultant material comes up short.

When the practitioners of MDM come together at conferences or in community forums, there is quick recognition that many of their MDM needs and initiatives are centered around the execution of fundamentally common practices and techniques with the variation only in the implementation approach and the adaptation of these practices and techniques to the specific environments, infrastructure, and business models within their company. Most practitioners will also indicate that had they garnered a better fundamental understanding of MDM practices along with more "under the hood" insight to guide their approach and techniques, their implementation and adaptation efforts could have been better focused and handled more effectively.

The main challenge with bridging this instructional gap is simply in determining a good starting point. Although MDM discipline can be applied to various data domains, any of which can present significant data management problems in a company, a common starting point where an MDM initiative is usually most critically needed, and will initially be considered, is with the customer data domain commonly referred to as Customer MDM.

Customer MDM is where we have cultivated our MDM experiences, perspectives, and solutions that we present in this book. Our backgrounds span many years of both business and IT experience primarily with Sun Microsystems and later with Oracle, and also reflect the data integration experience we have had in relation to companies Sun had acquired and from the acquisition of Sun itself by Oracle. As with all large multinational companies, there are huge data management challenges that emerge over the years as companies grow, constrict, acquire other companies, face new competitive challenges, transition from old system infrastructure to new platforms, and are subject to increasing requirements regarding security, information privacy, government regulations, and compliance.

Because any of these conditions can be very disruptive, companies that maintain a flexible and fluid dynamic between the business and IT roles will be most able to adapt quickly to address these challenges. The flexibility and adaptability needed here has to be an existing dynamic within specific roles and responsibilities, and doesn't just happen with initiating a new project or a consulting engagement. This dynamic needs to be demonstrated by dedicated managers, data stewards, and data analysts working closely together across business and IT lines under data governance authority to address these data management challenges while also minimizing disruption to the normal operational practices.

It has been our experience that an MDM initiative requires this type of a hybrid dynamic in order to be a successful ongoing practice. Customer MDM, in particular, will struggle to gain a successful foothold where traditional business and IT dynamics create a very rigid engagement model, has a mostly reactive break-fix approach, and generally is only focused on back-end oriented data management practices.

That said, we also recognize that this traditional business and IT dynamic has a clear purpose and serves a vital role in a company. For many reasons, there absolutely needs to be a strong charter for IT with clear distinctions and jurisdictions from the business organizations. However, we tend to repeatedly overstuff that model to a point that neither the business nor IT can effectively address many important initiatives that are pervasive and very time sensitive. Customer MDM is that type of initiative and, to really thrive as a discipline, it needs to be shifted away from a traditional business and IT dynamic.

As Customer MDM focus progresses, we see two implementation scenarios that reflect how this is actually playing out. One scenario is where the Customer MDM initiative has been launched and is subject to that traditional IT and business dynamic. In this scenario, the initiative often becomes bogged down by the constraints inherent to that dynamic. This causes delivery or execution issues to build up and results in significant delays or required course corrections. A Customer MDM initiative often does not thrive well in this scenario.

The second scenario is where early in the planning process, it is recognized that a Customer MDM initiative will require a more unique and flexible foundation and governing dynamic to be created. This recognition leads to the development of a more cross-functional and collaborative model with a management approach that better enables the ability to govern, maintain, and improve the customer master data without continual conflict and tradeoff with other business and IT priorities.

Obviously, this second scenario is considered the ideal approach, but requires more insight and availability of practical guidance in the planning stages. While outside consultants can certainly provide some of this guidance, a successful MDM initiative will ride on how well the business and IT owners can embrace the MDM discipline and resourcefully enable this across their lines of business. Note that we have broken out the topic of *ownership* into its own chapter before we take a deep dive into the topic of data governance. Although it is the data governance council who ultimately is the overseeing body of the stakeholders that are expected to be responsible for the management and integrity of the master data, because the dynamic of data ownership in a Customer MDM practice is sufficiently complex due to its cross-functional nature, we felt that this topic was important enough to address first. Ownership and governance need to be a carefully orchestrated dynamic in a successful MDM practice, but first it is critical to understand how the concept and delegation of data ownership should be approached to effectively set the stage for governance and the ongoing support of Customer MDM. This approach, coupled with the ability to define the right implementation plan, engagement model, roles and responsibilities, and enabling tools and techniques, is what will drive and sustain a successful Customer MDM practice.

With this in mind, we think that the four parts of this book covering the aspects of Planning, Implementation, Achieving a Steady State, and Advanced Practices will provide the logical order and insight needed for laying the foundation and establishing the ongoing management practices and success factors for Customer MDM.

We believe there is much efficiency and immediate traction to be gained in this MDM market if more ground-level orientation and generic guidance is provided. As this MDM market continues to emerge, so does the opportunity to deliver more guidance and instruction based on common approaches and techniques inherent to the MDM philosophy and disciplines. In other words, the ubiquitous nature of MDM is enabling us to provide this type of data management guidance and instruction in a more generic light.

 NOTE

1. Gartner, Inc., "Hype Cycle for Master Data Management, 2010," Andrew White and John Radcliff, November 2010, ID Number: G00206123.

PART ONE

Planning Your Customer MDM Initiative

CHAPTER ONE

Defining Your MDM Scope and Approach*

Success is not final, failure is not fatal: It is the courage to continue that counts.

—Winston Churchill

MDM APPROACHES AND ARCHITECTURES

Master Data Management (MDM) is about bringing master data together to facilitate the employment of master data management services—such as data governance and stewardship; data quality, metadata, hierarchy, and overall data lifecycle management—and ultimately, to serve as the single source of truth for the business. Customer MDM focuses on the *customer* data domain in particular and its associated properties, such as company name, tax ID, addresses, contacts, accounts, and company hierarchy.

In addition to data domains, such as customers, products, partners, and suppliers, data inside a company can also be classified as operational or

---

* Portions of this chapter are based on Dalton Cervo's contribution (Chapter 12: Master Data Management) to Phil Simon's book, *The Next Wave of Technologies: Opportunity in Chaos*, Hoboken: John Wiley and Sons, Inc., 2010.

nonoperational. Operational data is the real-time collection of data in support of a company's needs in their daily activities. Nonoperational data is normally captured in a data warehouse on a less frequent basis and used for business intelligence (BI). This particular classification of data is relevant in this context because it can be used to distinguish most common MDM initiatives.

Although the very essence of implementing MDM is in the appliance and fine tuning of MDM practices to fit the enterprise architecture and business model, MDM implementations as a whole can generally be categorized into three major types of initiatives based on its primary focus being operational or nonoperational data:

1. Analytical MDM: address BI
2. Operational MDM: address business operations
3. Enterprise MDM: address both BI and operations

Each has a somewhat different objective and carries distinct levels of complexity, risk, and impact. Companies should perform detailed analysis to decide which approach is required. At a minimum, an MDM program must take into consideration business and IT requirements, time frame, resource availability, priority, and the size of the problem to be addressed.

Deciding which approach to implement is dependent on the business case, which is explained in more detail later in this chapter. Because each of the previous approaches targets a different category of information, they ultimately impact a company at varying degrees. Figure 1.1 depicts the level of intrusiveness of each MDM approach.

Operational data is inherently more critical to a company than nonoperational data due to its usability and timeliness. Therefore, analytical MDM is the least intrusive approach, followed by operational MDM and obviously the all-encompassing enterprise MDM, which is a combination of both analytical and operational MDM.

Naturally, more intrusive MDM projects involve both higher risks and higher likelihoods of disrupting companies' daily operations. It is important to notice that the figure does not suggest a sequence or phases to be adopted when implementing an MDM solution. As a matter of fact, phased deployments need to be observed from two different perspectives. One is concerned with progressing from one approach into another, such as starting with an operational MDM, then an analytical one to complete the enterprise solution. Another way to look at phased deployments is within a particular approach. It is not uncommon to start an operational MDM integrating just a few legacy systems,

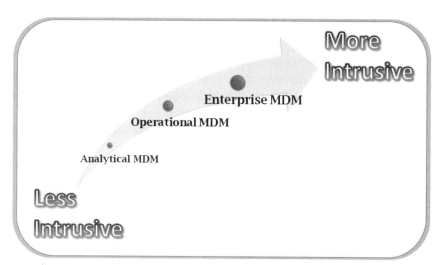

FIGURE 1.1 MDM Approaches

and slowly incorporate others. More about phased deployments will be discussed in Chapter 3.

Next, each of the approaches is explored further with the most common architectures employed for each of them. Keep in mind these are generic frameworks. MDM can be so encompassing and pervasive that the number of potential combinations can be many. Hybrid solutions are also very common. Finally, many subjects in the MDM arena don't have a universal terminology. What is called approaches and architectures in this book may be called styles, framework, or implementation in other books along with other varying definitions. What is important is to understand how the master data is integrated, used, maintained, improved, and governed.

Analytical MDM

Historically, analytical MDM has been the most commonly adopted MDM approach. This stems mostly from the relative simplicity of leveraging data warehouse projects. It is beyond the scope of this book to describe data warehouses in detail, but the following summary of the three primary data warehouse architectures might help you understand how MDM projects can benefit from this already existing integration:

1. **Top-down.** Major proponent is Bill Inmon. Primarily characterized by a data warehouse as a centralized and normalized repository for the entire

enterprise, with dimensional data marts containing data needed for specific business processes. Up-front costs are normally higher and it takes longer initially until common structure is designed, built, and sources are integrated, but it is more adaptable afterward.

2. **Bottom-up.** Major proponent is Ralph Kimball. Data marts are first created to provide reporting and analytical capabilities for specific business processes, and can eventually be integrated to create a comprehensive data warehouse. Provides results quickly to each independent business unit, but overall data integration is potentially harder to achieve.

3. **Hybrid.** A combination of top-down and bottom-up approaches, characterized by a high-level normalized enterprise model, more quickly integrated with business specific data marts for faster results.

One may ask: If there is already a data warehouse integrating the data from across the enterprise, isn't that MDM? The answer is: not necessarily. It actually depends what is being done with that data. Bringing the data together is just one piece of MDM. The other piece is applying MDM practices, such as identity resolution; data cleansing, standardization, clustering, consolidation, enrichment, categorization, synchronization, and lineage; metadata management; governance; and data stewardship.

Bottom line is a data warehouse, and data mart infrastructure can work as the conduit to a much larger and encompassing MDM program. Conversely, the business intelligence, analytics, reports, and other outputs relying on the data warehouse and data marts will greatly benefit from the additional practices imposed by MDM—above all, data quality and hierarchy management improvements. Keep in mind that in this context, a strategic or a tactical BI implementation is implied instead of an operational BI since the underlying data is nonoperational.

Figure 1.2 depicts a common architecture adopted by companies implementing an analytical MDM approach.

Figure 1.2 shows that an extract, transform, load (ETL) process gathers data from disparate operational systems. Ultimately, the data is stored on an enterprise data warehouse (EDW). EDW and associated data marts become the source of master data for BI and analytics. Since EDW is now a single source from an analytical perspective, it is also the centerpiece for what can be called MDM services.

Analytical MDM is the quick-hit approach. While companies can quickly make a tremendous impact with respect to reporting and BI, with the analytical MDM approach relatively minimal inputs yield corresponding outputs.

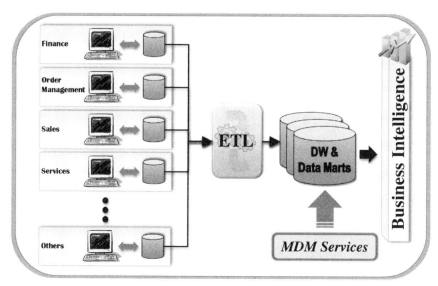

FIGURE 1.2 Analytical MDM

Specifically, companies fail to harvest the benefits of the MDM services back to their operational data. Remember, the data improvements are happening in the data warehouse, which is downstream from the operational systems. What's more, the analytical MDM approach does not enforce any regulatory or audit requirements since those are mandatory at the operational level.

Another drawback with this implementation is the possibility of adding one more fragmented and incomplete data system to the company. Obviously, the quality of the results will be directly related to the quality of the MDM services applied to the data. But a less obvious conclusion is the quality of the results is also directly related to the amount of data sources integrated. Certain lines of business (LOBs) are very sensitive about feeding data warehouses with their operational and strategic information, making it hard to achieve comprehensive integration.

On the other hand, it is possible for companies implementing an analytical MDM to influence the operational world. Analytical teams have access to an integrated view of the data and its underlying quality. They can recognize bad data and potential root-cause offending practices relatively quickly, as well as correlate discrepancies across LOBs. This is powerful knowledge that can be used by a strong data governance team to influence and improve data quality and business practices at the source. Be aware, however, that operational LOBs tend to be very resistant to this approach and to succeed with this practice, strong sponsorship from high-level executives is necessary.

Operational MDM

Operational MDM targets operational systems and data. It provides the opportunity to consolidate many, and ideally all, disparate operational data systems across the company, and become a true system of reference. This is obviously an enormous task. From a data integration perspective, the difficulty increases with the volume of data to be integrated along with the level of disparity among the systems to be combined. But it is much more than simply data integration. It is about business process integration and massive technological infrastructure change, which can impact virtually everyone in the company.

Depending on the size of the company, an operational MDM will likely be deployed in phases. Breaking down what is included in each phase can vary widely as well. One method for phased deployment is gradually migrating each data system into a single MDM repository until all systems in scope have reached end-of-life (EOL).

Another method for breaking down phases is gradually migrating portions of data from a single system. Sometimes this is necessary because it is not possible to promptly EOL a particular legacy system if not all its business processes have been transitioned to the new application yet. It may sound strange that there is a need to start transferring the data if the system is still operating. But that is sometimes necessary to support other already migrated systems that have dependencies on that particular legacy data.

Finally, a combination of both phased methods are not uncommon either, with systems and portions of data making their way to the single MDM source at contrasting techniques. The data integration component of MDM is obviously complex, and companies need to be very creative in finding the best method for consolidating legacy data.

The bottom line is that it can be very difficult to EOL a given operational system because it is not only a technical issue; it is a business issue, as well. Changing business practices that have been in place for years and years can be overwhelming. Besides, it could impact customer relations, and that is the last thing anyone would like to happen. Therefore, to avoid disruption of current business practices, a common practice is to implement a temporary interface between the legacy and the new system until the transition is finally complete.

Chapter 3 will get into more detail regarding phased deployments, data migration, business process reengineering, build versus buy MDM, and so on.

Nonetheless, once an operational MDM is implemented, companies can leverage it into the analytical world for a complete enterprise MDM solution with relative ease. Operational MDM can be accomplished via three different architectures:

1. Single central repository architecture
2. Central hub and spoke architecture
3. Virtual integration

Note that a service-oriented architecture (SOA) with an enterprise service bus (ESB) and business process orchestration is not required to make the MDM repository or the federation system available, but it is the most common and effective architecture.

Single Central Repository Architecture (SCRA)

In this architecture, a single central repository within the operational environment serves as the source of data to an integrated suite of applications and processes. Only one physical copy of master data exists.

It is important to emphasize that this approach may obviate the need for certain applications. In other words, after the consolidation of data, a company may not need all of its previous applications. Required applications dependent on that data might need to be rewritten, or will likely require some interface or other major changes to maintain integration.

SCRA guarantees consistency of master data. However, it can be very expensive—if not impossible—to implement due to potentially inflexible off-the-shelf applications in use (although, if reached, this could actually be the easiest and cheapest to maintain). SCRA could potentially require a massive data conversion effort, depending on the size of the company and the number of disparate systems.

In Figure 1.3, multiple legacy systems go through a data conversion step to bring data into a central hub. This conversion normally takes place in phases to minimize impact and lower risk of concurrently converting multiple legacy systems. When the central hub is operational, it is then used by application systems that would either replace legacy systems or add new functionality to the company. In this particular case, new application systems do not have their own versions of master data.

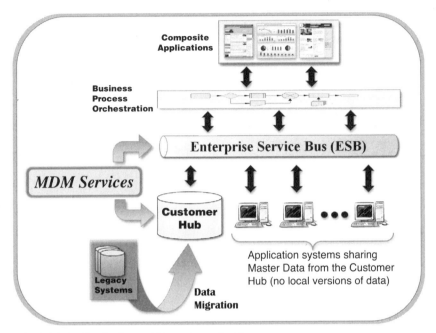

FIGURE 1.3 Single Central Repository Architecture

Central Hub and Spoke Architecture (CHSA)

This is a more common variation of SCRA. Like SCRA, CHSA has an independently deployed common repository. However, CHSA does not require that all applications and processes are fully coupled to the hub.

The major advantage of this architecture is the efficiency of a central hub hosting the master data, combined with the flexibility to support spoke systems operating relatively decoupled. This flexibility is important when integrating commercial, off-the-shelf (COTS) applications with an MDM solution.

Some of the applications can act as spoke systems with independent data models, but cross-referenced and synchronized to the central data. To be sure, CHSA alleviates some of the problems presented by SCRA, but CHSA can still require a massive data conversion effort and new interfaces between the hub and its spokes.

In Figure 1.4, multiple legacy systems go through a data conversion step to bring data into a central hub. Again, this conversion normally takes place in phases to minimize impact and lower risk of concurrently converting multiple legacy systems. When the central hub is operational, application systems then

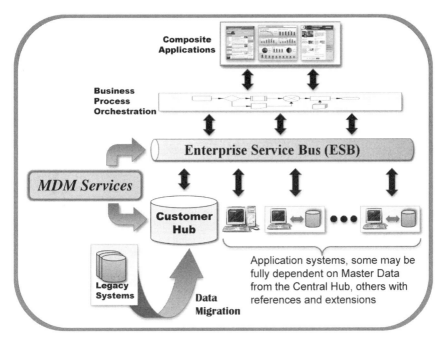

FIGURE 1.4 Central Hub and Spoke Architecture (CHSA)

access it to either replace legacy systems or add new functionality to the company. Spoke systems are synchronized and integrated with the central hub.

Virtual Integration (VI)

Virtual integration is a generic term to represent solutions that don't physically copy existing data into a new repository. This is a fundamental difference compared to the previous two methods. Registry and data federation (DF) are common VI architectures. A VI system aggregates data from multiple sources into a single view by maintaining a metadata definition of all sources. Data across multiple sources is collected in real time through some pre-established keys connecting the VI system and its sources. MDM services are applied to the dynamically collected data, becoming a new source of trusted data to downstream process applications. DF systems normally provide a more robust infrastructure than a simple registry implementation.

The biggest drawback with this implementation is the lack of data improvement propagation back to the source. VI provides benefits to consumers of its services, but not to the original sources of the data. Conversely, due to

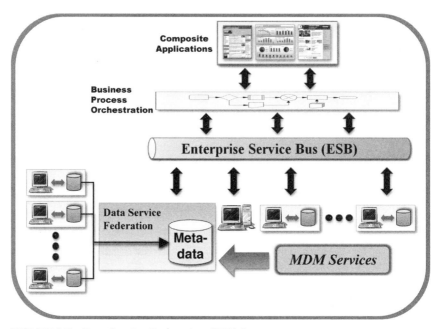

FIGURE 1.5 Data Service Federation (DSF) System

its nondisruptive nature, it is relatively simple to deploy. It could be a good first step before embarking into a central hub implementation.

In Figure 1.5, a data service federation (DSF) system collects real-time data from multiple existing sources. The data is not physically copied into the federated system. Information about the data in each source is stored on a metadata repository. It is further used to determine which system and data element to access based on requests performed to the DSF.

Enterprise MDM

Enterprise MDM is a combination of both operational and analytical MDMs. As such, it can be implemented by combining the architectures previously discussed.

A data warehouse solution could be added to any of the three operational MDM architectures. As an added bonus, most of the MDM services that would be needed in the warehouse are already functional in the operational system, making the maintenance of your data warehouse much easier. Furthermore, the ETL function of the analytical MDM should be much simpler since companies now maintain fewer systems from which to extract data. What's more, the data should be cleaner, standardized, and already consolidated.

Data federation offers another potential solution. DF could be expanded to provide a view into multiple departmental data warehouses in addition to operational systems. Through this method, DF becomes the single point to resolve complex BI queries. This solution reduces both companies' costs and complexity by lowering the need for an extra and expensive database server. However, there's no free lunch here.

DF technology takes a toll on performance of the operational and transactional data sources that it queries. It requires that transactional data sources are always on. This is in stark contrast to batch load data at preset and convenient times as normally done by data warehouse implementations—for example, at 4 A.M., while few users are accessing the system. BI queries can be quite complex and aggregate a multitude of data. Data warehouses are normally optimized to support those queries, making a DF implementation for this purpose potentially unfeasible. If companies go this route, then they should proceed with caution and perform extensive load testing to confirm viability.

Figure 1.6 shows one possible enterprise MDM architecture implementation.

In conclusion, the number of combinations of MDM approaches and architectures is large. The previous figures and categories are meant to be

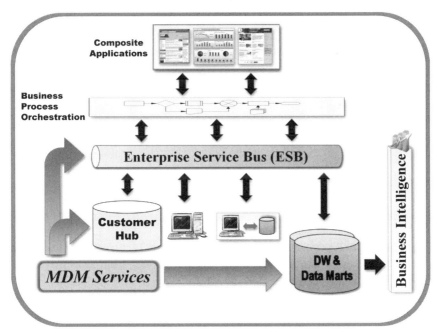

FIGURE 1.6 Enterprise MDM

general guidelines and the most common implementations. It is important to consider the data domain in scope (obviously *customer* in the context of this book), the purpose of managing the data (operational or analytical), and the technical architecture (central hub, data warehouse, virtual integration, hybrid).

Next is a description of the common business cases normally utilized to justify the deployment of a Customer MDM solution, followed by which approach(es) and architecture(s) best fit each of the business cases. Concluding this chapter is a discussion around the elusive ROI question.

DEFINING THE BUSINESS CASE

Why is MDM important? Quite simply, MDM not only gives companies the opportunity to better manage their key data assets and thereby improve the overall value and utility the data provides internally, but it also exposes internal process issues and business practices (or lack thereof) that are the underlying constraints to having and maintaining good data. Often, these underlying issues are generally known, but it's not until an MDM initiative is launched that the various business teams can or will start effectively addressing the issues. Looking at this from a Customer MDM point of view, the lack of having well-orchestrated data management practices will typically result in one or more of the following risks:

- Increased costs due to operational and data redundancies or differences across lines of business.
- Higher risk of audits and regulatory violations.
- Poorer BI and analytics, adding to customer frustration and missed opportunities.
- Customer/partner/vendor/employee dissatisfaction and consequently un-realized revenues.
- Possible overpayment of vendors and customers stemming from duplicate records.
- Over or under delivery of customer services due to inconsistent customer identity and tracking.

MDM does much more than just bring data together. It involves an entire set of processes, services, and policies that go along with it. Most MDM experts agree that the three main reasons used to justify an MDM implementation are cost reduction, risk management, and revenue growth, as shown in Figure 1.7.

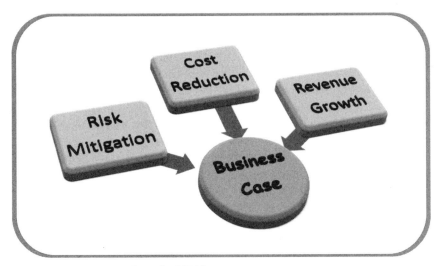

FIGURE 1.7 Business Case for MDM

Cost Reduction

From an information and knowledge perspective, customer data is the nervous system of a company. It is extremely pervasive and impacts virtually every LOB in the company. It is key information associated with transactions from order to shipment, and associated services before, during, and after a deal. Furthermore, proper management of information requires a complex infrastructure, trained personnel, and a set of well-defined and properly followed business processes.

There are costs associated with hosting and manipulating data, as well as costs associated with the activities relying on the accuracy of the information itself. Therefore, any effort targeted at any of those elements will help lower cost. Data hosting is about IT resources, data manipulation is about business processes, and accuracy of information is about data quality. MDM is a perfect fit because it addresses all these facets.

From a data hosting perspective, MDM emphasizes data consolidation through the elimination of redundant systems. This type of activity lowers IT capital expenditures, reduces costs associated with software licenses and maintenance fees, decreases spending on human resources due to having fewer systems to operate and maintain, and eliminates certain consulting fees as duplicated systems are retired.

From a data manipulation perspective, MDM stresses the need for more efficient and effective business processes. A strong data governance program facilitates the standardization of business rules, policies, and procedures, therefore increasing the predictability of data changes needed. Data steward-ship becomes better equipped to carry on data operations, lowering operating costs related to inefficient business processes, and minimizing the number of workarounds and redundant tasks.

Finally, data quality is a core competency of MDM. Data quality practices focus on cleansing, standardization, consolidation, and enrichment of infor-mation, therefore lowering costs related to incorrect business decision based on incomplete or wrong information. Better information also helps lower costs related to delivery errors, shipping fines, inventory management, wasted direct-marketing catalogs and other marketing initiatives, and so on.

Risk Management

Companies are susceptible to all kinds of risks. Large portions of them are dependent on having precise and timely information. For example, incorrect inventory management can lead to loss of customers, while improper compli-ance management can lead to lawsuits and hefty fines. Strategic objectives based on poor data quality analysis and results can have drastic effects, from missed targets to a total collapse of the company.

When looking at one aspect of risk, companies have legal and ethical obligations toward society. Law and ethics are intertwined, and a commitment to both is necessary to guarantee proper operations and successful business performance. Properly tracking and monitoring compliance to these rules requires active information management.

Obviously, the amount of regulation varies by industry, but just about every company will be subject to a multitude of labor laws and compensation, privacy at multiple levels, contract management, pricing, and so on. Addition-ally, regulatory compliances such as the Sarbanes-Oxley Act (SOX), U.S. Patriot Act, Basel II, and other financial related rules must be followed and flagged immediately if violated. These are all data-driven violations that threaten the survivorship of a company.

Looking at another aspect of risk, proper business decisions based on correct information will certainly lead to more opportunities and less waste related to mistakenly assigned and/or improperly executed activities.

Anyhow, the proper management of data as an asset will increase the probability of positive risks, such as better strategic decisions and increased opportunities, while minimizing the likelihood of negative risks, such as frauds, lawsuits, audit findings, loss of certifications, fines, penalties, and so on.

Revenue Growth

Companies are constantly looking for opportunities to increase revenue. While there are many strategies and variables to make it happen, it all usually starts with proper knowledge and understanding of the driving forces affecting that particular industry. These driving forces include: customer needs, market maturity, competition, partner relationship, product, price, distribution, promotion, and so forth.

A very common and effective strategy is improving customer relationships. However, this is easier said than done. Companies have been implementing Customer Relationship Management (CRM) systems to achieve that goal, but results are not necessarily optimal. A CRM system is just as good as the data behind it. If the data is siloed, and does not encompass the many LOBs across the company, it is difficult to have a clear understanding of the customer. This gap prevents a company from having a full insight into the customer information, or what is also referred to as a 360° view of the customer. This incomplete information is a double-edged sword, preventing a company from fully understanding its customer needs as well as preventing itself from being more efficient and effective when planning the next move. MDM and its practices address the root cause of those issues, consequently enhancing customer satisfaction, lowering customer churn, increasing sales, and ultimately improving revenues.

Better information will also lead to better marketing campaigns, improved partner relationship, and supply channel management.

Finally, an improved understanding of market forces, customer needs, and a company's own strengths and weaknesses will lead to enhanced strategic decisions, eventually culminating with a better focused company and potentially tactical mergers and acquisitions.

 SELECTING THE RIGHT MDM APPROACH

As discussed previously, companies typically use three main reasons to justify an MDM implementation: (1) cost reduction, (2) risk management, and (3) revenue growth.

But once a company selects its main area of focus for its business case, how does it decide which MDM approach to implement?

Enterprise MDM represents a combination of analytical and operational MDMs. To be sure, companies can use enterprise MDM to solve virtually any data and integration problem. Furthermore, if a company does want to address

TABLE 1.1 Business Rationale for Different MDM Approaches

Business Case	Recommended MDM Approach	Rationale
Risk mitigation	Operational MDM	The biggest concern is control. Implementing MDM on a data warehouse (analytical MDM) will not help, because operational data must be regulated to minimize risk and increase compliance.
Cost reduction	Operational MDM (maybe Enterprise MDM)	Most likely, the majority of costs are related to operations (see section on the business case for MDM). This means that an operational MDM is sufficient. However, inconsistent and incorrect data may also have a huge cost impact on wasted marketing campaigns. As a result, enterprise MDM may be required, depending on the situation.
Revenue growth	Analytical MDM	Revenue growth is mostly related to better strategic decisions. Analytical MDM only should suffice in most cases.

all three business cases described earlier, then obviously, an enterprise MDM implementation is the way to go. For some issues, however, enterprise MDM is simply overkill. This section aims to recommend the right solution to each problem, ensuring that companies do not attempt to kill an ant with a machine gun.

Note that Table 1.1 should be used only as a general guideline. Further, each of the three business cases overlaps the others to an extent; one does not start where the other ends. One could correctly argue that by mitigating certain risks, companies lower the costs of doing business. This, in turn, raises questions of whether this should be in the cost reduction category instead. Also, better data could reduce costs and improve marketing, and consequently grow revenue.

This book will highlight how the MDM practices and techniques described can apply to any of these architectures, or in some cases, may be more relevant to just a certain type of architecture.

DATA MANAGEMENT MATURITY LEVEL

While a business case for MDM will normally address one or more of the three reasons presented earlier, it is important to strengthen it with an accurate assessment of where the company is regarding the overall MDM spectrum. Two companies with the same business needs will not necessarily follow the same steps to get there because they might be at different maturity levels regarding what is necessary from an MDM practice perspective.

Several data governance maturity models exist and should be used as a frame of reference. Even though data governance in itself is just one of the components in MDM, it is perhaps the most pervasive one since it overlooks all other activities within MDM. That means a data governance maturity model can be used as guidance to understand where a company is and where it should be regarding the management of data as a strategic asset.

Multiple MDM vendors have their own maturity models, but most of the time their models can be used independently from their product lines. Besides, there are models from neutral companies such as Gartner, Data Management Association (DAMA), and the Data Governance Institute (DGI). "Data Governance Part II: Maturity Models—A Path to Progress,"[1] a paper authored by the National Association of State Chief Information Officers (NASCIO), provides a good overview into data governance maturity models, and a closer look into several existing models by multiple vendors.

The end state of a data governance maturity model is essentially when a company achieves a level characterized as being proactively governed, optimized, effective, standardized, and quality controlled at a global level. Everyone in the company will typically agree in principle with the merits associated with achieving this end state or at least with achieving a significant advancement toward this end state. Advancement consists of many individual objectives and achievements, with each one rooted to solving problems that generally everyone should be able to recognize and relate to in the current state. Addressing these problems becomes the heart of the business case. Relating these problems to "here is where we are" in the Maturity Model, and being able to express the achievable objectives that will drive advancement toward the end state, will be extremely important in establishing the business case.

Let's look at some examples of this. The intent here is to provide examples that will express undeniable customer data management problems and their risks along with a realistic course of action needed to mitigate the problem and to create ongoing practices for advancing in the Maturity Model.

These examples obviously need to be tailored to fit the type of issues and objectives that will be relevant to your company. Doing so will greatly help drive a shared perspective about the business problems, strategy, and direction needed to address them. This business case will also serve as a foundation for establishing the MDM model and creating the data governance charter that we

TABLE 1.2 Examples of Customer Data Management Problems

Problem	Risk	Action Needed
There is growing perception in our company that poor data quality is creating customer satisfaction issues, but we don't have any specific data quality measurements to qualify this.	Issues with data integrity, duplication, and fragmentation are going unchecked. This can definitely have an increasing impact on the customer transaction processes.	Data quality metrics and analysis techniques are needed to fully scope this problem in order to determine cause, effect, and a mitigation strategy.
The customer data in our data warehouses is inconsistent and cannot be trusted due to insufficient standards and lack of control at the data-entry level.	Without an accurate source of reference, operational reporting and customer analytics will be subject to error, interpretation, and cross-functional disagreement.	An overarching data governance process is needed to define and drive policies and initiatives that will establish the necessary standards, quality control, and trust of the data.
There is no single view of a customer, and each system has different representations and classifications of the same customer.	A 360° view of the customer cannot be achieved. Marketing, sales, and services cannot effectively synchronize on customer identity and continually are in conflict with customer reporting.	A customer data integration and hierarchy management strategy is needed to build a common customer view to be used as the foundation for consistent business intelligence and customer strategies.
Whenever we discover some major data management or data quality oriented issues, they always seem to require a major escalation followed by an inefficient and time-consuming process to define a focus team just to begin addressing the problem.	Data problems causing major business issues such as related to compliance, privacy, or operational performance, will be continually difficult to resolve and even further exacerbated if there is not a standard process with sufficient resources and roles for data quality management.	As part of a data governance model, an ongoing data quality management forum and process is needed to consistently and quickly address data-oriented issues that can impact business operations.

will cover in more detail throughout this book. The point here is to build a strong central business case that will drive specific, measurable, attainable, realistic, and timely (SMART) goals throughout the MDM initiative.

ADDRESSING THE ROI QUESTION

There is no one recipe for making the case for Customer MDM. Attempts to try to calculate and project ROI will be a swag at best and probably miss the central point that MDM is really an evolving business practice that is necessary to better manage your data, and not a specific project with a specific expectation and time-based outcome that can be calculated up front. Instead, consider all the business dependencies and decisions made that are associated with this data. If anything, the longer-term value of MDM can only be truly measured in real time as cohesive data management and sound governance decisions are made based on ongoing business needs and strategic plans. MDM practices driven by a governance process should certainly consider ROI where possible in making investment and data quality improvement decisions, but MDM, as a developing internal core competency, should be considered as an investment toward improving fundamental data management practices across the company.

Consider what we have identified as the fundamentals of Customer MDM practices. These are process and quality management investment areas that should be justifiable based on any number of existing business problems and data issues. Company A might suffer from such poor data quality that it can barely function. Company B may face severe strict government oversight. In any event, companies first need to recognize the strongest probable benefits of an MDM initiative and build the business case around that. Next, they should estimate how much they are losing by not realizing all the benefits of a having a timely, accurate, and consistent set of data delivered to the company. This is sometimes referred to as activity-based costing (ABC). Often, the best way to measure the potential benefit of MDM involves determining the amount of money that a company spends with reactive activities in place to compensate for a suboptimal set of processes and tools.

SUMMARY

Defining the proper business case is a critical requirement before deciding what Customer MDM approach and architecture to adopt. MDM is not exclusively a technology issue, but it is also a business capability. As such, companies need to align the proper MDM implementation with their overall strategy to address one or more of the following: risk mitigation, cost reduction, and/or revenue growth.

Not all Customer MDM implementations are the same. Analytical, operational, and enterprise MDM offer different challenges from both IT infrastructure and business model perspectives. Addressing analytical or operational data will lead to distinct levels of complexity, risk, and impact that need to be fully analyzed.

Customer MDM requires bringing many disparate data elements, systems, and processes into a common framework. But this involves a lot more than just data integration. It also requires aligning multiple business units into an integrated set of data, processes, rules, standards, policies, and procedures. It is about fostering collaboration to achieve a high level of success in overall data management, including: data governance and stewardship; data quality; data architecture, analysis, and design; data security; business intelligence; and reference and metadata management.

MDM is *not* a one-time project. It is a very pervasive program that requires executive sponsorship and complete collaboration from the many groups impacted. It also doesn't have a predefined formula. Current data management maturity within the company will dictate the proper steps to be taken, making it very important to position yourself properly from the beginning. Don't be discouraged, though. It is a long and tenuous road but very worthwhile in the long run. If done right, the outputs more than justify the inputs.

 ## NOTE

1. NASCIO, "Data Governance Part II: Maturity Models—A Path to Progress," www.nascio.org/publications/documents/NASCIO-DataGovernancePTII.pdf (NASCIO, 2009).

CHAPTER TWO

Establishing Effective Ownership

We accomplish all we do through delegation—
either to time or to other people. If we delegate
to time, we think efficiency. If we delegate to other
people, we think effectiveness.

—*Stephen R. Covey, The 7 Habits of Highly
Effective People*

THE QUESTION OF DATA OWNERSHIP

Who should own your customer data is perhaps the most controversial topic
you can expect will emerge up front, and a pivotal question that you will need
to address very tactfully because it's not really a question of who; rather, it's a
question of *how* ownership will be handled.

There are many valid perspectives about data ownership that are likely to
be brought to the table from the various line of business (LOB) organizations
such as Sales, Finance, Marketing, Services, or IT that exist in most companies.
The executive who will drive the MDM initiative, and potentially the data

governance process, is probably already associated with one of these LOBs. But from an operational perspective, we know that a customer master environment will still typically consist of data attributes that originate from the source systems and transactional processes that various LOBs already own and manage, as they should. These LOBs will naturally be very sensitive and potentially resistant to any unwelcome or heavy-handed sense of new governance control meddling in their specific business processes and data management practices. Handling this scenario is where top-down and bottom-up data management approaches meet at the crossroads. These are not mutually exclusive approaches, and if not embraced properly, they will lead to ongoing division across the LOBs.

There are those who may argue that you need a single *owner* of the data for MDM to work. In some companies this may work, but in many companies a single owner approach will not work and is not even feasible due to the dependence on a variety of business functions to manage and contribute to various elements of the customer master data. To really get your arms around implementing a successful cross-functional Customer MDM initiative, the concept of ownership actually needs to be addressed from both a data and process perspective and should consider a delegated approach.

There are two basic questions to consider:

1. How does the responsibility for creating and maintaining data need to be coordinated across the LOB functions?
2. Who will own and manage the actual MDM practice and its core processes?

An objective examination of these questions will probably identify existing business and IT dynamics that need to be part of the equation and can either be leverage points or create inhibitors for launching an MDM initiative.

It is necessary to clearly understand these leverage points and inhibitors in order to develop an effective MDM approach, especially considering that as a business practice MDM will need to be distinguished from the traditional business practices and operational processes such as Order Management, Accounts Receivable, Opportunity Management, Account Management, Marketing, Service Delivery, and so on. Fully considering the MDM distinction and its relationship to these existing practices is essential to identifying the right MDM ownership dynamic, which will need to be reflected in the design of your data governance model. Doing so will set the foundation around how governance as an operating process—not just a decision-making body—can embrace data ownership and vice versa.

EXECUTIVE INVOLVEMENT

It is in the initial planning state of the Customer MDM and data governance where executive involvement is most critical in order to establish the basic assumptions about ownership roles. As previously mentioned, often there is an existing executive role and organization that is already a strong advocate and well suited to drive the Customer MDM initiative and its ongoing practice. But assuming or suggesting this person will be *the* owner of customer data may be controversial and not at all practical. Why start a political battle that's not necessary? The point here is that in a cross-functional Customer MDM initiative, data ownership is not typically an autonomous role. If within a company there is a business climate and model that lends well to having the Customer MDM initiative and data owned by one organization, that's fine, too, but often this will not be the case because of the segmented nature of the business practices.

MDM with Segmented Business Practices

Although MDM is about the discipline and control of master data and its associated processes, this does not imply that create, update, and delete responsibilities for much of the data itself should be the responsibility of one central group. This would not be practical because in a typical business model the process flow and life cycle of customer data will involve various segments of the business. As noted previously, customer data typically consists of data attributes that originate from the various source systems and transactional processes that various LOBs own and manage. For example, the customer master data will likely have various entry points or touch points from Customer Relationship Management (CRM), Quoting, Order Management, Accounts Receivable, Finance, Services, Marketing, Partner Management, and possibly other functional process areas across a company. The LOB executives that oversee these functional areas need to be partners in the MDM model, buy into all expectations, and view the MDM initiative as an enabling proposition, not a disruptive one.

This partnership also implies that the executives must fully define and accept the concepts of shared data and master data. This means:

- They can't hoard data that needs to be shared in order to create a broader view of the customer.
- For the data attributes defined as master data elements that originate from their systems or processes, they are responsible to maintain these in accordance to governance policies and data quality standards.

A Customer MDM initiative is doomed to fail if it does not have broad and clear support. A healthy heartbeat of MDM is dependent on the successful reconciliation of data, standards, policies, and quality control—all of which can penetrate deeply into the business model. Executives, along with their functional directors and managers, are all accountable in the MDM scope. The executive driver for the Customer MDM initiative also needs to be recognized as the MDM program owner. That is, this executive should be responsible for establishing and overseeing the MDM program and processes associated with planning and strategy, budget management, team engagement, and the fundamental disciplines of Data Governance, Data Stewardship, Data Quality Management, Data Access Management, which will be covered more in the subsequent chapters.

A Top-Down and Bottom-Up Approach

By embracing the concept that an MDM initiative can be centrally managed along with having segmented data ownership, it should be easy to understand how the concept of top-down and bottom-up data management can come together in a very effective manner, as noted in Figure 2.1.

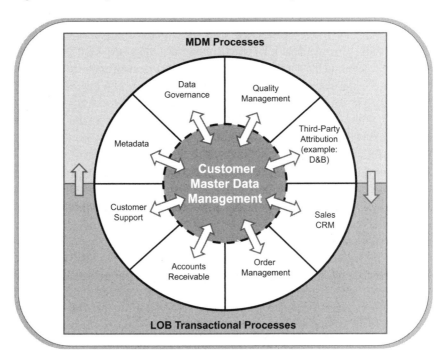

FIGURE 2.1 Example of Top-Down and Bottom-Up Customer MDM

The organization that drives the MDM model is less important than the organization's commitment and ability to establish a broadly serving MDM program and cross-functional governance process that enables appropriate authority and influence across the model. This is where the buy-in from the LOBs and the overall MDM partnerships begins.

As this dynamic moves into place, and once the initial strategic direction, priorities, and the governance framework have been firmly established, the emphasis starts shifting to the tactical management of governance and the MDM operating processes. At this point, the priorities become more focused on the ability of the program to facilitate data stewardship and drive a maintenance-driven model that allows for the various functional areas to still maintain the necessary levels of engagement, responsibility, and control of their specific process and data areas, while also staying in line with governance policies, standards, and expectations associated with the Customer MDM practice. Ultimately, it is the management of all of these dynamics that drives a successful MDM practice based on collaborative partnerships.

CREATING COLLABORATIVE PARTNERSHIPS

One thing to know up front is that for all the recognized end-state benefits and expectations associated with implementing effective MDM practices, achieving this can be a slow and deliberate process that needs to build on itself and will require some out-of-the-box thinking.

Can Your Current IT and Business Model Effectively Support MDM?

Data management initiatives, just like many other IT and business initiatives, have historically been subject to the imbalance between expectation and delivery—or what we all can relate to as an oversold but under-delivered project. Too often, we see that after the expectations are set and the go forward decisions have been made, there seems to be that reoccurring dynamic where the project becomes short on the expected resources and timely deliverables needed to achieve the end-state solution. We then start to see compromising that results in cutting or back logging of key pieces of the project, often causing ill will to emerge between the business and IT involved roles. While this scenario can occur across many types of business initiatives, delay or failure to deliver key aspects of a Master Data Management initiative can be particularly impacting because of the pervasive nature of master data across the business model.

This reoccurring dynamic is rooted in the inherent nature and ebb and flow associated with a traditionally stiff model between IT and the business. That said, we also recognize that this model has a clear purpose and serves a vital role in a company. For many reasons, there absolutely needs to be a strong charter for IT with clear distinctions and jurisdictions from the business organizations. However, there is a tendency to repeatedly overstuff this model to a point that neither the business nor IT can address many important initiatives that are pervasive and time sensitive. We have probably all seen where some initiatives and business practices won't or can't survive if constrained by this traditional model. For these cases, it's imperative that the business and IT can move away from the constraints inherent in this traditional model. MDM, and particularly the Customer MDM focus, is a poster child for this movement.

With just a bit more flexibility injected into the business and IT dynamic, a well-implemented Customer MDM initiative can be achieved that will definitely begin to stand on its own merits as a valued ongoing enterprise practice. Treat this initiative as an emerging business practice that needs nurturing. This is why we do not recommend that an MDM initiative be launched as an IT project bound by fixed time and delivery expectations. As we have been alluding to, a Customer MDM initiative is very likely to require some initial cultural and political changes to enable the cross-functional collaboration and investment required for this model. In general, implementing MDM is not just about implementing policies, tools, and processes; it also requires understanding and recognition of the softer and more intangible elements of a company's ecosystem.

The Acceptance Factor

Those who are familiar with the Change Acceleration Process (CAP) equation "Quality × Acceptance = Effectiveness"[1] will appreciate the Acceptance factor. In other words, a quality improvement strategy, in combination with a cultural and organizational adoption strategy, is critical to the success and effectiveness of an MDM implementation. As Tony Fisher, president and CEO of DataFlux, points out, "Data Quality and data governance should never be considered a one-time project. A quality culture must be established as an ongoing, continuous process."[2]

A well-targeted MDM practice also needs to be a well-grounded, ongoing discipline positioned broadly enough to capture the notion of Master Data

Management. Getting the acceptance and focus needed for this is the first challenge. Then, expect that maintaining MDM practices will be an ongoing exercise in creating and building collaborative partnerships in the enterprise data space. Even though the phrase *collaborative partnerships* may sound redundant, often in cross-functional initiatives teams are thrown together as business partners, but they still maintain a level of resistance and self-interest that can impede breaking down the organizational or political barriers that work against MDM practices.

To the extent that with this book we offer guidance, experience, and techniques for implementing MDM practices, we also know that an MDM initiative will have factors and challenges unique to a company's business model and line of business dynamics. A large part of MDM success lies in understanding that uniqueness and finding creative and collaborative approaches to address it.

Business Access to Data

A key ingredient in a successful MDM partnership is to recognize the need for appropriate business role access to data. In Chapters 4 and 5 we elaborate further on this topic, but early on, when the concepts and agreements around ownership and partnership are forming, the positioning of the data steward role needs to also be positioned within the MDM model. Consider how and where data stewards will operate, what authority they should have, what they can have access to, and how they are formally recognized in the company. There may already be some semblance and recognition of data steward functions as part of other business or IT job roles, but this can be fuzzy and these data steward functions are often just a secondary responsibility, which can easily be subjugated when attention is required for the primary job responsibilities.

MDM focus will suffer if the work and responsibilities are just tacked on to existing job roles that are already loaded with other responsibilities. If the data steward functions will be incorporated into other existing job families and roles, just be sure to fully recognize the time and skill sets needed to address the MDM needs, and ensure this work can be regularly performed by the individuals. Ideally, a clear and distinct data steward job family should be created in the business that is not competing with IT or viewed negatively as *shadow* IT. The business-oriented data steward role is a necessary complement to the IT roles in the overall MDM model. Not recognizing and sufficiently enabling this type of data steward role will significantly hinder the execution of the MDM practices by forcing too much expectation for MDM solutioning and delivery through the IT process or with other business roles that are not adequately skilled, resourced, or empowered.

Consider two general observations that most everyone can relate to:

1. Overburdening IT and creating unnecessary IT bottlenecks isn't conducive to improving business practices.
2. Where IT bandwidth is a concern, data management and data quality improvement projects will typically be considered as lower priority than the system, application, and business-sustaining demands for IT resources.

This backlog or lowering of priority translates to the project sitting in a queue and probably means eventual loss of momentum and business interest, or possibly forcing the project to be directed into a more expensive path using consultants or contractors. This is not to suggest that you should try to circumvent the IT engagement path for the implementation of Customer MDM tools, infrastructure, or solutions that should require IT to review, design, and deliver. But there are many aspects of implementing Customer MDM that we discuss throughout this book that can fully or at least largely be handled on the business side by skilled data steward roles and teams who are well versed in the business process areas and have authorized and controlled access to certain data.

Coordination of MDM Roles and Responsibilities

Value and purpose of the MDM roles and responsibilities needs to be recognized early on during the data ownership and partnership discussions. Spelling this out and planning for how these roles will coordinate with other business and IT roles will take any conflicts or jurisdictional issues out of the debate and enable the data steward functions to more formally thrive in a company's ecosystem and play a vital role in the MDM process and governance model. Figure 2.2 illustrates how these roles and relationships become the partnerships and executing dynamic of data ownership.

A well-defined and coordinated set of roles and responsibilities between the data governance and data steward roles becomes the focus point for the sponsorship and ongoing execution of MDM process. This data steward team will not only become the subject matter experts who have sufficient tools, skills, and responsibility to manage the MDM process across the enterprise, but also can work with specific functions to assist with many types of data analysis, standardization, or cleanup initiatives that are important to the LOB area along with benefiting many other customer data stakeholders.

For example, if addressed correctly, the reduction or elimination of data duplication can have a very positive cross-functional benefit, but it needs to be carefully planned and executed due to the widespread sensitivity around

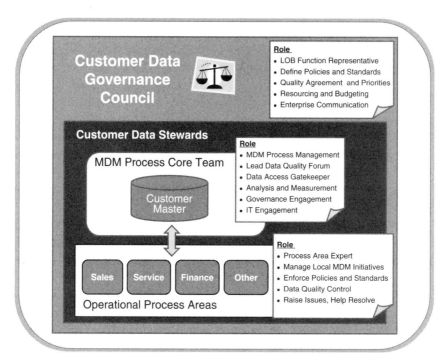

FIGURE 2.2 Customer MDM Roles and Responsibilities

eliminating customer records, with the merging of these records and the associated data, or with the linkage of this data with other data such as contracts, install base, service data, hierarchies, and so on, which all can be affected in the process. The planning and execution of de-duplication and record merge activity is much more than simple matching logic and backend clean-up actions. It will require not only a thorough study and testing of the inherent functionality and configurable rules available for actually performing duplication cleanup and record merging, but also will require the creation of a surrounding business process that addresses the various business rules, constraints, exceptions, manual research, timing, and support that are all elements of implementing a cross-functional data management process.

Getting this type of a data management process right and ensuring that all the stakeholders are appropriately engaged is what will create the underpinning needed to drive a common view of the customer and where the *source of truth* concept is actually rooted. We'll address these subjects in much more detail in the subsequent chapters, but it's important to recognize that it's through this type of collaboration and partnership that the LOB executives will appreciate the enabling value that the MDM practice and its core team bring. This becomes the bond for how the top-down and bottom-up approach to data management stays together.

SUMMARY

Although Customer MDM implementation and data governance plans will incorporate processes and structures aligned to the company's corporate operating model, it is extremely important that the basic principles described in this chapter regarding ownership, partnership, collaboration, roles, and responsibilities are thoroughly considered and are reflected in the implementation planning. Particularly for Customer MDM, it will be through this type of cooperative dynamic that the significant set of work and ongoing practice gets done. In the subsequent chapters, you'll see how most of the Customer MDM actions and solutions we discuss will rely heavily on the coordination across various aspects of this dynamic.

Let's recap the key points we have covered in this chapter:

- The concept of customer data ownership is a complex dynamic due to the segmentation of customer data across the business functions.
- Coordination of both top-down and bottom-up data management practices will create an ongoing collaborative approach needed to manage the MDM model.
- The cross-functional roles and responsibilities, particularly in relation to data steward functions, need to be clearly defined, distinguished, and complementary.

By carefully considering and addressing these key points early in the MDM planning and ownership discussions, the right foundation will be established that will enable the remaining topics in this book to be successfully addressed, coordinated, and positioned in your MDM implementation.

NOTES

1. CLOE of GE Capital Services, 2000.
2. Tony Fisher, *The Data Asset: How Smart Companies Govern Their Data for Business Success* (Hoboken, NJ: John Wiley & Sons, 2009).

CHAPTER THREE

Priming the MDM Engine

Success depends upon previous preparation, and
without such preparation there is sure to be failure.

—*Confucius*

 INTRODUCTION

The quote from Confucius says it all. Preparation is key. *Priming* the MDM engine is about proper preparation. It not only requires evaluating a multitude of vendors and solutions in the marketplace, but it also requires understanding your own company at many levels, including: company culture, objectives, and strategies; current state of data segmentation and fragmentation; data management maturity; technical infrastructure and competency; IT and business readiness; change management preparation; market pressure; and so on.

Customer MDM is complex because it brings together disciplines that were traditionally decoupled in the past. IT and business are now required to work even more collectively than before. Plus, business units have to collaborate at a higher level, too.

This chapter describes the proper considerations to be taken when analyzing MDM tools and making the final decision between build versus buy.

A huge step for MDM preparation is understanding and integrating existing data; therefore, subsequent sections discuss those topics in detail along with many techniques for data integration and migration. After that, there is a section to weigh the need for customer data consolidation while preserving the proper segmentation required by multiple LOBs. Finally, the chapter ends with sections about reference data and metadata management, which are also foundational concepts to a successful MDM program.

 POSITIONING MDM TOOLS

There is no question regarding how important technology is to MDM. Without technology, it is simply impossible to achieve the desired levels of automation, scalability, usability, reliability, time-to-market, and so on. Furthermore, and repeated over and over throughout this book, is the fact MDM is about people, process, and technology. The proper combination of these three elements is what makes MDM successful. Complementary is the fact MDM is constantly fine-tuning these elements for maximum benefits.

Figure 3.1 represents people, process, and technology and MDM as a pair of gears. As one is adjusted, the other is impacted.

As much as technology is clearly important, when companies start a Customer MDM program they are looking to solve a business need. It is a given business need that will drive what technology is required, and not the other way around. Obviously, in certain markets and industries, technology can be a strategic differentiator, and as such, it becomes a business priority in itself. In another example, a given company may become so ineffective due to an

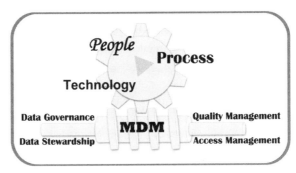

FIGURE 3.1 Reliance between MDM and People, Process, and Technology

outdated technological solution that it has no option except to upgrade. But again, it is not about the technology per se. It is about solving for the inefficiencies inflicted into the business operations.

In Chapter 1, the pervasive and encompassing nature of MDM was discussed, consequently impacting many organizations within the company. Business requirements can vary widely from one company to another due to differences such as culture, organizational charts, cross-functional relationships, industry types, operational practices, and so on. With that said, and considering the statement in the last paragraph, it is easy to see how it becomes difficult to find an existing technological solution that will fulfill all business needs on a large-scale program such as MDM.

In the early days of MDM, it was common to see companies opt to *build* their own solutions because vendor offers couldn't quite fulfill their needs. However, the pendulum is swinging toward the *buy* end as MDM solutions mature with improved products and considerable market consolidation through important acquisitions by major players.

Still, in a lot of cases, it will likely be necessary to buy from multiple vendors, as it is difficult to find a single one that can cover MDM practices from soup to nuts. Besides, most vendors and solutions have their strengths and weaknesses. Often, these solutions or particular product offerings are geared more toward one type of architecture and use case assumptions. Leveraging the right products can make a huge difference in overall deployment and effectiveness.

Even though vendor products have improved, and most of them allow for some customization on their own, it is practically impossible to anticipate every specific business need. Therefore, in addition to the possibility of having to combine multiple vendor solutions, it is also likely that it will be necessary to develop in-house components to achieve maximum customization.

As much as it is the business driving the solution, it is also about making the solution viable. Therefore, it is likely existing business practices might have to change to minimize the amount of customization required by a given technical implementation. Obviously, the goal is to meet the business need, but there could be multiple ways to do that. It is essential to find out exactly what is the ultimate goal being sought by the business. Chances are it is related to attracting new customers, enhancing customer satisfaction, improving the bottom-line, increasing sales, and so on. Hence, business practices can feasibly be changed without impacting what is really important. Besides, some existing business practices could be the result of years and years of unrevised practices, and not necessarily at an optimal level. Use this opportunity to review and improve them. Before jumping into extensive customization, look for opportunities to streamline existing inefficient or cumbersome processes. Technical tools will have built-in rules and recommended workflows that can be leveraged into the reengineering process.

In summary, start with the business requirements to identify the closest Customer MDM solution available. Customize and add in-house enhancements, but not without first looking for opportunities to change existing practices and avoid unnecessary costs.

Andy Hayler, founder and CEO of The Information Difference, has developed a webinar for the eLearningCurve (www.elearningcurve.com) to help companies evaluate vendors. The webinar is entitled "MDM: Selecting a Vendor."[1]

Next, we will discuss the common initial tasks when getting ready for Customer MDM. Typically, this involves the integration and synchronization of disparate data, with the need for data profiling and most likely, data migration.

 ## DATA INTEGRATION AND SYNCHRONIZATION

Just about every Customer MDM implementation will start with a data integration effort. Companies looking for MDM solutions probably have silos of data all over the enterprise. Therefore, it is necessary to look at the data as a whole to be able to identify duplicates, create relationships, build intelligence, minimize maintenance costs, control access, and everything else that is directly or indirectly related to maintaining a high-quality repository with trusted and governed data. For that reason, data integration is the foundation for everything else.

Data integration in itself does not necessarily mean physically moving data. As noted in Chapter 1, certain MDM architectures such as data federation and registration will simply create references to data that exists somewhere else. The concept of data integration in this book is about having an overall view into the entire company data, independently of where it is physically located. Nonetheless, physically moving data from one system into another is also very common, either as a one-time data migration effort, or on an ongoing basis, such as data warehouse systems. Data migration is explained further in this chapter.

Anyhow, on typical MDM programs, integrating data will likely encompass varying levels of physically and virtually joining data. Furthermore, Customer MDM is about having an integrated view into customer information. Other entities and/or transactional information dependent on customer data will have to be connected to the MDM repository, which, in itself, is another level of integration.

Next to the data integration challenge is data synchronization. Combining the data into a unified view is a very important part of the equation, but so is establishing consistency among data and its harmonization over time. Synchronization is obviously a bigger challenge the more the data is spread across multiple data systems, physically or virtually. That's why achieving the maximum physical consolidation into a single customer hub will be the most beneficial approach in the long run.

Data integration and consolidation are, therefore, extremely challenging and time consuming. From a data repository perspective, certain Customer MDM solutions include a customer data model along with a physical database, while others simply provide means for connecting existing data sources. The former option will require more data migration with more up-front costs, but should be easier and cheaper to maintain. The latter will be less intrusive, but will not be as effective if the business case is built on eliminating redundancy and lowering maintenance costs, for example.

Nonetheless, no matter the amount of integration, migration, conversion, and synchronization needed, it should all start first and foremost with understanding the data very well. Data profiling is an often overlooked activity, and even when it is carried on, it is usually not done at the necessary level of depth. Understanding the data helps in understanding the dynamics of the business, which are not always evident from processes, rules, and procedures. Besides, data integration efforts require clear knowledge of structural constraints and semantics of the information since meanings and dependencies might vary widely in a potentially newly defined business purpose of entities and attributes.

Let's take a closer look at this important activity of data profiling, followed by data migration. Concluding this section is a deeper discussion into the effects of data consolidation and when segmentation might still be desired.

Data Profiling

Data profiling is a critical activity whether you are integrating and synchronizing disparate systems, migrating a data repository, incorporating a new source into a data warehouse, or just trying to measure and improve the quality of the data. It helps to uncover facts about the data and associated dependencies, constraints, relationships, usage, and integrity.

Data profiling can also help set the right expectations on a data integration or migration effort. It is not uncommon for business users to expect the data will be magically better once it is moved into a new system. Granted, newer systems may have higher levels of constraints and integrity rules that will automatically enforce adherence to certain standards. But, bottom line is: garbage in, garbage out (GIGO). If a legacy system is impregnated with bad data, the new system will be, as well, if little or no cleansing is done as part of the migration effort. But to find out how much should be done, it is necessary first to understand the condition and fitness of existing data.

Lastly, the assessment of the state of the data will help estimate the amount of work necessary to adapt and/or convert the current data into a new model. At the same time, it will also help identify potential gaps and prepare and communicate necessary changes to existing practices in a timely manner to avoid adverse business impact.

Even though the benefits of data profiling are quite clear, the actual activity in itself is quite often unique, unconfined, and unpredictable. It is unique because of the wide variation of data system structures, data conditions, and pre-established goals. It is unconfined due to its mostly exploratory nature. It is unpredictable because the result of one step can dictate what needs to happen next. Therefore, data profiling is quite an art.

Examples of data profiling techniques are pattern analysis, frequency distribution, domain analysis, type identification, interdependency verification, redundancy analysis, and a multitude of other statistical measurements. It takes time and experience to master the techniques and to combine them effectively since data profiling is so broad.

When creating a data profile plan, it is important to consider how much is already known about what the data is or about what the data should be. We like to call this *prior knowledge*. Since the data elements to be analyzed have so many associated properties, such as type, content, pattern, association, conformance, business rules, and so on, the pre-existing knowledge about each of them varies extensively even within the same data source. In the case of data integration or migration projects, there is quite a bit of prior knowledge about what the data should look like in the new structure.

Figure 3.2 depicts a Data Profile Spectrum, which is used to convey the concept that data profiling is influenced by how much is known about what the data is or should be, and therefore, dictating how the data profiling techniques should be employed.

The geometric figures composed of four squares, aka *tetrominoes*, are used to represent the techniques. That is just to call attention to the fact that data profile techniques are pieces that can be applied and/or combined in a variety of ways to accomplish what is needed. For example, the data distribution technique can be used during discovery just to understand what random values exist at what percentage. However, the same technique can be used on a

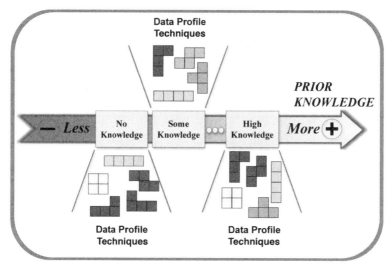

FIGURE 3.2 Data Profile Spectrum

country code field to identify the percentage of valid values. It is the same technique applied slightly differently dependent on the location in the spectrum. In another example, there is no need to verify uniqueness when a primary key constraint already exists in the database for a particular field. Different attributes could be at different parts of the spectrum, thus the spectrum is per element being profiled, not per data source as a whole.

Let's take a look at three different data profiling scenarios to understand the spectrum:

Scenario 1. Explore a fairly unknown data source, with no documentation, looking for any useful customer information. In this case, there is practically no prior knowledge; thus, it is toward the beginning of the spectrum. In this situation, the data profile techniques should be employed to understand the data structure, explore data fields to understand their contents, and look for patterns and trends in the data, relationships between attributes, and so on.

Scenario 2. Convert customer data from a relatively known data source into a new well-known MDM customer data hub. In this case, there should be quite a bit of understanding around the target source structure and accompanying rules and constraints. This information should be used to frame the data profiling activity to be performed on the legacy system being converted. Consequently, this is at a higher level in the spectrum. The data profile techniques should be used to validate the old data and will fit into the new structure both lexically and semantically. Questions, such as the following, should be answered: Can this data be moved without fallouts due to tighter integrity checks? Is the new field(s) for this information of proper type? Does the old data need to be transformed before it is loaded? Is a business process going to be impacted by the conversion?

Scenario 3. Convert customer data from a relatively known data source into a new and unknown MDM customer data hub. In this case, not much is understood about the new structure, and one would assume a profiling activity toward the beginning of the spectrum is needed. But there is a failed premise here: One should not start a profile activity until there is a good understanding of the target system. It is inefficient to profile a source system to be converted if there is little knowledge about the constraints to be faced. Therefore, before profiling even starts, it is necessary to heighten the knowledge level and place the activity where it properly belongs in the spectrum.

The first two scenarios are relatively straightforward. But, from the third scenario, you can conclude it is necessary to consider not only where you are in the spectrum, but also where you should be based on the request at hand. Before you start a data profiling activity, think about how much you should know already. Sometimes the proper amount of information is provided because the request came from a very specific requirement, but sometimes it is not. Being able to make that distinction is critical.

There is a multitude of data profiling tools offered by MDM and data quality vendors, as well as open source options. We highly recommend you adopt one. As much as it is possible to use database languages and/or other reporting techniques to profile information, these do not offer nearly as much sophistication as the more specialized tools.

Jim Harris, blogger-in-chief at Obsessive-Compulsive Data Quality (OCDQ), has written an outstanding multi-part blog series titled "Adventures in Data Profiling."[2] Jim describes in detail a multitude of data profiling techniques and common functionality provided by data profiling tools.

Data Migration

Data migration, in simple terms, is about physically copying data from one repository into another. The need for a data migration effort is highly dependent on the MDM architecture chosen, as explained in Chapter 1. If there is no physical copy of data involved, then there is no need for data migration.

Let's first take a look at some data migration categories, followed by data migration considerations and strategies.

Data Migration Categories

Data migration normally falls into three main categories:

1. **One-time data migration.** Data is migrated from a legacy system, which is EOL'd after the task is completed. This is very common in many MDM architecture solutions.
2. **Ongoing data migration.** Data is indefinitely extracted from an active source system on a regular basis. This is very common when implementing an Analytical MDM in a data warehouse.
3. **Temporary ongoing data migration.** Data is extracted from an active source system on a regular basis until its EOL is possible. This is very common when implementing a phased MDM program with many business processes dependent on a particular set of legacy systems. It could be too risky to perform a one-time migration and completely EOL these key system(s) until all business processes are properly transitioned and validated.

Data migration in all three categories is often performed via an Extract-Transform-Load (ETL) process. Normally, what differs is the amount of integration and synchronization necessary after the migration.

Obviously, in one-time migration efforts, there is no post synchronization required since the legacy system is EOL'd. In ongoing migration, the synchronization is normally one way, with the source system(s) feeding a downstream repository such as a data warehouse, for example; therefore, the initial ETL process can be leveraged for scheduled transfers.

Temporary ongoing migrations are trickier because they could require a two-way synchronization based on how business process operations are divided between the two dependent systems and what data needs to be moved from one place to another. In this case, there is an ETL process for the initial bulk transfer and a custom interface is typically required to maintain the two systems' consistency.

The goal of MDM is to eliminate redundant systems and have a single system-of-record. Therefore, it seems contradictory to have a temporary ongoing data migration, which is, in essence, maintaining multiple systems and having to write additional software to keep them synchronized. Why would companies do this and what are the consequences?

There could be multiple reasons why companies opt to delay the EOL of a particular system, but they are all most likely related to minimizing the risk of disrupting a given set of business processes. After all, companies want to avoid at all costs the potential to upset existing customers and/or break contractual agreements. Transferring all business processes and training everybody involved accordingly can take a long time. Consequently, it is safer to operate with redundancy for a while. But it does come with a price, which we will discuss shortly.

Here are a couple sample scenarios where a company might start migrating data into a main customer hub, while still keeping the legacy system operational:

- A new company is acquired. Customer data from the acquired company needs to be integrated. However, the acquired company has very disparate customer business practices due to strategies and operations of a different product line.
- A company is doing a massive MDM program, but one of the systems to be integrated is used by many global teams, and is critically related to financial aspects of the company. EOL of this system would require all global teams to be fully trained on the new system without any risk of causing financial incompliance of any kind. The company decides to phase out the old system incrementally instead of all at once to give employees a chance to get used to the new system, while slowly transitioning all business processes.

Looking at the two scenarios, it is understandable why companies would maintain redundant systems to avoid potential issues. There are direct costs associated with keeping multiple systems operational, and those costs are normally easy to predict. But what are some other not so obvious impacts?

Sometimes companies fail to fully analyze the impact to the quality of the data when keeping a legacy system operating in parallel to a new customer hub. Chances are the upgrade has happened because the business has outgrown the legacy system limitations. It certainly depends on a multitude of design decisions, such as which of them is the system-of-record, what information is synchronized, where CRUD operations occur, and so on. But it is very likely the legacy system can become an overall constraint preventing new functionalities in the new system from being applied properly, consequently perpetuating outdated practices, and increasing the number of exception scenarios to be managed.

The lesson here is be very aware of those situations, and fully analyze the impacts of your data migration strategy. Physical data synchronization certainly is a complicated issue, but even more complicated is business process synchronization when spread among multiple systems. Remember that certain LOBs may be fully migrated, while others are still operating in a semi-integrated legacy system. Proper coordination of all data and processes can be overwhelming. If parallel operation is a must, please do so with a well-thought-out plan, with clear dates on when transition can be fully completed, and as soon as possible. Long-term usage of old practices can have a long lasting effect on the quality of data, even when operating in a new system. A new system is just as good as the business processes around it.

Data Migration Considerations

Data migration is very complex and influenced by many factors. As a result, there is no single correct way to do it, but certain considerations should always be made.

As stated earlier, data migration is typically accomplished by applying an ETL process. The challenge is to determine what needs to be extracted and how much transformation should be done before loading the data into a new repository. Another method that is sometimes used is Extract-Load-Transform (ELT). The primary difference between ETL and ELT is where most of the transformation occurs: before or after it is loaded into the final repository. The samples in this chapter assume an ETL methodology since it is the more mature and the more common approach.

Data structures are certainly going to be different between legacy systems and the new customer repository. That means a certain amount of transformation will be required to allow the data to be moved without any fallouts. It is the bare minimum necessary to adhere to the new constraints without leaving any important data behind. It is, in essence, a mapping exercise: data elements from the old system are mapped to where they will reside in the new structure. As usual, it is easier said than done, because it is not always a simple mapping. The following are just a few samples of potential issues:

▪ Data normalization between the two systems could be different, requiring values to be copied into one place, and at the same time, a foreign key added to another location. For example, account type in the old system may be a free-form field. In the new system, it may involve a normalized table for account types, and all accounts need to reference it through a foreign key.

- Length of fields or actual number of fields could be different, requiring values to be truncated or broken down into multiple elements. For example, a legacy system may have fewer but longer address lines. To avoid losing any data, it may be necessary to break the information into more address lines in the new system. Ideally, the new system will have more capacity, but it may not always be the case.
- New systems may have stricter constraints, requiring migrated attributes to be corrected before they can be loaded. For example, a new system may have a reference table for country codes, meaning only valid country codes are accepted throughout the repository. If the old system had no country code validation, any invalid record will be rejected. Consequently, during conversion, all country codes have to be fixed to avoid fallout.
- The semantics vary between systems. Elements may look like they serve the same purpose, but that is not necessarily true. For example, in an old system, *customer* is a single entity, while in a new one, customer may be the combination of a *party* with an *account*. Party in itself could store a customer name, or a prospect, or an employee, and so on. However, only parties with accounts constitute what was previously defined as a customer. Therefore, when transferring a true customer from the old system, it is necessary to create both a party and an account in the new system.

There are many more examples. But the point is, all transformations in these cases are necessary. There is little controversy about them since if they are not done, data won't make it into the new system, or even if they do, they will be useless. IT can normally identify the amount of fallouts, and validate with the business what level is accepted or not. But it is, obviously, a business responsibility to assess the usability of the data in the new system.

Next is the type of transformation that is not necessarily required, but is related to data quality improvements. Repeated throughout this book is the GIGO principle. A massive amount of transformation may be done during data migration, but if none is related to data quality, previous dirty data will pollute the new system. As a matter of fact, problems can even be exacerbated, as we will see next.

Companies with many disparate systems suffer from two types of data duplication: intra-system and inter-system. Intra-system duplication is data redundancy existent within the same repository. Inter-system duplication is data redundancy existent across multiple repositories. As disparate systems are moved into a single customer hub, data duplication can be amplified since it now combines previous intra- and inter-system duplication in a single place.

When users are searching for a particular customer, they may have to look through a lot more records than before, giving the false impression the conversion made it worse.

Data migration does sound like a perfect opportunity to apply data transformation to improve the quality of the information for the following reasons:

- An IT structure is in place to support and execute data changes.
- Business is mobilized to specify requirements and test modifications.

But more often than not, companies do a very poor job improving the data during migration. They normally adopt the "migrate the data as soon as possible, and clean up later" mindset. Unfortunately, the cleanup rarely occurs at the level needed afterwards. Why do companies miss out on this opportunity? There are many reasons and it also depends on the type of data migration and its category. Ongoing data migration into a data warehouse, for example, is normally not as critical as a one-time or temporary data migration into a new operational hub. Typically in ongoing migration, it is possible to regularly refine and improve the logic for better data quality in subsequent extractions. But when the number of migration opportunities is small or single, the quality usually suffers.

Making matters worse is the fact that the more critical data migrations are usually one-time and/or have to be completed in short cycles because they impact important operational systems. This calls to mind the old cliché of fixing a plane while flying it, since data creation and maintenance can't stop during the transfer. Data quality becomes one more thing in addition to adjusting business processes, completing the minimum transformation to avoid data fallout, training personnel, communicating changes, and so on. It is truly overwhelming, and since data quality is usually the least apparent of the problems, it becomes an afterthought. Another common rationale is: "We have been able to operate with the data as is; hence, we should be able to continue to do so for a while without any quality improvements."

Following this premise can have long-term devastating effects on the quality and usability of the information. Granted, sometimes companies have no option but to adopt a *clean later* approach. But if they do so, it should be a carefully analyzed situation with a very detailed risk analysis and data quality plan to be implemented as soon as possible. It is also important to remember how confidence in the new system on the part of its users is directly related to the quality of the information. If users perceive a lack of quality, they lose trust and will start engaging in unapproved practices to get around what they see as an already corrupted system.

Now, there is one particular scenario where it might be desirable to wait until the data is in the new repository before it is corrected. It happens when the new system provides powerful functionality to perform a given set of cleanup. For example, a new system may have a customer *merge* functionality that automatically combines all associated attributes from the duplicates into a unique view. Duplicating the same functionality during migration may be expensive and time-consuming, making it viable to do this afterwards.

The general rule of thumb should be to clean the data as soon as possible, and to refrain from underestimating the opportunity to do so during the migration. Next, we will take a look at some strategies to organize the data for cleansing and de-duplication during migration.

Data Migration Strategies

As stated earlier, data migration is required in many situations. Strategies will vary widely according to those situations. This section uses some sample scenarios for data conversion to convey some fundamental practices, but it is not meant to be comprehensive since the amount of variations can be quite broad. Companies should consider hiring consultants to help in creating their data migration strategies. It should be a coordinated effort between IT and the business.

One sample scenario assumes multiple operational legacy systems are being migrated into a single customer data hub. All legacy systems involved should be profiled in detail with a clear understanding of the new system structure and associated new business practices.

The first step should be to profile the data and identify what needs to be migrated. Within the data to be migrated, some will only have to go through minimal transformation, while others will require cleansing, either to fit into the new structure, or simply to improve quality. Another set is data that should be consolidated to avoid data duplication to reach the new system. Figure 3.3 is a graphical representation of how data elements can be organized. Notice the term *cleansing* is used generically to signify scrubbing, enrichment, and standardization.

The classification in Figure 3.3 is useful when writing the conversion logic. It is important to have a clear understanding of the data elements to be converted as well as the type of transformation required to convert them. It may be necessary to break down the classification even further. For example,

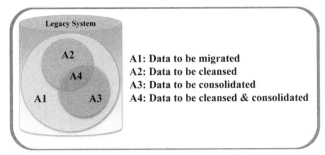

A1: Data to be migrated
A2: Data to be cleansed
A3: Data to be consolidated
A4: Data to be cleansed & consolidated

FIGURE 3.3 Organizing Data for Migration

the type of cleansing varies widely; therefore, there will be very specific requirements for each data element. But the coarse classification suggested is a great starting point that can serve as guide during profiling and when estimating the amount of work necessary to convert and test if the migration is successful.

The actual data transformation typically occurs on a staging area, which is a data repository environment set up by IT. The staging area can be organized in many ways. Data warehouse projects normally include a permanent staging area. One-time data migration projects will usually have a physically independent temporary data source as the staging area. The logical organization of the staging area varies, as well. When migrating operational systems, it is normal to have multiple logical staging areas. The first one is very similar to the legacy system to be migrated, and the last one is very similar to the final data source structure. There could be multiple structures in between to support the many required transformations. The reason for this is to minimize the cycle time to extract and load the data. Since the majority of the time during migration is spent doing transformation, it is better to avoid much of it during extracts and loads because those activities may tie up operational resources.

Figure 3.4 shows a possible organization of a staging area during data migration. Notice the first stage structure is usually similar to the source system to avoid the need for much transformation during the extract process. Intermediate stages should be created as needed to allow for multiple steps of data cleansing, enrichment, standardization, and consolidation. Finally, the last stage resembles the target customer hub very closely. Most of the transformation should be completed by then to allow for intensive testing to be completed and assure the data is ready to be loaded into its final destination. Obviously, the number of stages is dependent on the volume of data to be converted and amount of transformation required.

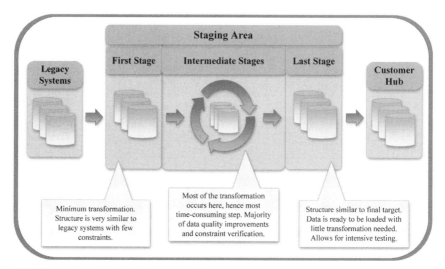

FIGURE 3.4 Sample Staging Area Design

Data storage is relatively cheap. As such, it is recommended to have more data tables than not to track transformations more closely. If too many data manipulations happen between one stage and another, it may be difficult to debug the cause(s) of a potential problem. And the more stages, the better for analysis and proper lineage. Please note also that throughout the entire migration and within the new system, a reference linkage should be maintained to allow for a record, at any given point, to be mapped back to its source uniquely.

Figure 3.5 depicts a possible organization of the intermediate stages to handle the many data quality aspects required during data migration. This is meant as a general guideline only. As stated before, data cleansing, as a whole, can be very encompassing; therefore, further breakdown may be necessary depending on the particular situation.

Data migration is indeed a complex project. It is common for companies to underestimate the amount of time it takes to complete the data conversion successfully. Data quality usually suffers because it is the first thing to be dropped once the project is behind schedule. Make sure to allocate enough time to complete the task maintaining the highest standards of quality necessary. *Migrate now, clean later* typically leads to another source of mistrusted data, defeating the whole purpose of MDM.

With that said and in addition to the considerations previously stated, it is necessary to deal with the fine line between what should be consolidated and

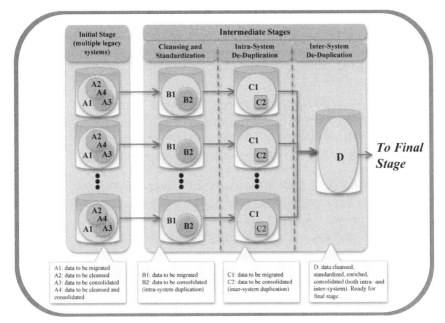

FIGURE 3.5 Organizing the Intermediate Stages within the Staging Area during Data Migration

what should remain segmented to address certain business needs. The next subsection deals with this conundrum.

Data Consolidation and Segmentation

While the overarching purpose of Customer MDM is generally aimed at achieving that single source of truth, often there are, in fact, significant limits or unanticipated negative outcomes concerning the structure of the customer master data. Within an integrated environment, particularly where there is a hub or spoke customer master within a transactional model, not only is the master data controlled and shared across these integrated transaction processes, but so is the structure of that master data. This means integrated functions such as order management, accounts receivable (AR), opportunity management, agreements/contracts, install base (IB), customer support, marketing, partner management, suppliers, and so on, will be largely bound to how this data is segmented or consolidated in the customer master.

Unfortunately, how opportunity management, IB, or customer support would like to segment the customer data can differ from how order management, finance operations, and other AR-oriented practices want to do it. Consider that in a decentralized model where more independent systems existed to handle various business functions, the organization and structure of the customer data has usually been optimized with each system to support the segmentation and consolidation needs for that particular function. Moving to a centralized model means that only one underlying structure will generally prevail. Therefore, in the early planning stages, it is critical to accurately understand the inherent design of the customer master data model. Following are some of the questions to pose and considerations to be made:

■ Is the primary design of the customer repository AR-centric, or is it Customer Relationship Management (CRM)–oriented, or does it offer a highly configurable approach?

■ What are the options, extents, and cross-functional technical dependencies associated with the given structure?

■ How will additional segmentation or consolidation of data, such as merging of parties and accounts, impact the work of integrated functions?

Without proper consideration and a thorough cross-functional impact assessment, the segmentation and consolidation aspects of the customer master data can and probably will be a major ongoing business issue across these various functions. Not carefully examining and addressing this area of impact can easily create deep-seated division among the customer master stakeholders, which can undermine or erode the partnership and support needed for MDM and data governance to be successful.

This is *not* to say that one size can't fit all and that the single version of truth is a myth. As long as the system implementation and MDM planning process carefully examines the various segmentation and consolidation needs across the integrated scope, legitimate differences and various requirements can be functionally and technically addressed as part of the overall implementation to enable all ends of the customer engagement and customer management spectrum to successfully share one customer master. Consider the following examples of challenges common to a centralized customer master model that should be addressed and solved:

■ AR requires customer name to be the company legal name, while customer support requires department information included in the name, therefore breaking the legal name requirement.

■ Marketing requires a primary address to be the company headquarters' address, while finance needs a bill-to site as the primary address.

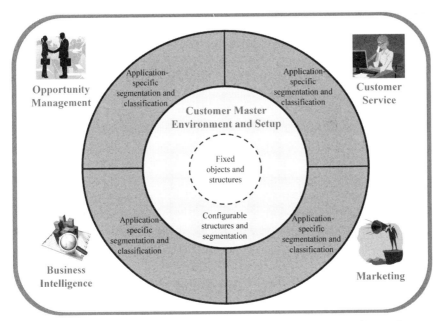

FIGURE 3.6 Customer Data Segmentation—Customer Master and Boundary Applications

- The segmentation and consolidation rules for customer accounts support sales and finance requirements, but may not be granular and flexible enough to support customer service requirements.

Being able to identify and solve for these challenges is an essential acid test for successful Customer MDM planning. Addressing this will also serve as a preamble to a better understanding of the MDM ecosystem and the data governance dynamic, which will be covered more in Chapter 4.

Figure 3.6 depicts a possible way to consolidate and segment customer information as needed by the many integrated functions.

Keep this important topic in mind when looking for vendor solutions and when going through a data integration phase within your Customer MDM program.

REFERENCE DATA

Interestingly enough, there are several definitions of reference data, and even articles and debates about differences between reference data and master data. Please see the following sources for more about it:

Chisholm, Malcolm. "Master Data versus Reference Data." *Information Manage-ment* (April 2006), www.information-management.com/issues/20060401/1051002-1.html.

Loshin, David. "Master Data and Reference Data—More Thoughts." *DataFlux Community of Experts* (July 2010), www.dataflux.com/dfblog/?p=3391.

Mosely, Marty. "What ARE 'Master Data'?" *Initiate* (June 2010), http://blog .initiate.com/index.php/2010/06/10/what-are-master-data/.

We actually have a very simple definition of reference data: Reference data is data used to validate other data. According to this definition, just about any data could be a reference at some point. Therefore, it is not actually the intrinsic content of the data that makes it a reference, but its usage. Obviously, caution should be taken when using *any* data as a reference to avoid inconsistency and misinterpretation.

Certain data sets are likely to be used as reference always, because they were created specifically for that intent. For example: a list of ISO country codes, or list of states and/or provinces within a country. Now, let's use customer name as another example. There is very little argument that customer name is one critical master data attribute of the entity customer. However, if a company is trying to analyze whether a new customer coming into the system is a duplicate, that company will be using the distinct set of existing customers in the comparison. Therefore, the list of existing customers is the reference data in this particular analysis. Granted, customer name by itself may not be sufficient to resolve the identity of a customer, but the example was simplified to make a point.

Even country code, which sounds very undisputable, may be context dependent. For example, the comprehensive list of ISO country codes is not necessarily always appropriate. It is possible that a company is trying to associate only countries where it is currently doing business. In this case, the reference data is *not* the entire ISO list, but the distinct list of countries with transactions. Needless to say, the shorter list of countries should ideally contain only valid ISO codes to avoid other types of accuracy and consistency issues.

Reference data are always likely to suffer from accuracy, either due to how it was compiled or due to how often it is refreshed. Very few, if any, strict references are undisputable. Some are more static than others, which facilitates its management. Let's take a look at three examples to illustrate the accuracy and currency of reference data:

1. Country codes do not change very often, and ISO will certainly keep its references very up-to-date. But most company systems don't actually feed

from ISO online. It is normally an offline snapshot in time of the ISO reference that is captured locally in the company, and used throughout the application. Therefore, a newly valid country according to ISO standards is not valid in the company until the reference copy is refreshed.

2. Postal code references all over the world are constantly changing. Updates could happen at many levels, such as street name, street number, city, county, postal code, and state/province. There is a currency issue here just as it exists for country codes, but it is exacerbated because it is more dynamic information. There is also the risk of accuracy. Postal services deal with huge amounts of data and are susceptible to human or technical mistakes just like any other company.

3. Customer reference information provided by vendors, such as D&B and OneSource. The number of mergers, acquisitions, spinoffs, legal name changes, and so on, is overwhelming. Keeping all this information accurate and up-to-date is a challenge to those vendors. The way a company uses the information provided by them also varies. If an online portal provided by the vendor is used to validate a customer, the issue of currency is smaller, but there is risk of accuracy due to a potential mistake. If an offline copy is maintained inside the company, the currency risk is higher.

Even though the previous examples are from external references, there are internal references, as well. What determines the internal or external nature of a reference is its source, not where it is maintained. An ISO list of country codes is an external reference even if it is maintained as a local normalized table. Internal references include a multitude of information, with many of them maintained as normalized reference tables for internally created attributes such as party and account type, address usage, contact preferences and roles, and so on. Internal reference information can also be compiled dynamically, such as a list of existing prospects, or list of countries where the company has existing business.

Offline references, either external or internal, will age and need to be refreshed properly. Online references are typically refreshed through their normal maintenance process. Companies should have a clear reference data management strategy to maintain up-to-date information.

The following are some examples of situations that should be avoided when dealing with reference data:

■ Software developers have a tendency to create offline references hardcoded into their software to facilitate validation, or as a workaround due to a lack of access to the repository containing the online reference. This practice should be avoided because it is expensive to change, test, and release a newer software version. Reference data is hard enough to be kept up-to-date when it exists in a data repository, let alone when it is coded inside an application.

- Companies deal with a series of one-time data migration projects as a series of unrelated events. This practice leads to duplicated and probably mostly manual types of work. Companies should strive to create an evolving reference knowledge base for the purposes of data migration and data quality practices in general. Even though data migration projects are quite unique, a lot of validation rules using reference data can be generalized and instituted to support a learning paradigm. With time, the more migrations a company performs, the easier, more efficient, and more reliable it becomes. It may take longer initially, but the long-term benefits are worth it. Even companies that won't be doing a lot of data migration can benefit from leveraging that knowledge base to other data quality projects.

- Not having a well-defined reference data management strategy. This sounds pretty obvious, but numerous companies start well with external references, but forget to plan who, how, and when the updates will be applied. Some dynamic references might need a monthly refresh, others quarterly, and some yearly. Sometimes they need to happen on demand based on a business need. It is important to plan and communicate this accordingly.

A given data element is just as good as the reference used to validate it. It does not matter how much validation is performed if the source of the reference is dubious or outdated. Reference data should be unique within a Customer MDM program to avoid inconsistency and synchronization issues. Duplicating reference data should be avoided at all costs, even for temporary usage. It is not unusual to see reference data maintained in spreadsheets throughout the enterprise, and exchanged via e-mails. It is very easy to lose track of their validity when this happens.

 ## METADATA

Metadata can be defined as data describing other data. It varies from simple catalog information, such as tables in a database, their names, sizes, columns, type of data, and number of rows, to more complex information, such as purpose of the data, who uses it and why, who owns it, who created it and when, who is allowed to change it, and so on.

It is very common to see different LOBs have different and sometimes conflicting definitions of apparently simple data elements. The more cross-functional data integration there is, the higher the possibility of misinterpretations and disparate understanding regarding data elements. Metadata management becomes more important as repositories are integrated and shared among multiple LOBs within the company.

Before a Customer MDM type of data integration, the many LOBs operate in silos. This often generates disagreements, but a common understanding and a unified jargon typically prevails. Moreover, the combination of many years of operation and a somewhat more specialized type of communication lowers the chances of misinterpretations and inconsistencies.

However, there are differences among the multiple siloed systems within the enterprise. Besides, a new Customer MDM repository will generally have its own nomenclature as well. As an example, a customer in a legacy CRM system may be either a prospect or a current customer, while the concept of prospect may not exist in the legacy AR system at all. When both CRM and AR are migrated to a customer hub, a prospect may be a party only, while an existing customer is the combination of a party and an account. Further classification of party and account types can complicate understanding and usage even more.

The previous example is just the tip of the iceberg. Many business processes and associated data elements will be impacted by a Customer MDM program, making it extremely important to properly document the many aspects of the data and its usage.

A particular type of metadata is data lineage. Data lineage handles the tracking of data: where it comes from, where it goes to, and how it is transformed. It is a particularly important component of data migration since understanding the source of the data and applied transformations can be critical when interpreting information in the new repository.

Companies typically underestimate the importance of metadata management in general, and more specifically during data migration projects. Metadata management is normally postponed when data migration projects are behind schedule because it doesn't necessarily provide immediate benefit. However, in the long run, it becomes critical. It is common to see data issues later, and without proper metadata or data lineage it becomes difficult to assess the root cause of the problem.

Metadata itself is data, thus it is commonly maintained in a data repository. There are specific metadata management products that may or may not be

TABLE 3.1 Examples of Metadata Management Problems

Problem	Comments and Mitigation
Not providing the foundation for or encouraging metadata management as a routine activity.	Metadata is a type of documentation. As such, people approach it as a hurdle. Companies need to provide a viable infrastructure for metadata management to facilitate the practice. Furthermore, it needs to communicate and demonstrate its need as an incentive to make it part of the culture.
Using people familiar with the metadata repository to document the information instead of people familiar with the actual data and business rules.	A metadata repository or whatever else is used to create metadata is just a tool. Familiarity with it is obviously important, but no more than the knowledge about the data. It is a lot easier to train somebody familiar with the data to learn the tool than the other way around.
Expecting that one person or one particular LOB can do the job alone.	A Customer MDM repository is likely the integration of many data sources, and it is used by many LOBs. Therefore, it needs to be documented from all facets. This exercise in itself can be the foundation for creating a common understanding of data elements, their business purposes, and reconciling any differences.
Expecting to go from 0 to 100 within a single massive metadata management project.	Everything must have a business purpose, and metadata is no different. Simply creating metadata for the sake of it can lead to frustration, skepticism, and consequent failure. It is important to establish a goal, and prioritize what needs to be documented. Requiring every single element to be documented may be ideal, but not viable.

already included with an MDM solution. Sometimes those products can be cumbersome to use or take a long time to set up. Companies can implement their own metadata repository using a normal set of database tables, but that can take even longer. As usual, a diligent analysis should be performed before deciding on the best alternative.

Metadata management projects have a relatively high rate of failure. It happens usually because companies don't correctly define scope, set the correct expectations, and/or engage the right people. Table 3.1 presents some common problems faced by companies along with comments and suggestions for mitigating the issues.

Most companies are behind with their metadata creation, and as such, will likely require a dedicated project to catch up. But do so wisely. Understand the business needs and how the metadata repository can support the existing business processes, data governance, and data stewardship. Don't bite off more than you can chew.

For a metadata management program to be successful, it needs to be accessible to everybody that needs it, either from a creation or a consumption perspective. It should also be readily available to be used as a byproduct of other activities, such as data migration and data cleansing. Remember, metadata is documentation, and the closer it is generated to the activity affecting it, the better.

 ## SUMMARY

Companies need to approach MDM with an ecosystem mentality. Ecosystem definitions typically include *living species*, *habitat*, and their complex *interaction*. Analogically speaking, that is *people*, *technology*, and the complex *processes* around them. Proper balance and harmony is critical, and companies capable of adaptation will have a better chance of survival.

Admittedly, we got fairly technical in this chapter, but that's because there are a lot of technical decisions involved in preparing for and executing the transition to an MDM model. As stated in the introduction to this chapter, the line between IT and business is blurry, and requires deeper collaboration.

Understanding existing MDM tools as well as understanding your own data and how to integrate and maintain them are all critical steps that set the foundation and quality baseline for your master data environment. In the next chapters, we'll focus more on the people and process aspects involved in the implementation and ongoing management of the MDM practice, but for the implementation to start off soundly and become a successful initiative, it depends on how well the MDM engine has been primed with data that is well organized, structured, and supported by good tools.

 ## NOTES

1. Andy Hayler, "MDM: Selecting A Vendor," http://ecm.elearningcurve.com/Online_Selecting_MDM_Vendor_Course_p/mdm-03-a.htm.
2. Jim Harris, "Adventures in Data Profiling," www.ocdqblog.com/adventures-in-data-profiling/.

PART TWO

The Implementation Fundamentals

CHAPTER FOUR

Data Governance

Whenever the people are well-informed, they can
be trusted with their own government.

—Thomas Jefferson

INITIATING A CUSTOMER DATA GOVERNANCE MODEL

While you can initiate data governance without having an MDM practice,
you can't have an effective MDM practice without data governance. Data
governance is the glue in MDM. Without it, MDM will not be a cohesive sustainable practice. In a 2010 study conducted by The Information Difference,[1]
88 percent of the respondents felt that implementing data governance either
prior to or together with MDM and data quality is critical to the success of an
MDM initiative.

Defining and planning a Customer Data Governance (CDG) model should
start with an initial assessment and the groundwork necessary to drive a sound
charter and implementation proposal for your governance model. The assessment and proposal should predominantly be a business-driven initiative with
sponsorship at the vice president (VP) level to ensure strong commitment and

advocacy exists for establishing data governance. Within the sponsoring organization, there should be an existing director or senior manager appointed by the VP to lead the tactical aspects of the initiative. The sponsoring VP along with this tactical leader will be the driving force needed to get the data governance ball rolling.

Involvement of a consultant in the planning phase of your governance initiative can also be a major benefit. A consultant with a good track record in the MDM and data governance space can greatly assist in best practice evaluations, initial process or data quality assessments, gathering of metadata, evaluation of third-party MDM tools or services, preparation of reference material, or facilitation and planning of meetings. But always keep in mind that CDG needs to be developed as an organic business-driven function within the company. Consultants should only be leveraged in very specific roles to help establish the foundation for CDG or to help accelerate the implementation of CDG. Overuse of consultants will actually become a limiter and an ongoing cost factor that can potentially kill the program if budget constraints or reductions occur.

As a general rule, planning and initiating a CDG model is something that should be done early on, but data governance should never be implemented hastily. A bad model and charter will probably fail. There is an excellent white paper authored by Jill Dyché and Kimberly Nevala of Baseline Consulting entitled "Ten Mistakes to Avoid when Launching Your Data Governance Program."[2] We highly recommend you refer to this as you plan your governance initiative. The guidance and practical approaches we cover in this chapter should help to greatly avoid those mistakes. If your governance plan considers and implements a well-balanced approach across the aspects of data ownership, decision making, data stewardship, and data quality and control, a successful governance model will ensue and will be well equipped to handle the operating challenges and course corrections that can emerge in any company.

In the long run, data governance becomes less about the big decisions and macro-level control of the data, and becomes more about institutionalizing the consistent micromanagement of the data. Of course, the decision making, big rules, and the overarching influence of a data governance council are still critical, but over time the influence and mechanics of data governance should settle into the business fabric to form more of a day-to-day operation and quality management process that is comfortably interacting with the various LOB and IT functions.

Let's first take a look at an example of a high-level CDG process design and implementation approach shown in Figure 4.1. This will help explain the

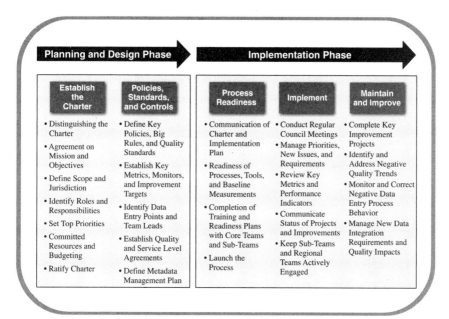

FIGURE 4.1 Example of CDG Process Design and Implementation Approach

overall planning and execution needed to achieve the end state. Then we'll break this down further to discuss the planning and implementation components.

PLANNING AND DESIGN

One of the first and most serious mistakes commonly made with implementing a data governance plan is that it is not considered and planned for early enough. The need for data governance usually emerges only after there has been widespread recognition and executive consensus that data quality and integrity problems are at a sufficient level of impact to warrant a governance focus. A lack of standardization and control of the data will eventually raise its ugly head during data integration or migration projects, or if compliance, privacy, or data security issues are creating risk factors, or if poor data is sufficiently hindering the ability to produce good business intelligence.

Often, large IT projects involving data migration and integration are planned, budgeted for, and launched without a data governance plan, only to quickly realize that there are many business issues with the data definition, usage, standards, mapping, and the acceptable level of quality that need to be resolved before the data migration requirements and integration processes can be completed. Had these issues been better anticipated and a governance forum created early on in the plan to address these issues, the project would have proceeded far more smoothly.

Early consideration and planning for data governance will pay its dividends later. Let's look at how to get a CDG planning and design process started.

Establishing the Charter

There can be any number of reasons why companies begin to recognize the need for data governance, such as:

- Historically, the management, quality, and control of a company's data have been lacking and that now is being acknowledged as causing significant operational, reporting, marketing, or customer satisfaction issues.
- Cross-functional discord due to quality problems, distrust of data, hoarding of data, or lack of a source of truth.
- Issues or risks related to legal or compliance requirements.
- Hardships with data migration and integration related to mergers or acquisitions.
- System infrastructure changes are driving need or opportunity for implementing data governance.

Whatever the drivers are, be sure to zero in on the fundamental needs along with how and where implementing data governance can effectively address the needs. Don't overshoot and assume that data governance can solve or control all the deep-rooted legacy data management or quality issues that have existed, or undershoot with doing just a test pilot focused on some low-hanging fruit that offers little challenge and will hardly exercise the intended governance process. A data governance initiative needs some meaty issues to be in scope, but also needs a realistic sense of approach. Success will be dependent on the governance council having both a dedicated MDM core team and aligned LOB-oriented data steward type teams who can address various tactical needs, data analysis, front-end tasks, user training, or clarification needs that are identified by the CDG process.

Distinguishing a Data Governance Charter

Data governance needs to be clearly distinguished from other types of governing bodies and steering committee charters that typically exist in a company.

Don't be surprised if in the initial discussions about data governance there may be some confusion or a perception of overlap with existing steering committees or change control processes that already exist in the LOB and IT practices. To distinguish and advance the data governance dialog, it will be necessary to firmly establish the fundamental positioning and purpose of an enterprise data governance initiative and how it will coexist with other type decision-making charters and processes. When positioned correctly, a data governance function can nicely fill a data management authority void and serve a very valuable role with an existing IT decision-making process and design methodology, as illustrated by Figure 4.2.

In general, building the data governance charter should start with gathering together the Customer MDM executive sponsor, as we discussed in Chapter 2, to define and agree on a clear mission, set of objectives, scope and jurisdiction, top priorities, key operating assumptions, the representation and commitment expected, and the budgeting and resource needs. Covering this

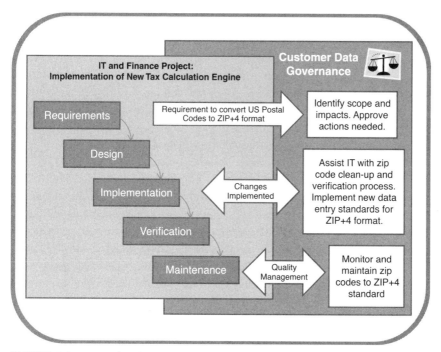

FIGURE 4.2 Example of CDG Interaction with IT Projects and Standard Design Methodology

may require a facilitated process and will likely take several meetings to iron out. In the next sections of this chapter, we provide more context and examples for the charter building and ratification process.

Mission and Objectives

For a CDG initiative, start by considering what will be the fundamental purpose, what will need to be controlled, and what are the key objectives. Answers to these questions will be the foundation of the charter. Following are some examples of statements that describe a Customer MDM charter:

- Establish processes, policies, and organizational principles around managing and protecting customer data as a corporate asset.
- Establish the authority and control board for the decisions related to managing the fitness, quality, and standardization of the targeted data assets.
- Establish Customer Data Governance as a core competency in the company.
- Implement Data Steward and Data Maintenance practices with clear accountability and responsibilities to ensure there will be comprehensive data management and quality management in place for the data assets.
- Enable data governance interaction and influence on the design of data management solutions (e.g., tools, processes, services) and the improvement or resolution of data quality issues (e.g., driving cleanup initiatives, sponsoring Bugs and RFEs, providing a help desk).

For the charter discussions, be sure you can put these statements and objectives into a realistic business case context to help sufficiently qualify the intent so that the executive can easily relate to the underlying data governance issues and needs. This will help enable the executives to more specifically provide their perspectives and expectations regarding these objectives. This is also a critical step in the process to establish executive buy-in and acceptance (remember the CAP equation: Quality × Acceptance = Effectiveness). Be sure there are no hidden agendas. This effort should truly be about implementing data governance practices and not an adjunct to, or reliant on, delivery of other specific business objectives.

Don't assume that the executives will just rubber-stamp your proposed charter. Do assume that you may just initially receive a lot of feedback indicating more clarification or detail is needed before decisions can be made.

As we said, the process to nail down and gain approval on a data governance charter will likely require a few rounds.

Scope and Jurisdiction

In preparing the charter, carefully consider, and be able to clearly express, what is in scope and what is out of scope. What is in scope should include the type of data assets and characterization of the types of decisions, policies, standards, systems, and process areas within the data governance jurisdiction. In addition to establishing policy, rules, and direction, governance needs to be both analytical and actionable, so be sure that the scope expresses this aspect, as well. In general, expect that any aspects of the scope could receive a lot of scrutiny and require refinement before gaining approval. Be clear about what is out of scope so that there is no confusion or charter conflict with other decision-making bodies or steering committees.

The scope of your CDG model can vary depending on the approach and positioning of your MDM initiative and how the executive sponsorship falls into place, but in general here are some statements that are examples of how to define and distinguish scope:

In Scope

- The definition and implementation of a customer data governance model.
- Defining and managing policies, rules, and standards governing the quality and integrity of the customer master data including the data entry and data maintenance practices, customer classification, segmentation, relationships, and hierarchy structure.
- Defining policies, standards, and rules related to definition of customer life cycle or 360° reporting views.
- Oversee the IT and business support practices associated with the quality, integrity, and maintenance of the customer master data assets.
- Ensure that the integrity and design of the common customer data model and structure is maintained. Ensure that no particular business practice can alter or compromise this design to accommodate their business needs while adversely impacting other practices and stakeholders using this same functional design and integrated model.
- Define and oversee customer data quality standards, goals, and measurements.

- Oversee all access to this master data. Ensure audit and gatekeeping processes are in place in that meet security, privacy, and other compliance requirements.
- Resource and budget planning for the ongoing customer governance process and core Data Steward and Data Maintenance functions.
- Oversee third-party tools and data or services necessary for enabling the governance practices or management and enrichment of the customer master data (e.g., D&B or other third-party data quality and enrichment services).

Out of Scope

- Data residing in other boundary system or processes areas that may be linked or associated with the customer master data but considered under the control and governance of other data entity or transaction process areas (e.g., products, suppliers, partners, employees, agreements, materials).
- Other transaction systems' or boundary systems' business rules, metadata, configurations, and policies defined for those processes that are not directly associated with the assets, rules, policies in scope of Customer Data Governance.
- Design, implementation, release management, or Change Control Board (CCB) functions related to specific infrastructure, applications, or processes that may utilize or interact with this master data. This data governance role and function should align and have influence with other IT or Business program functions or steering committees but will not be a replacement or overlapping management function for those other charters and jurisdictions.

Roles and Responsibilities

The charter should clearly define the roles and responsibilities expected in the governance model, but should not necessarily get hung up on dictating that only specific titles and job levels be engaged in the governance team. Yes, it is very important to involve the right leaders and influencers in a governance model, but equally important is to engage the *doers*, who are empowered to act on what needs to be addressed. Who is in command and control of the data can vary greatly across different business functions. This can typically vary between director, manager, analyst, functional lead, or IT consultant roles. Ensure that the person representing a business or IT function who has the best

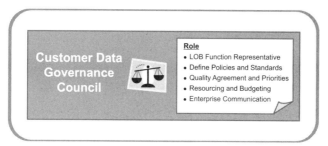

Role
- LOB Function Representative
- Define Policies and Standards
- Quality Agreement and Priorities
- Resourcing and Budgeting
- Enterprise Communication

Customer Data Governance Council

FIGURE 4.3 Customer Data Governance (CDG) Roles

ability to engage, understand, and execute governance actions is part of the team. Title is less important.

In Chapter 2, we presented an MDM roles and responsibility model (Figure 2.2) that presented a high-level list of the governance roles, which are shown here in Figure 4.3.

In the remaining sections of this chapter, we'll touch more on the context for each of these role descriptions, but as we discussed in Chapter 2, we want to reiterate that ownership and governance need to be a carefully orchestrated dynamic in a successful MDM practice. Because a Customer MDM practice is sufficiently complex due to its cross-functional nature, it will be necessary to plan and implement an effective cross-functional engagement model in combination with a well-defined and coordinated set of roles and responsibilities as part of the data governance process.

Most importantly, a LOB representative—typically a director or senior Manager—on the CDG council will need to have sufficient authority and influence with the functional team or teams that enter customer master data. Establishing a close and beneficial relationship with the functional teams is key to MDM success. A LOB representative who does not have sufficient authority and influence with these functional teams will not provide much value to the MDM initiative and CDG process. Insufficient authority and influence may also reflect a lack of genuine engagement or commitment from that LOB with regards to the MDM initiative and governance charter. Getting the right type of LOB representation on the CDG council may actually take a few attempts. Often, it is not until the CDG process has been initiated and the priorities and expectations are more fully vetted out, that the right type of representation will settle in.

Council members with sufficient authority and influence will typically need to work closely with designated data stewards or team leads in the LOB processes areas where the data entry occurs. These data stewards or leads will provide the ground-level eyes, ears, and task management focus needed to monitor, coordinate, and carry out specific actions driven from the CDG council.

Set Top Priorities

Set top priorities initially for activities that support immediate, actionable, and foundational needs that also align well with the overall CDG objectives and roadmap activities or are needed to help support critical operational problems that have been identified. Avoid setting top priority for interests that are too ambiguous, have too many dependencies, are not of immediate need, or simply don't have the right underlying foundation in place yet to realistically be addressed.

Let's again refer to the example we used earlier in the Figure 4.2 where there is a requirement to convert all U.S. postal codes associated with ERP activity from the current five-digit format to the nine digit (ZIP+4) format in order to support implementation of a new tax calculation engine. Let's just say that there is a six-month window to complete this conversion. In order to meet that goal there are a number of actions needed, such as to analyze the current state of the zip codes, determine the scope, impact, and amount of existing codes that need to be converted, use a U.S. postal code reference for address and zip verification, and ensure the data entry teams and BI teams are oriented and preparing for this change.

Each of these actions needs to be prioritized against each other so that the right sequence of actions and dependencies are addressed. For example, to initiate the data analysis and scope activities, there may be a concurrent set of immediate actions needed, such as a dependency on a reporting team or data analysts to run some current state reports, a business impact assessment needs to be conducted, and a need to immediately identify the method and cost for doing the postal code verification against the U.S. postal code reference. These actions become top priorities because of their immediate need and other activities being dependent on this. Once these initial top priorities are addressed, the next set of top priorities will emerge, and so on.

The CDG council needs to be very interactive and able to quickly address a variety of business- and IT-involved actions that will typically be part of MDM projects and issues.

Let's look at another example involving data migration and integration. A company-wide systems infrastructure initiative is underway where processes and data from various legacy systems are being migrated to a new integrated application suite that will be sharing a common customer master. The processes and data from the legacy systems will phase in over a two-year period. A similar situation may also exist in a merger or acquisition scenario. In either case, a CDG council may have to set top priority on support of the data migration plans and defer initiatives to improve various quality aspects of the customer master data until all or most of that data migration phases are completed and the data is in a fully integrated state.

In general, a CDG charter needs to be broad and specific enough to allow the council to always balance focus and decisions between efforts to improve data and quality management needs and with efforts to help address operational needs or issues related to data.

Resourcing and Budgeting

The formal interactions and decision making expected from the CDG council will be largely based on need, priority, time, and budget considerations similar to other business decision processes. And like all business functions, the CDG council will need to weigh new initiatives versus other priorities, support of ongoing functions, and possibly consider spend reduction in conformance with the fiscal plans of the company and the sponsoring organization. Because many Customer MDM activities, particularly data cleanup projects, will often require a cross-functional effort, the CDG executive sponsor and the other members of the CDG council will need to plan for and facilitate cross-functional budget planning and resourcing needs. This will be a critical success factor.

Inability to sufficiently anticipate and coordinate this dynamic can severely limit or even kill the ability for MDM to execute effectively. As an example, consider how your CDG council will need to handle these types of budgeting or resourcing scenarios:

- An annual budget is required for third-party services and licenses that are needed for customer data enrichment, credit management, customer research, customer entity matching, hierarchy management, or other needs.
- Incremental budget is needed to evaluate and potentially purchase some new data profiling and analytical tools that now are emerging in the MDM market that could greatly assist areas such as data analysis, quality assessment, and metadata management. These tools would give your data analysts and stewards the ability to get their jobs done more efficiently and effectively and with less dependency on IT support.

- Consultants are needed for a six-month project to help scope, define, and pilot a data quality dashboard requiring standardized validation rules and measurements that the CDG council will use to evaluate data quality and target where improvement needs to be focused.
- Some data security and compliance issues have been identified that require immediate attention and remediation by IT and certain business teams. Some resources will need to be temporarily shifted off of some existing projects to address this problem.
- Corporate spending has tightened up and each LOB is tasked with cutting back on projects and expenses. This will impact CDG-related projects and resources. The CDG council needs to reprioritize their plans and coordinate changes in line with the cutback expectations.

Be sure that the CDG council has the charter to be able to effectively address these types of scenarios.

Ratify the Charter

Once the charter has been fully defined and discussed by the CDG council, be sure that all executive sponsors and council members formally declare their approval for the execution of the charter. This ratification is critical for the communication and ongoing legitimacy of the CDG process. A clear and solid charter in place with an active and effective council will continue to demonstrate its value within the company and in coordination with other steering committee and decision-making processes.

Over time it may be necessary to adjust the charter and council member roles in line with organizational or other corporate changes that will typically occur in a company, but adjusting what has been a good existing charter should be a much easier task than having to build a new one.

Policies, Standards, and Controls

With the charter ratified and the council engaged, there are still some important CDG process planning and design activities that need to be addressed before preparing to launch the process.

Define Key Policies, Big Rules, and Quality Standards

Customer master data is largely a fixed asset with only a limited amount of ability to maintain, change, enrich, or cleanse it. Therefore, its value is highly dependent on how accurately the data is captured and how relevant that data is in context to its usage. The responsibility for this primarily falls on the data entry processes. These data entry processes are where the governance council needs to have sufficient influence to ensure that data standards, validation rules, and quality control expectations are actively involved in the process.

The ability to accurately capture customer identity info such as name, address, contact info, and tax IDs may seem to be a rather straightforward task, but then consider that it is often dependent on how and where a person enters this data and to what degree this data entry event is subject to a fixed format, validation rules, field length limitations, and so on. Local data entry behavior is typically influenced by the requirements and limitations associated with the particular application and business process being used. Then consider that these types of data entry conditions can vary by system, application, region, or country.

The net result is that the aggregate quality and consistency of this data from these various entry processes will undoubtedly be poor unless common rules, standards, and controls have been applied to these data entry processes by a governance process. This is where governance influence matters most. The extent that governance rules, standards, and monitoring capability can directly influence master data entry practices and specific work behavior— but without undue burden that could negatively impact transactional performance—will reflect how well data governance is effectively in motion with a company. Governance policies, rules, and standards will have little impact if they are not appropriately positioned and effectively enforced. Figure 4.4 reflects how data entry practices in an integrated environment need to be bound by common rules and standards.

Define Key Metrics, Monitors, and Quality Improvement Targets

There is nothing worse than a new governance council getting out the door only to find a blind alley. Once the charter and expectations are set, the CDG council and process will be expected to begin demonstrating effective monitoring and governance of the customer master data. To do this, there needs to be at least a baseline level of information available about the current state of the data and its quality. Therefore, before launching the CDG process the council needs to establish the necessary baseline information and ability to begin tracking this.

Key metrics—often called Key Performance Indicators (KPIs)—as well as a tracking process will need to be defined and initially implemented to start

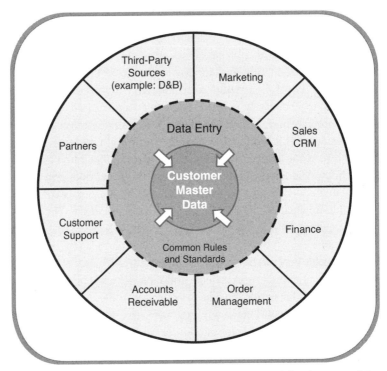

FIGURE 4.4 Common Standards and Rules with Entry of the Customer Master

serving as the Customer MDM baseline metrics and monitors when the CDG process is launched. These key metrics should generally cover at least the basic volume and quality measurements needed to report and monitor the fundamental statistics and incremental changes (at least weekly or monthly) associated with the customer master data. Chapters 6 and 8 will cover this in much more detail, but suffice to say that having a baseline understanding of the makeup, volumes, and quality of the customer master data is fundamental for the CDG council to operate effectively. This baseline data will also be necessary for setting any immediate priorities associated with quality improvement. With this baseline data, the CDG council should be able to at least start seeing the obvious quality issues or other concerns that should become targets for further analysis and improvement plans.

Once CDG is launched, it can be expected that there will be a need to further expand on the metrics and monitors in line with CDG objectives to drive more standardization, improve data quality, or monitor critical process events that can impact data integrity. Expansion of such metrics and monitors is a natural and ongoing aspect of an MDM practice.

Identify Data Entry Points and Team Leads

Similar to establishing metrics and monitors to at least ensure a baseline understanding of the customer master data and its quality, a CDG council needs to have a clear understanding of the customer master data entry points and what processes have create, update, and delete capability with this data. You can't begin to govern this if you don't know who is touching the data and where this is occurring.

As part of the CDG planning, an exercise needs to be conducted to identify these entry points, what business functions are involved, and who the team leads are for those processes. This is an exercise where a consultant can be very helpful with gathering and summarizing this information. The summarization of this can create a very valuable and maintainable matrix that will serve as a fundamental roadmap indicating who, how, and where in relation to the entry and change of customer master data. Table 4.1 provides a very basic example of this matrix. This type of matrix can, and probably should, be expanded to add other useful details related to the processes, rules, and maintenance teams associated with the data element and its touch-point conditions.

As we'll discuss and illustrate in more detail in the next chapters, establishing this type of roadmap and entry point detail will serve as a common and underpinning thread across Data Governance, Data Stewardship, Data Quality Management, and Data Access Management.

Quality and Service Level Agreements

There are essentially two levels of quality agreement that should be addressed. First, as part of the ratification of the CDG charter, there should be high-level agreement across the CDG board that ensures each board member is committed to the CDG mission, objectives, and the data quality management goals. Second, at the operational level it is good practice to implement service level agreements (SLAs) where appropriate with IT or between business teams where data maintenance expectations exist.

It's important that an SLA reflect reasonable expectations and corrective action time or it will quickly become an ineffective instrument that may have only resulted in creating contention between the parties if the expectations cannot be reasonably met. Also, consider that it is far better to allow some latitude and demonstrate some patience with regard to getting the support

TABLE 4.1 Example of a Data Entry Point Matrix

Master Data Attribute	Description	Entry Point	Contact	Capability (Create, Update, Delete)	Process Reference Info	Governance Reference Number
Customer name	Represents the customer legal entity name	Opportunity Management Process	[Contact Name]	C	[Reference number or URL to info]	[Reference number or URL to info]
		Customer Data Management Team	[Contact Name]	C,U,D		
Customer primary address	Main address or corporate address for the legal entity.	Opportunity Management Process	[Contact Name]	C,U	[Reference number or URL to info]	[Reference number or URL to info]
		Customer Data Management Team	[Contact Name]	C,U,D		
Taxpayer ID	Taxpayer identification number that serves as a unique identifier of this legal entity. The type of ID and format can vary by country.	Order Management Process	[Contact Name]	C,U,D	[Reference number or URL to info]	[Reference number or URL to info]
		Finance AR	[Contact Name]	U		
DUNS#	The DUNS number, a unique, nine-digit identification number assigned to business entities by Dun & Bradstreet	D&B Interface	[Contact Name]	C,U,D	[Reference number or URL to info]	[Reference number or URL to info]
		Marketing	[Contact Name]	U,D		

needed than to regularly disparage a support team for not always meeting the SLA terms and conditions. Support teams generally do want to meet their obligations and have happy customers, but backlogs, resource issues, and shifting priorities are all realities in the service delivery business. Quality improvement needs will typically compete with, and often take lower priority to, operational support needs. So keep this in mind and be prepared to accept or make adjustments to SLAs from time to time.

What's most important is to maintain a good flexible relationship between the data users and the support teams that will continue to enable support and address data maintenance needs as part of the ongoing ebb and flow between operational and data management practices.

Define Critical Metadata Management Needs

In Chapter 3, we spent some time on the topic of metadata management, including some of the challenges and problems associated with organizing and managing it. Although pulling together, managing, and maintaining metadata with a comprehensive cross-domain solution—usually requiring an IT solution—can be one of the more complicated and hard to achieve aspects of MDM, from a customer data governance perspective, there are a few areas of metadata that will be critical to focus on and ensure that this information is accurate and easily available for reference by the CDG council.

Entity Relationship Diagram (ERD)   Often, this is metadata that only the IT or business reporting teams are familiar with or have access to. Being at least generally familiar with the conceptual representation of the customer master data should also be a requirement for the CDG Council, MDM core team, and other associated data steward teams that are engaged in overall MDM practice. Having an ERD easily accessible, or even printed in hard copy and posted on your office or cubicle wall, is a great way to stay familiar with the data model.

Data Dictionary or Attribute Listing by Entity Type   Again, this is also metadata that isn't often generally available to the business teams, but typically will exist somewhere along with the ERD. If a formal metadata repository exists, there should be some form of a data dictionary there. Depending on what work went into creating the data dictionary, the level of detail may vary significantly. What's most important is that for each data element associated with a data entity (as represented by the ERD), there is at least the name, definition, size, type, and any relevant comments related to use and ability to modify the data element. In some cases, not all of these data elements will actually be implemented, and there should be information in the application setup documentation indicating what data elements were actually implemented and if any custom elements were defined and implemented. An accurate and well-maintained data dictionary, or other form of data attribute listing by entity type, is must-have reference information for a data governance process. In the Data Stewardship and Data Access Management chapters we'll see how this type of reference information is utilized in the various data management tasks.

Data Element Business Definition　The previously mentioned data dictionary or attribute listing will typically just reflect the generic out-of-the-box data definitions and descriptions. As the applications that use these data models are set up and implemented there is typically some form of adaptation to business practices and business definition that will replace or add to the generic data definition. Capturing and managing this business definition should be a key responsibility of the data governance process in alignment with IT and any general metadata management practices. All business definition of the data should be maintained directly with the existing data dictionary or data attribute listing so there no confusion or conflicting references to the data definition.

Policies and Standards　A data governance council and process need to ensure that data governance policies and standards are well documented, communicated, and enforced. The governance council needs to define a simple method where such policies and standards can be easily referenced. If a company already has a flexible metadata management solution in place, then adding or linking to policies and standards information should be able to be accommodated, but often that will not be the case. Short of that, the CDG council and the MDM core team should determine what other documentation and posting methods can best serve this need. In many cases, the policies and standards will relate to specific data entity areas or even specific data elements (e.g., customer name or address standards, DUNS or SIC code standards, data privacy policy and rules). In such cases, the CDG council should consider how to cross-link policies and standards with the data dictionary or data attribute listing. Being able to identify the policies and standards associated with specific data entities or elements is, quite simply, good governance practice.

Mapping and Cross-Reference Information　Some form of data mapping and system cross-reference tables will typically exist in an MDM environment. In Chapter 1, we covered various MDM architectures where data mapping and cross-reference tables are involved. Whether that is in relation to how converted data was mapped to the master data model, how data is mapped over a systems interface, or how a systems cross-reference table is maintained to express how entities such as parties and sites are connected between systems and what the original source of data is, understanding this mapping and cross-reference data is critical to understanding the integrity, origin, and reach of the data. Not being able to understand this mapping and cross-reference can lead to uninformed decisions that can severely impact many stakeholders in the food chain of the master data.

Additional types of reference information related to data quality, volumes, users, types of usage, and access to or maintenance of the data, is also critical information that the CDG Council will need to be able to reference and potentially associate to the previously mentioned metadata areas, but because we don't consider this additional information to necessarily be considered metadata—as opposed to just being metrics or type of operational information—we cover the description and need for this additional reference information more specifically in other chapters.

Since the common types of metadata can represent a large amount of detail about the data, what's most important is to zero in on—and to more conveniently summarize if needed—the metadata that will frequently be needed to accurately understand the structure, definition, policies, standards, and where applicable, how the customer master data is mapped or linked to other data in the overall architecture and boundary system model. Understanding and being able to easily reference this key metadata is essential to developing the core knowledge and underlying awareness that a CDG Council and the associated data analysts and stewards must possess. This type of metadata should not be buried or restricted to just IT access.

 ## IMPLEMENTATION

As indicated in the prior section, there needs to be a reasonable amount of planning and design focus before a CDG process is ready to implement. Assuming that due diligence has occurred in the planning and design phases, let's now go through the key components of the implementation phase.

Process Readiness

Once again, there is nothing worse than a new governance council getting out the door only to be caught unprepared in a blind alley. In fact, it is very possible that once the CDG charter is communicated there will be an abundance of data quality and data management issues that emerge, which have been fostering for some time but have previously lacked an appropriate process into which they could be channeled. Be prepared to demonstrate the value and effectiveness of CDG on day one. To do this, the following readiness areas need to be addressed.

Communication of Charter and Implementation Plan

As with implementation of any major business process, there needs to be a communication plan to sufficiently broadcast the purpose and launch of the process. With the charter approved, it should be able to be internally posted and summarized for general communication purposes. Communication of the charter along with the expected implementation dates should come from the Customer MDM executive sponsor or sponsors. The executive sponsors, CDG Council members, and the MDM core team should all be clearly identified in the communication. The communication should also include or point to a clear description of how to engage the CDG process. It is important to emphasize any key scope and jurisdiction points in the body of the communication, so that the audience clearly understands the CDG purpose. For example, it may be important to emphasize that the CDG process is not a replacement for other existing IT and business decision-making bodies or steering committees.

Readiness of Process, Tools, and Baseline Measurements

Some process readiness checks may be necessary to fully validate how the process will be engaged, executed, and how various outcomes will likely occur. First, consider how issues and requests should be submitted to the CDG process. For example, what level of information and qualification will be required with the request? Can anyone fill out and submit a formal request or should a request be first reviewed with an organization's representative in the CDG council and only that representative can submit and sponsor the request? Either approach may be valid, but these types of process questions need to be considered and the expectations set correctly.

In any case, what's most important is that the CDG process will receive a well-qualified request that has business justification which can be acknowledged and further represented by a council member. Submitting issues that the council members cannot clearly understand, recognize, or consider sponsoring will only either demonstrate a disconnect between the council members and the requesting parties, or indicate a submission process problem where the detail and prequalifications needed to construct a solid request are lacking or not being enforced. Receiving well-articulated and qualified requests is a necessary first step to enable a good review and decision-making process. It's okay for the CDG process to reject poorly prepared requests, but always try to provide some feedback or further instructions that will help the requester understand the requirements for submitting a request.

Upon receiving a solid request, the CDG council should give the request appropriate review and quickly provide next step expectations to the requester. The request may require additional analysis or measurements to which often only certain data analysts, stewards, or IT roles can respond. This is another example of why an MDM core team and the regional data stewards all need to be part of the CDG network. These analyst and steward roles need to have sufficient tools and data access capability to conduct their assessments and provide accurate information related to the request. Chapter 6 will take a deeper dive into the actual process and tools used within a data quality management forum. That forum will typically be a sub-team function of the CDG process where many of the CDG requests will eventually go so that more specific analysis can be conducted or action plans initiated.

As the CDG process is ready to launch, be sure the necessary sub-teams, tools, data mining capabilities, and quality assessment measurements are ready to utilize as needed. Not being prepared with these capabilities could cause weeks if not months of delays while attempting to get other functions and resources to assist with these sizing and analysis needs.

Completion of Training and Readiness Plans with Core Teams and Sub-Teams

The council members, the MDM core team, and any related sub-teams or regional data stewards are likely to need some form of training or orientation to any new policies, standards, processes, tools, environments, documentation, metrics, metadata, or other collateral associated with the implementation and ongoing operational aspects of the CDG process. Ensure that all associated teams and key stakeholders are sufficiently familiar with the CDG related terminology, practices, and team members, and can easily get to CDG reference info.

Launch the Process

If all the prior mentioned elements related to planning, communication, and readiness have been sufficiently addressed, then the actual launching of the process should simply be a matter of having the executive sponsor send a final communication about the CDG process launch and generally thanking all sponsors, stakeholders, and team members who have contributed to the planning and implementation process. The various council members and any regional data steward teams can assist with any local channeling and launch communication needs.

Implement

Be sure that the implementation and ongoing process reflects good habits, maintains awareness of data quality trends and operational events that can impact or enhance the customer master data, continues to inform stakeholders of CDG actions and events, and keeps team members actively engaged so that the process of data governance is a continuously active and vital component of the overall Customer MDM practice. Next, we'll cover some of basic guidelines to follow.

Conduct Regular CDG Council Meetings

CDG should not be an as-needed process. In a Customer MDM environment, there are going to be more than enough challenges, need for policies, standards and quality improvement, ongoing data management and maintenance tasks, and so on, that should keep a CDG council, process, and associated teams continuously busy. Ensure that cross-functional and regional interests are being well served. Don't become focused on one region or one business area. There certainly will be issues and priorities that are associated with specific functions or regions, but in general, a Customer MDM initiative depends on the data governance process to drive global standards and consistent data management practices.

Over time, MDM and CDG influence will hopefully become well embedded in the company's business model with various processes and teams operating in self-monitoring and self-correcting modes. This will reflect that data governance has reached a mature and steady state. In this state the CDG council may not need to meet as frequently, but should always continue to keep a strong pulse going and clear focus on the Customer MDM environment.

Manage Priorities, New Issues, and Requirements

A robust CDG process should be regularly revisiting existing priorities and putting them into context with any new issues or requirements that have emerged. New needs come into play frequently that shouldn't be ignored or just added to the bottom of an existing queue. Expect that some new items may be of high priority and that some existing items may become less important or drop out of focus due to a change of need or circumstances since that item was initially submitted. In all cases, be sure to maintain an up to date list, ranking, and status of the items in the CDG queue, and regularly review this with the CDG council members and any other key stakeholders associated with the open items. In some cases, a large task or project in the queue may need to be broken out into smaller projects due to dependencies, resource constraints, or to better manage any associated impacts.

In general, when considering items for prioritization, make sure these fit within a reasonable time frame and expectation of execution. For example, for large data integration or data cleanup projects, there are often multiple phases associated with the overall execution plan. In such cases, it would be reasonable to focus CDG attention and priority just on the immediate needs and priorities associated with the current phase and perhaps the preparation needed for the next phase. Longer-term objectives often need more vetting out and are likely to be dependent on the execution and status of the current and nearer-term priorities.

Regularly Review Key Metrics and Performance Indicators

We previously mentioned that setting up key metrics and performance indicators is a necessary step in the CDG readiness phase in order to avoid the blind alley problem at implementation. And similar to having regular reviews of the CDG priorities and new requirements, the CDG council needs to keep a watchful eye on the key metrics and performance indicators from both a volume and quality perspective. In Chapters 6 and 8, we'll get into much more detail regarding quality management and the type of measurements needed, but it will be incumbent on the CDG council, and likely a data quality forum, to track the throughput and quality of the customer master data to fully understand and appreciate how people, process, and system events impact this data. And as is often said, it's very hard to control what can't be seen and measured.

We opened this chapter stating that you can't have an effective MDM practice without data governance. To add to that perspective, you really can't have effective data governance without having good measurements. So, be sure that key metrics and performance indicators are established and regularly reviewed in the CDG process.

Communicate Status of Projects and Improvements

Establish a broad and regular cadence of CDG communication to the sponsoring executives, core team, extended team members, and other stakeholders who will have interest or be impacted by projects and decisions. If anything, initially over-communicating about CDG is probably a good thing in order to raise awareness and to gauge who the interested audiences really are. Keep general communications succinct and well organized using a standard format as much as possible, and provide references or links to where more detail can be easily found if needed. Communications may need to be tailored for different audiences, but as a general rule don't inundate the audience with too much detail and be sure the audiences know who represents them on the CDG council or other sub-teams should they need to inquire about anything.

Communicate good and bad news quickly to ensure that awareness and opportunity for feedback is immediately available. Communicating about data quality improvements, project plans and achievements, new policies and standards, and so on, will generally be well received where the audiences have been advocating for and anticipating these results. But keep in mind that CDG actions or decisions can have a far-reaching effect and it's always possible that someone wasn't previously engaged sufficiently and may still have inputs or issues to raise that require a response.

Keep Sub-Teams and Regional Teams Actively Engaged

The CDG process needs to be active and participatory from the council members down to the front-end teams who enter the customer master data. That's not to say that CDG meetings should be conducted as large community gatherings allowing everyone from all levels to have their say. Rather, an enterprise-wide CDG process should consist of a top-level council supported by various interactive forums or sub-teams, which allow the extended teams and regional data stewards to participate effectively in the planning and execution of CDG initiatives. It's this active network of engaged data management–minded folks that creates the channeling and community framework that enables the whole MDM practice to thrive.

Because in Customer MDM there are typically many regional and local aspects to the data, processes, policies, and standards, there has to be a solid connection and level of interaction throughout the governance process with the regional and local teams.

Maintain and Improve

So far we have stressed the need to carefully plan, prepare, and implement a CDG model that will have sufficient recognition, reach, and impact across the enterprise. Achieving this objective is only half of the end state equation. Being able to also maintain a steady state, drive improvement in data quality, and increase data management effectiveness is the other half of the equation. Our next chapters will cover the details and techniques for maintaining and improving customer master data, but as with most everything that makes up and enables an MDM practice, it's the data governance team and process that has the responsibility to navigate this, make any necessary course corrections, and to ensure the MDM motor is well tuned and reaching its destination. Let's review some of the basics for maintaining and improving.

Complete Key Improvement Projects

While this may seem to be pretty obvious advice, in the data management arena it is not unusual for projects to be dropped or only partially addressed. As we have already mentioned, in the grand scheme of things data management and data quality improvement projects will typically take lower priority than other system, application, or operational projects. A key aspect of the CDG charter is to raise the visibility and level of importance for data management and data quality improvement projects. A well-established CDG council should be able to establish this, but will also need to demonstrate value by ensuring that these projects are well planned, funded, resourced, and executed in a timely manner. Successfully achieving this will depend on having those data analysts, data stewards, and sub-teams ready and able to be engaged.

Not having these resources and processes ready to be engaged will put the viability of the project into question or will create critical path issues that are likely to delay the project or reduce its scope. Failure of MDM projects to get initiated or sufficiently completed are signals of either an underlying issue with a company's commitment to MDM or ineffectiveness of the CDG council and process.

Success always breeds more opportunity, so be sure that the overall value proposition associated with the Customer MDM initiative and its data governance component can be successfully demonstrated through good planning and completion of projects that achieve the expected results.

Identify and Address Negative Quality Trends

Particularly in a large company, there is typically an expected amount of change or shift with customer-oriented operations. This can come from new systems and processes being introduced, organizational change, change in call center operations, change in partner models or vendors, mergers or acquisitions, or simply employee turnover. Any of these types of changes can impact what has been standard operating practice, which can have any number of impacts on the quality and integrity of the customer master data. If good data governance practices have already been well institutionalized, then many types of changes will still be subject to standards, training, and requirements that at least continue to maintain, and not degrade, the quality level of the customer data.

But where data governance is just getting off the ground and creating awareness, it will probably not have the proactive influence yet on many of these types of changes. This means that data governance will initially need to take more of a reactive stance when these changes occur and rely on its ability to monitor and respond accordingly if any negative data quality trends start to occur. This point further emphasizes the need to have good metrics, monitors, and regular reviews in place. Quick identification of a negative trend will allow the best opportunity to analyze the root cause and initiate corrective action plans.

Monitor and Correct Negative Data Entry Process Behavior

We talked earlier in this chapter about creating a data entry point matrix (see Table 4.1) that will indicate who, what, and where in regard to the process and authority to create, update, and delete specific data. This type of matrix in association to specific reports or monitors should serve as a guidance to determine if and where unexpected data entry behavior is occurring. In subsequent chapters, we'll provide more specific discussion and examples of this, but generally expect that either because of training issues or insufficient data access control, it will not be unusual to find authorized users who knowingly or unknowingly are not following data entry rules and standards.

Where the CDG council and the data stewards are already aware of where bad behavior is occurring, they should be prepared to address this quickly. However, being able to recognize these conditions and patterns is not often easy and may be a competency that develops over time. As long as there are sufficient baseline metrics, monitors, and reporting capabilities as part of the CDG process, the core team and extended data steward roles will begin to recognize bad behavior associated with the data entry points and practices. Recognizing this behavior is essential to developing control mechanisms that need to become part of an effective and mature CDG model.

Manage New Data Integration Requirements and Quality Impacts

Earlier in this chapter (Figure 4.2), we touched on how data governance can interact and serve a valuable role in the design and implementation of IT and business projects. And as we covered in Chapter 1, in an MDM initiative there is invariably some form of data integration that results in the creation of a master repository or system of reference. The CDG process should be highly engaged in the migration planning and integration process for any project that involves customer master data. Data integration efforts are one of the very best opportunities for data governance to become engaged and set the stage for data quality and integrity.

In Chapter 6, we discuss the dynamic between data governance with data quality management (Figure 6.4). This dynamic can be highly leveraged during large data migration and integration projects because these projects involve mapping of data from one source to another that will usually require business interpretation of the data and standards to be adopted where differences exist. A CDG council should ensure that any external data that will be integrated into the customer master data must meet certain data quality and integration standards. This is necessary so that the overall customer master data will not be significantly degraded by the integration of new data. Some quality and integrity compromises are likely to exist with integration of new data. The CDG council needs to be fully aware of this and engaged in decisions about such compromises.

 SUMMARY

Let's use a simple analogy to help summarize the need for and benefit of good data governance. Think of cases where you have seen good city and community planning, such as where a municipality has done well to improve roadways, parks, alleviate traffic issues, has initiated better trash and recycle programs, and improved the water and sewer systems to ensure cleaner, healthier water. These are improvements that better all the communities and make day-to-day life more pleasant and rewarding. These improvements all take planning, budgeting, commitment, execution, and maintenance over the long term, but are recognized to be vital to the health and welfare of the residents.

Good data governance is very much the same. Understand what data is vital to the health and welfare of the business, drive improvements to the quality and availability of the data to make these assets more valuable and utilized, and ensure there is ongoing budgeting and caretaking to maintain the health and integrity of these assets.

NOTES

1. The Information Difference Company Ltd., "How Data Governance Links MDM and Data Quality," August 2010.
2. Jill Dyché and Kimberly Nevala, "Ten Mistakes to Avoid when Launching Your Data Governance Program," Baseline Consulting Group, White Paper, 2009.

CHAPTER FIVE

Data Stewardship

If you care enough for a result, you will most certainly attain it.

—William James

FROM CONCEPT TO PRACTICE

In previous chapters, we have touched on the importance of data steward roles. Whether these roles will exist within a formal data steward job title or within other job titles, most important is that these roles will truly support the concept and practice of data stewardship as an underlying discipline and success factor for MDM.

Data stewardship runs deep through all of Customer MDM, therefore the MDM plan needs to develop a firm concept of how a data steward model will look and function, where the data steward roles will be most critical, and how the right resources will be identified and engaged. Once the concept of data stewardship is fully recognized and a model is defined, it boils down to a combination of the people, processes, and a data caretaking focus that will establish the practice of data stewardship. These three critical elements are where we'll focus most of our time in this chapter.

But before we dive further into these elements, it's important to recognize that exactly who, where, and how data stewards will be engaged will be highly dependent on how the overall MDM and data governance practices will be defined and executed. Earlier in this book, while discussing the planning aspects of MDM, we pointed out that implementing a successful Customer MDM initiative starts with choosing the right approach that will drive the proper fitting of the MDM practices to an enterprise architecture and business model. The existing enterprise architecture and business model will consist of many specific functions, processes, teams, and job roles that already interact with the customer master data. Therefore, the concept and practice of data stewardship needs to be clearly embedded in the key junction points between the entry and management of the master data.

In this chapter, we will discuss many opportunities where these data steward roles can be applied, but it will be critical for the MDM core team and data governance council to sufficiently understand their business model, the ebb and flow of their customer data, and where to best inject data stewards so that the practice of data stewardship has a broad foothold to support a Customer MDM model. In any MDM model, data stewards cannot just be agents for data governance policy and standards; they need to also be closely aligned to the touch points and consumers of the master data where data entry, usage, and quality control can be most influenced.

 PEOPLE

Customer MDM has a lot of layers of complexity and cross-functional involvement. As these layers become better understood and reveal the coordination needed to successfully drive data quality improvement initiatives, it will be the data stewards who will make the difference between poor and successful execution of the initiatives. For example, it should not come as a surprise if in the analysis of a significant data quality issue, the mitigation plan will require a number of orchestrated tasks from a number of committed resources from across business and IT functions. Often, the IT expertise and resources will already exist—although they may not be immediately available—but on the business side, the resources, skills, and the time commitment needed are often nonexistent or will only partially exist. Business functions or geographies that are most impacted by the problem may try to offer some resources on a short-term or part-time basis. In other situations, use of contractors may have to be considered, but often the cost associated with that has not been planned in

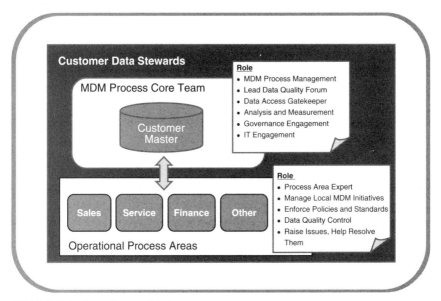

FIGURE 5.1 Data Steward Roles

anyone's budget—all of which makes it repeatedly difficult to get data management and quality improvement projects underway and fully completed.

Now, contrast that with a scenario where data steward roles have been considered and positioned across the business in key functional and regional areas, are sufficiently skilled and empowered, and can immediately help support the projects and priorities determined through the data governance process. This scenario demonstrates that there is process readiness and business commitment to data management and quality improvement.

In Chapter 2, we presented an MDM roles and responsibility model (Figure 2.2) that included a high-level view of data steward functions and roles shown in Figure 5.1.

Let's take a more detailed look at these functions and roles.

MDM Process Core Team

These are the data steward resources focused primarily on the business support and data quality management of the actual customer master environment. This core team and its management layer should be considered the owners of the overall Customer MDM process as well as the caretakers of the customer master environment with a focus across various roles and responsibilities, which we'll be describing further.

MDM Process Management

The fundamental disciplines of a Customer MDM implementation (governance, data stewardship, quality management, and data access management) will contain the majority of the ongoing processes that make up the MDM process model. In addition, there will be other more incidental and discrete processes related to planning, budgeting, vendor management, data integration, and so on. The coordination and management of all these processes, such as when they are engaged, how well they are performing, and where to adjust the dials on them so that the overall MDM goals and objectives are being supported correctly, will be a key focus of the manager and lead data stewards on the MDM core team.

This core team is where executive dashboard formats should be developed and maintained that reflect the performance, quality, and operational well-being of the Customer MDM practice as a whole. These dashboards will typically summarize key status or statistical trends related to governance, data quality, data volume, and budget spend, as well as highlighting the top issues and accomplishments.

This type of status provided or presented by the MDM core team should be part of a regularly scheduled review process between the core team and the CDG council. Outside of the CDG council, there may also be other executive or stakeholder teams that will request similar types of presentations as part of their business review processes or simply due to interest in the Customer MDM initiative. It is good practice to always be prepared with timely and accurate information that can be readily presented regarding the Customer MDM operations.

Lead the Data Quality Forum

In Chapter 6, we will cover the purpose and the content of the data quality forum. This forum should be led by a role we describe as the *data quality lead*. This lead role should be a part of the MDM process core team, and in addition to facilitating the data quality forum, should also drive the creation and reporting of the data quality metrics and may often need to participate in the CDG council meetings to drive data quality agenda items. The person in this role will work closely with other data quality specialists or analysts in the data quality forum who are representing their functional or regional areas, and this person may also need to represent Customer MDM as part of a broader data quality interest group within the company.

Data Access Gatekeeper

System and data access control has historically been an IT-directed task, and usually carried out in response to a user-submitted and manager-approved request, which may also be subject to security or system access rules that IT will check before granting the permission. In some cases, a user may automatically be provided certain default data access capabilities based on his job role. Unfortunately though, and all too often, this is where awareness and control of user access to the data starts and stops. A lack of sufficient ongoing review and management of user access capabilities will contribute to poor data management and accumulation of excessive capabilities by users, and will make it increasingly difficult to quickly spot and prevent unexpected access or changes to the master data.

In an MDM environment with a customer master that is shared across an application suite and can involve other interfaced systems, there may be a complex variety of data access needs from various user groups involving different combinations of create, update, delete, or read-only type requirements. Often, the customer master application will only provide generic and default data access capabilities and user roles that do not necessarily align well with a company's actual operational practices. In other words, these generic capabilities and roles may be too narrow or too broad and often hard to customize to better fit the business model. If these are applied as defaults, there may be some immediate data access issues that emerge such as users complaining of too little access and not being able to get their jobs done; or if too much access is granted, this can lead to overexposure and ensuing change control problems with the data.

In a broadly used Customer MDM environment, the methodology and control practices related to access management need to be more rigorous and should involve a business gatekeeper function associated with the MDM core team. This gatekeeper function will be expected to define and manage a more robust set of checks and controls in the process that will maintain a tighter and more accurate management focus on who has and receives authority for direct access. This gatekeeper process will be an additional layer injected into the overall access control process which will typically still require a user request, manager approval, and IT to fulfill the request. In Chapter 7, we will go into greater detail on the topic of data access management, along with how to define and manage a gatekeeper function.

Analysis and Measurement

Data stewards need to be analytically minded and need to largely function through the ability to measure, monitor, and maintain various data management and quality elements within a targeted or acceptable range of performance. Previously, we have stressed the importance of having metrics, monitors, and reporting capabilities in place to immediately support data governance and data steward functions. In most cases, it will be the MDM core team that will keep a close eye on these measurements and their trends in accordance with the MDM objectives and CDG standards.

Through regular review and analysis of these measurements and monitors, subtle behavioral aspects of the operational process will be discovered, which can often have significant impact on the integrity and quality of the master data if not managed correctly. Like many things, the more you study something and watch its behavior, the more you learn about how the microaspects support or impact the overall system. Following are a few such examples from a Customer MDM perspective:

- **Example 1.** The customer master data quality metrics are showing an unexpected increase in customer account duplication following implementation of an interface with a new partner management application. Upon further analysis, it appears that on the partner management side a country code attribute was not set up as a mandatory field. This code is necessary to help determine the legal entity and country specific distinction for accounts under the same parent company. When this country code is not entered, there can appear to be duplicate accounts. Changing this to become a mandatory field and updating existing accounts that originated from the partner application resolved the duplication problem.
- **Example 2.** In the initial phase of a data migration plan, the customer master volume metrics are showing a disproportional ratio of new accounts versus account sites being created. The rule is that all customer entities being migrated should have at least one site designated as the account site, but the migration volumes are showing more accounts than account sites. After further analysis, it was discovered that in some of the data sets being migrated, there were special internal accounts or other exception cases that may not have account sites. The migration logic was corrected to exclude these cases, and any such cases were removed from the customer master.
- **Example 3.** A monitor is in place that reports cases where the customer name in the customer name field has been changed. There are specific

rules and standards that apply to name changes, and only certain authorized groups are allowed to make such changes. The monitor is indicating that some non-authorized users have made name changes. After further investigation, it was determined that a new customer service group had the ability to update the customer name field and was unaware of the control process that should have been followed for name changes. The training for this customer service group was updated to cover the name change process, and the capability to update the customer name field was removed from their data entry forms.

In Chapters 6 and 8, we will dive further into the implementation of data quality management, monitoring, and maintenance practices, but it is these practices that are a central part of the MDM core team's role and analytical focus. From this, the core team will be able to better understand the checks and balances needed in a successful Customer MDM practice. That includes not only understanding how and where to work with the operational process areas and regional data stewards to address corrective action needs, but also—very importantly—to recognize and praise where good quality management practices are occurring in the regional and local teams.

Governance Council Engagement

The MDM core team will generally be the primary engagement point for the CDG council. Although the council members will be expected to directly represent their operational or regional business function, if at the data steward level there is a well-functioning relationship between the MDM core team and the operational process teams, most any significant quality and governance issues should already be visible at the data steward layer with active dialog or analysis in process before the CDG council is actively engaged. In other words, the data stewards associated with the MDM core team and operational process areas should be constantly checking pulse, communicating, and pre-evaluating the open issues and needs prior to engaging the CDG council. In many cases, these data steward teams can address the issues without even needing CDG involvement.

In cases where CDG should be engaged, it will be through this pre-evaluation process that CDG agenda items will need to get properly prepared and presented to the council. Remember, the council will not typically want, nor be able to act on, any items that are not well prepared for their review and decision-making process. In Chapter 4, we discussed how the CDG process should provide a clear set of submission guidelines, a standard format for providing content, and what the process expectations will be.

The MDM core team manager can serve a valuable role in having the responsibility to monitor CDG submissions, ensure guidelines are met, and to facilitate these submissions as part of the CDG council meetings. With these types of roles and responsibilities in place, the MDM core team should become the primary engagement point for the CDG council. This makes sense because the majority of CDG decisions that will require further support will usually be directed back to the MDM core team to act on or define more specific action plans. Therefore, the MDM core team should play an active role in the CDG process.

IT Engagement

Similar to what we just described regarding the core team's role with the CDG process, this team should also be actively engaged in the IT engagement process. Because this MDM core team is providing the business representation for the customer master data and its associated processes, this team needs to be highly involved in IT activities or requests that are related to the customer master data or can have impact on the overall customer operational process. In most cases, this will involve IT-oriented service requests or change requests that are targeted at the system or process points where the customer data is entered or maintained.

In the previous chapter, we pointed out how having data touch-point mapping will greatly assist with identifying where the customer master data is entered or maintained. This mapping will also largely represent the system and process points for any service requests or change requests where the MDM core teams needs to be engaged. In a best case scenario, one or more members of the MDM core team should be formally engaged in the review and approval path for these types of requests. Usually the IT engagement process, similar to the CDG process, will require specific detail and business justification before the request can be further acted on. The MDM core team should be engaged as needed in the preparation of this. Although many general types of IT service requests or change requests can often be handled without CDG council involvement, it is important for the IT process, the CDG council, and the MDM core team to collectively determine the guidelines for how and when to engage CDG with these types of requests.

Operational Process Areas

A comprehensive customer data stewardship model should include data stewards representing the operational teams in sales, marketing, finance, services, and potentially other business functions that are the primary creators, updaters, and consumers of the customer master data. These operational area data stewards work closely with the MDM core team to form an extended customer data steward team responsible for the day-to-day quality focus and data management practices associated with the customer master data. Depending on the makeup of data governance council and the data quality forum dynamics, these data stewards may also be closely involved in those processes.

What is most important is that these operational areas are represented and highly engaged in the Customer MDM model in order to create that top-down and bottom-up data management dynamic discussed in Chapter 2. Let's take a closer look at the responsibilities associated with an operational area data steward role.

Process Area Expert

As we often point out, data stewards need to be dedicated to the MDM mission, have specific roles and responsibilities, and be actively engaged. A passive data stewardship model will not offer much value. Active engagement is accomplished through having specific, data management oriented processes and participation expectations that enable the process area data stewards to be continually engaged. This essentially boils down to two types of expertise that are needed from the data stewards:

1. Being well versed in the overall operational process area they represent, the local business practices associated with it, and the specific process points (e.g., tools, forms, interfaces, reporting, and so on) in that process area that interact with the customer master data.
2. Being fully aware of how the local data entry and management practices can influence or impact the larger MDM picture, and vice versa, how MDM practices or changes can influence or impact the local operational practices.

The ability to leverage this type of process area expertise within a data management context is extremely valuable and necessary for a successful MDM practice. In the past, this type of expertise and context was often only recognized and leveraged by local business reporting teams, or simply may not have been utilized at all. With the emergence of MDM disciplines, this type of expertise can be highly utilized via the data steward roles.

Manage Local MDM Initiatives

From the CDG process and Data Quality forum there will be various initiatives that emerge that can range from complex data migration and integration projects to fairly simple and one-time data cleanup projects. Most such initiatives will have some level of impact to the operational or reporting processes, or at least should require the need for an assessment to determine if there are any impacts. In either case, the process area data stewards—in conjunction with the data council member who represents that business function—will be the point persons who will need to help manage the initiative or at least be accountable for specific action items.

These data stewards will usually work within a specific protocol or action plan framework that the MDM core team, CDG process, or data quality forum has defined, depending on from where the action is being driven. Depending on the depth and complexity of the actions needed, the data steward may need to engage with various teams in the operational areas. Any issues or concerns that emerge with planning or executing the activity should immediately be discussed between the data steward and the CDG council member to determine how to best address the situation. The actions taken or mitigation plans related to issues should all be part of a closed-loop process with the initiating team. Not having effective accountability and closure with local initiatives and actions can often result in later discovery that all expected actions were not fully or properly executed, accompanied by an inability to trace those steps or the root causes of the situation further.

Enforce Policies and Standards

As discussed in Chapter 2 with the topic of ownership, local enforcement of policies and standards is critical in the ecosystem of MDM. Enforcement is a key responsibility of the process area data stewards. Through the governance process, the data stewards should be given sufficient orientation and reference information to understand how and where policies need to be applied and enforced within their process areas. In addition to that, the data steward will also be expected to provide input or feedback with regard to the creation and implementation of policies and standards. Policies and standards need to be realistic and able to be applied locally without causing undue hardship or disruption to the operational processes. If any execution or enforcement issues emerge with regard to these policies and standards, the data steward should immediately review them with the data governance council representative.

Lack of enforcement is one of the primary causes of the garbage in, garbage out (GIGO) issue we often bring to attention throughout this book. Although the GIGO problem is widely recognized, there generally seems to be a lack of focus on addressing this persistent issue. And that, historically, may very well be due to the lack of having MDM and data governance practices in place. It is important to recognize that enforcement of policies and standards is a critical function of the data steward role. In a good MDM model with a solid governance process in place, the ability to declare and enforce policies and standards should be a natural course of action.

Data Quality Control

A constant complaint from the reporting teams or business intelligence teams is along these lines: "Why can't the front end enter the data correctly and consistently so we can trust this data and don't have to keep spending or scrubbing it to make it more useful?" While there is usually truth in this type of statement, it also reflects a shallow perspective with a tendency to place easy blame on the front-end teams. Historically, there has been a disconnect between the front-end and back-end teams. With a broader understanding of the front-end processes and drivers, the complexities and sensitivities that are involved with driving quality improvement become more apparent, and it also becomes clear that data quality will not improve without an end-to-end quality control plan that can enable front-end functions to effectively get on board.

It should be the job of the data governance council in conjunction with a data quality forum to define a reasonable quality control plan. This plan should utilize the process area data stewards who create that quality management connection between the front and back end. As such, these data stewards need to be highly engaged in the data quality management forum and must be prepared to manage action items directed to them. This responsibility will require the data steward to be involved in the analysis, planning, execution, and monitoring of data quality activities associated with their process area. The data steward will also likely need to coordinate with the MDM core team and CDG council to determine what specific areas of data quality are most important to monitor and control within their process area. Ultimately, it is assignment of quality control responsibilities and a shared focus across the process area data stewards that will enable an end-to-end data quality management process.

Raise Issues, Help Resolve

And finally, in addition to having the process expertise and quality management focus we have already described, these process area data stewards need to play a key role in the incident management process. In the next section, and again later in Chapter 8, we will discuss how a company's internal support model needs to support the data management process. With that model in place there needs to be a network of people who are actively involved in that support process, both as a submitters of problems and as persons who can help resolve the problems. Data management and quality improvement is often a circular process. A person who discovers or submits the problem will often also need to help solve and manage the problem. Following are two examples of this:

1. A regional order management team lead submits a service request ticket indicating that a number of customer accounts they have created seem to later be deactivated and merged into another account associated with the same customer. Upon review of this by the process area data steward and MDM core team, it is determined that this regional team has been creating duplicate accounts due to insufficient instruction regarding how to search for and select existing accounts that should be used. These duplicate accounts are eventually identified in the back-end account merge process causing them to be merged into what is considered the master account for these transactions. The data steward and the regional order management team lead work together to correct the team's work instructions to prevent the creation of these duplicate accounts.

2. In the data quality forum, a process area data steward raises the issue that there does not seem to be a consistent standard for how customer names should be entered. This is causing problems for the process area reporting teams who are constantly complaining they have to frequently edit or normalize customer names in order for them to create clean reports for management. The data quality forum and governance council recognize this problem and define standards for entering customer/company names, but because these standards will need to be phased in, the data quality council requires the process area data stewards to complete an implementation plan so that a phase-in schedule can be defined. The data steward completes an implementation plan that is approved.

There can be any number of scenarios like this that will require this type of two-way engagement. A dedicated data steward or process team lead will usually be quite happy to participate in any way possible to help define and resolve the problem as long as there is a support process that is responsive and able to identify sound solutions.

 ## PROCESSES

Similar to having committed people, there need to be processes and channels available that are geared to the recognition and support of data management or quality issues. In the previous topics, we have given a number of examples of data management issues where data stewards have been involved, and so far we have talked about how CDG, the data quality forum, and the incident management processes need to involve the data steward role. But let's discuss what triggers the engagement of these data stewards.

This actually goes back to the point we made in Chapter 4, where ideally, data governance involvement should be considered in the design and implementation of systems and business processes. When engaged in the design process, data stewards' roles and engagement points can be formally identified in the process model and flow. But since many systems and processes will already exist before data governance practices emerge in a company, getting data stewards plugged into IT and business processes will usually require the MDM team and governance council to actively pursue how and where to get this type of data steward engagement into place. Here are some examples of where process area data stewards can get plugged in to existing processes to better establish data management support and to begin demonstrating the data steward value proposition:

- **Incident management and service request processes.** Set up specific customer data management and data quality labeled queues or service request paths associated with system or process areas where the data stewards can be formally engaged in front-line or back-line support process with expectations to monitor and respond to the issues or requests.
- **Change management processes.** Often resulting from bugs or enhancement requests reported through the incident management or service request process, there will typically be an IT-driven change management process that controls release of fixes, enhancements, or upgrades to systems and applications. Most of these change management processes will require a certain amount of business involvement with regard to justification, testing, process verification, or sign-off that the fix or enhancement

is working correctly. Where change management actions can affect specific process and data areas, data stewards should be engaged with responsibilities to assist in the review, test, verification, or sign-off where appropriate. This will ensure that the data management and quality impact aspect of change management is not overlooked.

- **Data access management process.** We'll cover this more in the next chapter, but this is another important process area where data stewards can work closely with the data access gatekeeper to assist with monitoring, verification, approving, or auditing of the user data access process. This type of involvement will give the data steward a clear sense of who in the process area has access to the customer master data, which is key to the successful management and control of master data.

- **Governance and quality management processes.** In the prior chapters, we have pointed out how data stewards are integral to the data governance and quality management process. And similar to what we have previously mentioned in the other process examples, there needs to be formal interactions and responsibilities in which the process area data stewards are engaged. This can cover analysis, planning, testing, verification, readiness, support, or other types of tasks. All of these types of tasks should be expected in the execution of governance and quality management initiatives; therefore, you should ensure that these types of expectations are properly set in the data steward job role.

These are just some process engagement examples where data stewards can add value. Every company will have its own flavors of these processes, but check closely to see how well these processes are actually distinguishing and supporting the data management area. If these processes are very system- and application-centric and act as a pipeline primarily for IT support, then most likely the concept of data stewardship and focus on data management has not been well established in the company.

DATA CARETAKING

Good caretaking is the result of genuine interest, aptitude, and appropriate skill sets being applied to what needs to be cared for. Caretaking is the more intangible aspect of the elements that make up data stewardship.

Being able to demonstrate genuine interest in data management and quality management practices should obviously be a key factor in who is appointed to the data steward roles. Such interest will usually stem from a person with a past history with and ongoing passion for data management, or perhaps someone who has been in other functional roles and recognized the value of good data. Either way, a data steward needs to have genuine interest in data and its integrity to fuel the right caretaking mind set.

In the planning stages of the MDM initiative when a steward model is being defined, the MDM project team should look closely within the existing business functions to identify good data steward candidates. Often there are a number of well-qualified internal candidates who will exist within the ranks of IT analysts, business reporting teams, process area leads, and support organizations. If they can be leveraged, they can bring a wealth of existing operational knowledge that can translate well to a data steward role.

Aptitude and appropriate skill sets should come from a combination of past experience, new orientation and training related to the data steward role, and having sufficient processes and tools that enable the data steward's ability to analyze and support the customer master data. There is nothing more frustrating for a data steward-minded person than to have a role and responsibility for data management and quality control, but lack an effective process or the tools that are needed to help support them. A data steward that can't dig in is a data steward who is not likely to stay very long in that role.

Caretaking also needs to be a common denominator across the data steward teams. While the people and process aspects of data stewardship can vary depending on global, regional, and local roles, the aspect of data caretaking is ubiquitous. The data governance council will set the high-level priorities, policies, and standards, but it will be the responsibility of both the core team and process area data stewards to execute the day-to-day coordination and quality management practices that require having a shared sense of a data caretaking.

 ## SUMMARY

We have discussed that data stewardship is defined by the combination of the people, processes, and a data caretaking focus, and provided examples of how and where these three key elements can be applied in a Customer MDM model.

From a people perspective, we pointed out that there needs to be business resources commitment to data management and quality improvement, and that this should be driven by data governance through a data steward model involving an MDM core team and process area data stewards. From a process perspective, we talked about how incident management, change management, and gatekeeping processes needed to sufficiently recognize and support data management and quality control, and how data steward roles can be engaged and add value to those processes. And from a data caretaking perspective, we indicate how this is the more intangible element of data stewardship, but also the common denominator that makes for good data stewards.

In general, we have stressed the importance of data stewardship and how the data steward roles can make the difference between poor and successful execution for many initiatives. In essence, it is the ability to execute MDM with a data stewardship approach and through the data steward channels that will make for a cohesive MDM model.

CHAPTER SIX

Data Quality Management

Courage is the first of human qualities because it is the quality which guarantees the others.

—*Aristotle*

IMPLEMENTING A DATA QUALITY MODEL

Data quality is likely the single most important reason why companies tackle MDM. Trusted data delivered in a timely manner is any company's ultimate objective.

However, there are many aspects of data quality, including, among other things, the source of bad data as well as the actual definition of what bad data really is and its associated representation. Let's take a look at a couple examples to illustrate this further:

- There is no contention about what the two acceptable denominations are for the attribute *gender*. However, one system may represent it as *M/F*, another with *1/0*, another with *Male/Female/MALE/FEMALE*, another without any validation whatsoever, with a multitude of manually entered

111

values that could be missing, correct, or incorrect. Furthermore, it is possible to have a correct gender value improperly assigned to a given person. In the end, this information can be critical to companies selling gender-specific products. Others, however, may not be impacted so much if a direct mail letter is incorrectly labeled *Mr.* instead of *Mrs.*

■ Some data elements may not even have an obvious definition, or its definition is dependent on another element. An expiration date, for example, has to be a valid date in the calendar as well as later than an effective date. In another scenario, some customers are eligible for a certain service discount only if they have a *gold* account.

The previous examples show just one facet of data quality or lack of it. Data suffers from a multitude of problems including fragmentation, duplication, business rule violation, lack of standardization, incompleteness, categorization, cataloging, synchronization, missing lineage, and deficient metadata documentation.

One may wonder why companies get in such a mess. It is caused by a multitude of factors, some potentially more avoidable than others.

Certain companies grow at an incredible and sometimes unpredictable pace. Mergers and acquisitions are very common vehicles to increase market share or to tap into new business endeavors. Every time a new company is acquired, it is necessary to integrate its data. That means more quality lacking data is added to the pile. As discussed in Chapter 3, companies usually don't have time to cleanse the new data coming in as part of the migration process, except when it is absolutely required to make them fit into the existing structure. *We'll cleanse the data later* is a common motto and rarely achieved.

Additionally, software applications have historically been developed to solve a particular aspect of the business problem. That has led to years of multiple distributed software and business applications with disparate rules. Different systems might contain multiple instances of a customer record with different details and transactions linked to it. Because of these reasons, most companies suffer from fragmented and inconsistent data. The net effect is that companies face unnecessary and increased operational inefficiencies, inconsistent or inaccurate reporting, and ultimately incorrect business decisions. Even enterprise applications, such as ERP and CRM, have remained silos of information, with data being constantly duplicated and laden with errors.

There is also the business process as part of the equation. It is human nature for people to look for creative ways to solve their problems. That means when users have technical problems or run into business limitations during data entry, they will find ways to do it, even if it means breaking business rules or overriding well-defined processes. From a data quality perspective, this is not a good thing, but should the users be blamed? After all, they may be facing a particular customer need that doesn't fit an existing business process, or a system bug that is delaying a high-profit transaction.

Let's assume a company does have all the correct elements in place, such as data governance, data stewardship, data quality, IT support, and so on. Users are less likely to engage the proper teams if their confidence in the support process is low. They may think: "By the time I get this problem resolved through the proper mechanisms, I'll have a customer satisfaction issue beyond repair." Therefore, for the benefit of the company, they act with imagination and solve the immediate problem with non-approved solutions. Making matters worse, these out-of-spec practices and associated data issues are usually difficult to monitor, detect, and correct.

With that said, the primary goal of a company should be not only to have the proper elements of a well-governed entity, but have them working effectively, as well. This comes with maturity, and a constant focus on process improvement. Simply improving the data entry process alone is not enough. It is necessary to improve the support process around it. Just about everything is constantly changing: business needs, business landscape, technology, people, and so on. The only hope is to have an efficiently adaptive model that in spite of all these changes can continue to deliver results quickly.

The bottom line: Data quality is both a technical and a business issue and it requires tackling all three elements of the people/process/technology triangle. From a *people* standpoint, it necessitates the combined effort from both business and IT when addressing the myriad of quality issues throughout the enterprise. From a *process* perspective, it also demands IT and business to engage in a truly collaborative effort, without so much of the commonly seen politics and obstacles generally imposed in their relationships. Finally, *technology*, when applied properly, can expedite the problem resolution as well as make it viable to establish a mature and repeatable process.

This chapter discusses in detail the need for business and IT engagement. To start, a data quality process is presented with the objective to show how to connect the many players inside the enterprise into an overarching and repeatable methodology to foster recognition and action upon data-driven issues.

Described later in this chapter is a methodology to assess the current state of the quality of the data and establish a baseline to define the need for immediate actions as well as to gauge future improvements.

When reading through this chapter, it is important to take into account the type of MDM approach being implemented. For the most part, the discussions will assume an enterprise MDM solution since that is the most encompassing of them all. Therefore, adjustments will be necessary when implementing a different solution. For example, chances are an analytical MDM will not impact as many LOBs in the company as an operational or enterprise MDM, which may lead to a different decision-making process from that which is presented here. However, readers should be able to make the proper adjustments according to their particular situations.

 ## A PROCESS FOR DATA QUALITY

There is no one-size-fits-all model for data quality. When creating one, it is necessary to take into consideration a company's culture, the MDM approach being implemented, how multiple LOBs interact with each other, the maturity level of the data governance and stewardship teams, the degree of management engagement and sponsorship, technology resources, and personnel skills.

Figure 6.1 depicts the major roles involved in a data quality process and how they interact with one another to create a flexible and effective model to

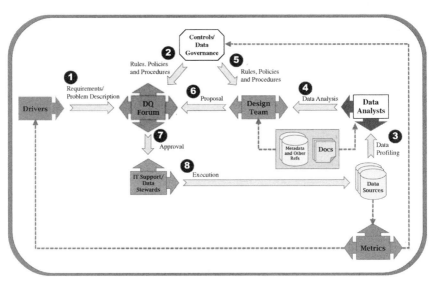

FIGURE 6.1　A Data Quality Process

address data quality issues. The arrows represent events or dependencies, while the numbers represent the sequence of activities.

A description of each of the elements presented in Figure 6.1 is provided next.

Drivers

Drivers are essentially the initiators of a data quality activity and the means by which they bring data quality issues to proper attention. A company with a mature data quality practice should be able to support a multitude of drivers. Not only that, it should also demand that everyone across the company participate in improving the overall quality of the data. After all, data quality is everyone's responsibility.

Continuous training, both formal and informal, is essential to achieve everyone's participation and strengthen a culture of focus on data quality. Actually, several studies have shown informal learning can be more effective than formal learning. With that in mind, companies need to find creative ways to disseminate information, such as mentoring and coaching programs, brown bag sessions, lessons-learned reviews, and so on. Technology should be leveraged to increase collaboration. Social media, generically speaking, still has a long way to go in the workplace, but needs to be considered as a mechanism to increase collaboration and promote information sharing. There are multiple categories of social media applications, such as: blogs, microblogging, social networking, wikis, webcasts, podcasts, and more. Striking the balance of what resources to use and to what extent is a challenge. Companies in certain industries may have less difficulty in adopting some of those applications. As an example, it is likely that high-tech companies are more prepared than healthcare companies to embrace and spread the use of social media in general. When defining what will be most effective in a company, it is necessary to take into consideration the company culture, computer resources, and human resources and skills.

Essentially, data quality initiatives fall into two categories: (1) reactive and (2) proactive. In general terms, proactive initiatives are measures established to avoid problems from happening or getting worse, while reactive initiatives are measures adopted after the problem has already occurred and needs correction. Drivers throughout the company, acting on their particular roles and driven by specific business needs, will either be reacting to data quality problems, or will be proactively preventing new problems from happening or existing problems from getting worse.

Users following a particular business process for data entry, for example, may detect irregularities with the data due to a system bug, a bad practice, or weak enforcement of business rules. The users will not necessarily know the root cause of the problem or the best way to resolve it, and that is expected. But they need a mechanism for presenting the problem and requesting a correction. Most companies will implement a type of trouble ticket system that will allow users to communicate the problem they see. These trouble tickets are then categorized and routed to a suitable team for proper actions. In this scenario, the problem entered by the user in the trouble ticket becomes the *requirement or problem statement* represented by arrow number 1 in Figure 6.1.

Trouble ticket is just one mechanism by which a company should support requests for data quality improvements. Special projects and certain activities commonly carried out are very likely to have data management impacts, and should be supported with proper engagement of the data quality team according to pre-established level agreements. Here are some examples of activities that will require close data quality participation:

- Migrating data from one system into another due to mergers and acquisitions or simply to consolidate multiple systems and eliminate redundancy.
- Changes in system functionality, such as a new tax calculation engine may require a more complete, consistent, and accurate postal code representation than previously.
- Regulatory compliance, such as new financial reporting rules, Sarbanes-Oxley Act (SOX), U.S. Patriot Act, or Basel II.
- Security compliance, such as government data requiring particular access control rules.

The drivers behind the previous activities will vary depending on the organizational structure. Even within a company, the same category of change could come from different organizations. For example, an IT-initiated system consolidation task may be the driver to a data migration activity, while a merger or acquisition is a business-initiated activity that will also lead to a data migration effort. In another example, a regulatory compliance requirement can come either from a financial organization or from an enterprise-wide data governance initiative.

Nonetheless, what is important is that the data quality process supports all data-driven requests, no matter what the driver is. Remember, the goal is to create a culture of focus on data quality. If a company is too selective about its drivers, it will create skepticism regarding its true objectives, which could ultimately lead to a company-wide data management failure.

When evaluating the requirements of one driver, it is necessary to consider the implications on the entire company. This is where the importance of establishing a data quality forum comes in (which is described next). In essence, a driver, through some established process and procedure, will provide the forum with a set of requirements or problem statement.

Data Quality (DQ) Forum

MDM is about bringing data together in a meaningful and fit-for-purpose way. An important consideration for MDM is assessing the effect a particular data change will have on all dependent parties in the company. A data quality forum can efficiently analyze the impact of data changes if it encompasses liaisons from the multiple LOBs that are contingent on that particular source of data.

Most of the activities are carried out by the lead of the forum, also known as the data quality lead. Depending on the size of the company, the data quality lead may need help from other data quality specialists to form a full-time data quality team. The representatives of the multiple LOBs act as liaisons meeting the data quality lead/team on a regular basis to evaluate requirements, review solutions, and issue approvals. Figure 6.2 shows the data quality forum.

The data quality lead/team will be in charge of most of the following activities, but obviously will bring in the liaisons according to agreed expectations, roles, and responsibilities:

FIGURE 6.2 The Data Quality (DQ) Forum

- Analyze and review requirements with associated business driver(s).
- Evaluate data governance rules, policies, and procedures and make sure the required changes are not in violation of any of them, or if a particular change might be necessary to existing data governance directives.
- Perform data analysis and profiling to fully understand data issues and provide alternatives for resolution.
- In addition to data analysis results, also take into consideration data governance rules, policies, and procedures when architecting potential solutions.
- Review solutions and determine the impact of the changes with data governance, the multiple LOBs, and other potential stakeholders.
- Obtain proper approvals and carry out execution of the changes with necessary team(s). The resolution could be a combination of activities to be performed by the business only, by IT only, or both.

Figure 6.3 shows a flowchart depicting the sequence of the major activities performed by the data quality forum as a whole. It should be clear when the

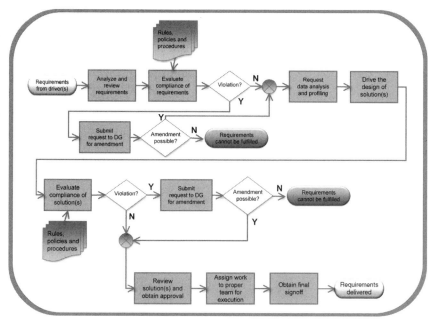

FIGURE 6.3 Data Quality Forum Flowchart

LOBs' liaisons are involved or not according to the nature of the activity itself and the explanation presented earlier.

Since data quality and data governance are tightly coupled, it is beneficial for the data quality lead of the forum to be a member of the data governance council, as well. This way, when a data quality issue requires data governance attention, the data quality lead can properly convey the issues and advise on alternatives for resolution.

Controls/Data Governance

Companies have multiple types of controls, such as business rules, policies, procedures, standards, and system constraints. Furthermore, company culture and amount of regulation in a particular industry will also dictate the quantity of controls imposed. However, the fact that companies have a lot of controls doesn't necessarily mean they are more mature from an MDM perspective. The maturity comes from having data governance more engaged on the multitude of controls across the company. As data governance matures, more controls are likely to be added. Put simply, more controls don't necessarily indicate more MDM maturity, but more MDM maturity will lead to more controls.

Companies will be subject to controls regardless of whether they have a data governance program. Data quality management is impacted by the controls, not necessarily by who manages them. Therefore, without a data governance team managing rules, policies, procedures, and standards, it means the data quality team will need to be responsible for validating all changes with the many diverse teams imposing or subject to all the controls. But forcing such onus on the data quality team is not efficient, because a data governance role is much better equipped to achieve this task.

The bottom line is this: Data governance and data quality should be complementing entities, with data governance a bit more strategic and data quality a bit more tactical, but both growing together as data management matures within the company. Plus, the higher the maturity in data governance, the less effort is needed in data quality, since better-governed data needs less correction. Figure 6.4 depicts this relationship.

Looking at Figure 6.4, keep in mind that data quality management will always be required no matter how mature a company's data governance program is. As a matter of fact, certain components of data quality will increase as governance efforts mature, such as monitoring, dashboards, and scorecards. One unit increase of effort on data governance doesn't mean one unit decrease of effort on data quality management. As companies become better governed

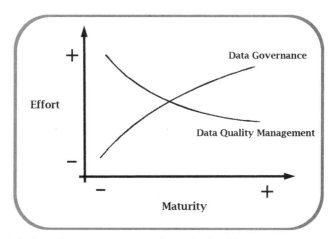

FIGURE 6.4 Data Governance versus Data Quality Management

and more controlled with quality engineered into the processes, the data quality initiatives are more predictable and require less work.

Obviously, a data governance program can only go so far. Eventually, it will end up reaching a point of diminishing returns. But most companies are far from that point as the majority of them still struggle with implementing data governance. For a more in-depth data governance review, recall that Chapter 4 covers this topic in detail.

Data Analysts

Many companies underestimate the amount of data analysis they need to perform before writing their requirements or proposing a solution to a particular data problem. Data projects need to be supported by data.

The Storage Networking Industry Association (SNIA) has the following definition of information lifecycle management (ILM), sometimes also referred to as data lifecycle management:

> Information Lifecycle Management: the policies, processes, practices, services and tools used to align the business value of information with the most appropriate and cost effective infrastructure from the time information is created through its final disposition. Information is aligned with business requirements through management policies and service levels associated with applications, metadata, and data.

The life cycle aforementioned would normally include creation, distribution, use, maintenance, and disposition of data. Notice the definition is very rigorous regarding governance, documentation, and business purpose of the data. These are all solid concepts, which would work perfectly in a company if they were being followed meticulously from the beginning. But that is very unlikely. The majority of companies do not have a good understanding or documentation about all their data elements and business purposes.

To make matters worse, an MDM project is normally the result of many consolidations of multiple repositories, or bringing in data due to mergers and acquisitions. All these activities will lead to fragmented, inconsistent, nonstandardized, and potentially inaccurate data elements.

In his book, Tony Fisher provides a more encompassing data management life cycle.[1] He calls for five steps: (1) discover, (2) design, (3) enable, (4) maintain, and (5) archive.

The last four steps in this lifecycle model (design, enable, maintain, and archive) are very similar to the more traditional steps: create, distribute, use, maintain, and dispose. But the very important first step, *discover*, is a clear indication that companies and experts have recognized the significance of understanding the data before deciding what to do with it.

Data profiling is one key component of data discovery. Therefore, data profiling should be sought at multiple stages of the data quality management program. Sometimes data profiling is necessary to help the business define or clarify certain business rules, and consequently, their requirements for a data quality improvement project. For example, contact duplication may be impacting the business by creating inefficiencies in business processes, poor business intelligence decisions, and/or increasing marketing campaign costs. However, simply stating in the requirements that contact data needs to be consolidated may not be sufficient. The actual definition of what a duplicate really is has to be stated by the business. It could be contacts with the same phone number, or the same e-mail, same first name/last name, belong to the same company, or combinations of these. Before profiling the data, it is highly likely that the business doesn't understand the true degree of completeness of these attributes in the system.

In data projects, there is a balance of how much business requirement is needed and how much data analysis is necessary to support the requirements and achieve the objectives. One can't assume there will be a clean set of requirements ready to be executed when there is a chance the business has no clue as to the condition of the data. When the data quality forum gets a request from a driver, it is important for the data quality lead/team to work with the data analysts to ensure a comprehensive data profiling exercise is completed before the requirements are finalized. After all, it is very likely data itself will support or even dictate the business rules.

A seemingly simple question: Who performs data profiling? Data analysts from the business side—or data analysts from IT? The data must be evaluated from a business perspective, because data must have a business purpose to be useful. If a business purpose does not exist, one needs to question the request for the data quality improvement.

A challenging situation can occur, however, when the person with the business perspective may not have the proper technical skills to do the data profiling, or potentially may not have the proper data or system access permissions.

Several vendors provide tools that tremendously facilitate the data profiling activities and allow for collaboration between the business and IT. Some tools are easier for a business person to use than others. A careful evaluation should be done before deciding what tool to buy. Some MDM solutions will have better data profiling/data quality capabilities than others. As stated previously in the book, it may be difficult to find a single vendor providing all the MDM components to satisfaction.

Data access can also be a limiting factor. Business users obviously have access to the data they need, but the access is normally limited to a front-end screen that gives them a view to a small number of elements or records at a time. This type of access is usually not sufficient when running data profiling. Most likely, it will be necessary to have back-end access to the repository to be able to query data in bulk. Certain companies are very sensitive about providing this type of access to business teams, even on a read-only mode.

Considering all these factors, here are the options regarding the selection of a data analyst:

- **Business person with technical abilities and proper data access.** This is the most efficient scenario because the business data analyst can more effectively work with other business teams regarding the data profiling needs and results, and quickly make the proper adjustments.
- **Technical person with business abilities and proper data access.** This is the second best option assuming there is somebody who can fill this role. Normally, technical people don't necessarily have the inclination to be more engaged on the business side of the company, but this role can be fostered.
- **Business person working together with a technical person with proper data access.** This is likely what most companies do, although it is

probably the most inefficient method. Data profiling can be a very iterative process. Normally, there is no clearly defined path to follow. It is common for the results of one data analysis to dictate what needs to be analyzed next. If there is a dependency on the technical person to collect the data and the business person to do the analysis and make the decisions, a lot of time will be spent back and forth between the two of them.

When deciding on a data analysis team, take into consideration the company structure, culture, and political issues. But this shouldn't deter you from looking toward the best interests of the company. Challenging the status quo is a healthy practice in any company as long as it is done in a constructive manner and with an end goal of improving the business. Tough choices require courage—hence the use of Aristotle's quote at the beginning of this chapter.

Design Team

Once the problem is clearly understood and the requirements clearly stated, it is time to move on to designing solutions. As stated earlier in this chapter, data quality requests can either be reactive or proactive. As companies mature, it is expected the total number of data quality issues will go down. Not only that, the number of quality requests should shift from the reactive to the proactive category since mature companies are better about predicting potential issues with their data before they impact the multiple LOBs.

Companies can definitely improve regarding the prevention of issues from happening, but reactive data corrections will never go away as data variables and complexities will always exist.

Figure 6.5 shows what is likely to occur as companies mature regarding reactive versus proactive data quality projects. Reactive issues go down as a percentage of total data quality problems identified, while proactive measures go up.

Data quality requests can lead to a multitude of activities. Reactive data issues will likely need a data correction step and potentially some action to prevent the offending code or practice from causing more of the same issue. This also depends on how well prepared a particular company is regarding managing data. Immature companies might fix the current problem but not make the necessary adjustments to prevent the very same error from reoccurring.

Data correction will normally fall into one of the following categories:

- **Data cleansing or scrubbing.** Encompasses correcting corrupt, invalid, or inaccurate records. For example, eliminating invalid characters or extra spaces from a set of records.

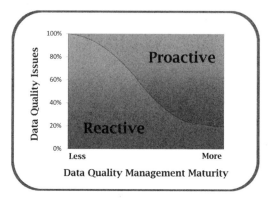

FIGURE 6.5 Reactive versus Proactive Data Quality Issues as a Percentage of Total in Maturing Companies

---

- **Data standardization.** Includes conforming the data to a list of established rules and standards. For example, replacing all variations of *Incorporated*, including *Incorp*, with *Inc.*
- **Data enrichment.** Involves augmenting the data by adding some new required information. For example, adding +4 to U.S. zip codes, or adding province information to a particular European country.
- **Data consolidation.** Encompasses eliminating duplicates. This particular data correction activity is likely the most time-consuming within a company. Data duplication is one of the major issues causing operational and business intelligence inefficiencies throughout the company. Before duplicates can be identified, it might be necessary to cleanse, standardize, and enrich the data so proper comparison can be achieved.
- **Data validation.** This refers to preventing bad data from entering the system by performing some type of validation at the data entry level. For example, accepting only *M* or *F* values for gender on an employee or a contact.

In addition to identifying the type of data correction required, categorizing the data quality issue is also significant. Data quality issues can be categorized into quality dimensions. Data quality dimensions are explored further later in this chapter, but for the purpose of the following example, understand the *completeness* dimension as the level of data missing or unusable.

It is important to categorize the type of issue to ensure the correct data analysis measures are taken and to ensure a comprehensive correction plan can be mapped out. For example, a request comes in to add +4 to zip codes in some U.S. address records. An advanced data quality management program would identify this as a *completeness* problem and provide the recommendation that this request requires data enrichment. Furthermore, it would engage data governance to understand whether this rule applies to all U.S. addresses. If applicable to all, a data profiling activity is performed to measure the degree of completeness of ZIP+4 in all U.S. addresses. Lastly, three activities would be spawned: correct the records initially requested, correct the remaining records in the system, and prevent users from adding new U.S. addresses without the +4 information. The last activity could be achieved by adding validation at the data entry point, by changing a particular set of business processes, or if prevention is not possible, by establishing scripts to correct the data on a regular schedule.

Deciding who is on the design team can also be a challenge. The data quality forum and data stewards should certainly be highly engaged in the proposed solutions. The same considerations made to the data analysis team are applicable to the data design team. The data design team needs a combination of business and technical skills. Business skill is important to propose a solution that satisfies the needs of the multiple LOBs, and technical skill is important to propose a solution that is feasible.

When proposing a solution, it is necessary to take into account the potential rules, policies, and procedures that could be impacting the compliance of the resolution. Only conforming solutions should be considered when searching for final approval. If none of them are compliant, an amendment to existing controls should be requested to the data governance team. If an alteration is possible, the solution can move on to the approval stage. If not, the data quality lead/team will need to work with the driver(s) and impacted LOBs to search for alternatives.

Once approval is issued for the solution that best fits the business need, it is time to move on to the proper team(s) for execution.

IT Support/Data Stewards

In the previous section, a description was provided for how a data correction request can turn into a data correction activity plus a root cause analysis and consequent action for error prevention.

The proposed solution and accompanying actions will dictate who needs to be engaged during the execution phase. It is possible that business data stewards need to be involved, or IT, or both. If the data issue is a consequence of some system bug, IT needs to be involved to implement the fixes. IT may also need to be included to write some sort of automated data correction script. Data stewards will likely be involved most of the time. As described in Chapter 5, data stewardship is a business function; therefore, they are ultimately responsible for assuring the data fitness for use. Even if IT is fixing the problem, data stewards should be engaged in testing the fix and supporting the drivers throughout customer acceptance.

In Figure 6.1, the targets of step 8, *execution*, are represented as *data sources*. That is a generic representation. Depending on the MDM implementation, there could be a single source or multiple sources of data. Many operational data sources may exist during the transition to MDM to achieve the ultimate goal of establishing a single system-of-record for a particular set of information. Therefore, the location varies where the data correction and/or associated prevention activity is executed. For example, when transitioning to a central master data repository, the action to fix the data could be changing it in the legacy system before the data is migrated to the new repository. In another example, a bug fix could be required to a particular interface that is bringing the data together. Even on a complete MDM solution implemented with hub and spoke architecture, it is possible the fix is not at the hub, but in one of the spoke systems, or the underlying interface. Companies need to trust the data quality forum team members to obtain a clear understanding of where the correction should take place and engage the proper support teams to execute it accordingly and in harmony.

Metrics

Data quality metrics measure the quality of data so proper actions can be taken to prevent a recurrence of previous issues and a deterioration of data quality over time—especially as new data enters the company at exceedingly rapid rates. Metrics can be separated into two categories: (1) monitors and (2) scorecards. Monitors are used to detect violations that usually require immediate corrective actions. Scorecards allow for a number to be associated with the quality of the data and are more snapshot-in-time reports as opposed to real-time triggers.

Data quality metrics will be described in more detail in Chapter 8. At their most basic definition, data quality metrics are resources to be used by drivers and data governance to support requirements, prevent degradation in data quality, and address compliance issues.

ESTABLISHING A DATA QUALITY BASELINE

"If you cannot measure it, you cannot improve it." This quote by Lord Kelvin is as relevant today for data quality as it was when it was first written in 1883 regarding sciences in general.

Many companies have no idea about the quality of their data. Most of the time they recognize their issues, but they don't realize the extent of those issues. Furthermore, they continue to make wrong assumptions and incorrect business decisions because they are relying upon incorrect information.

What companies need is an assessment of the quality of their information combined with a strong process for continuous improvement. The first step is to get situated by establishing a data quality baseline. This section will discuss what needs to be considered when creating this baseline, while Chapter 8 will describe a data maintenance model for continuous data quality measurement and improvement.

Many companies fail to scope their data quality projects with an emphasis on business needs. It is not data quality for the sake of data quality. It must serve a purpose, and as such, the business must be driving what needs to be measured—and why—on a traditional top-down approach.

It is easy for business teams to get overwhelmed with their day-to-day activities and lose sight of data quality improvements because they may not see immediate benefits. It is not uncommon for data quality projects to take a while before they start showing results. That's why a culture of emphasis on quality is so important—and why executive sponsorship is an absolute requirement for success. Furthermore, to overcome a potential *business paralysis*, or lack of business support, it might be necessary to combine a bottom-up approach to achieve quicker results.

Before providing an example for organizing a quality baseline for customer data by combining a top-down with a bottom-up approach, let's take a look at three elements that need to be considered when defining, qualifying, classifying, and cataloging a measurement baseline. They are:

1. Context
2. Data quality dimensions
3. Entities and attributes

Context

Bear in mind that quality of data is *context* dependent. That means a particular data element may be of sufficient quality in one specific context, but not in another.

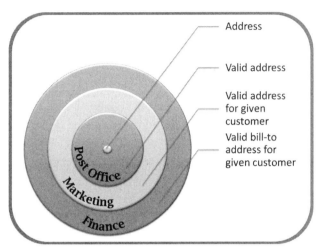

Address

Valid address

Valid address for given customer

Valid bill-to address for given customer

Post Office

Marketing

Finance

FIGURE 6.6 Context in Data Quality

Figure 6.6 shows an address element in multiple contexts. An address may be accurate from a postal code perspective because it is a valid location, but if it is not a valid address for a given customer, it could be of little use to marketing, for instance. From a finance perspective, it is very important that the address is the correct bill-to location in addition to being a valid address for the customer.

The actual technique for assessing the quality of the data will differ according to the context with varying degrees of difficulty. In the example in Figure 6.6, determining if an address is a valid location can be achieved by comparing it against a reference provided by the postal office for that particular country. Validating an address for a given customer will require other references, such as Dun & Bradstreet or OneSource, for example. Finally, validating if the address is indeed the correct bill-to location may have to be done through inspection, or with an integrated invoice system that can flag incorrect addresses based upon proper confirmation from the customer.

Another very important context to consider is country or region/territory. Countries have their own address formatting peculiarities and requirements for proper postal delivery. A lot of rules and regulations are country specific, with business units in large corporations operating differently depending on the country where they are located or where their customers are located. Sales and marketing are normally territory driven from a customer operations perspective as well as from a sales force concentration and compensation perspective. All of these factors impact how to evaluate the quality of the information.

The need for contextual understanding will certainly dictate how much work is necessary to break down the evaluation of the information. For example, a postal code validation is typically required by country. If a finance team has different tax rules dependent on a particular address element, it may be necessary to separate that information by region or territory. All of a sudden, Figure 6.6 becomes a matrix of possibilities, such as: Post Office/U.S., Post Office/CA, Post Office/JP, etc; and Finance/Americas, Finance/EMEA, Finance/ APAC, and so on. The number can grow exponentially depending on the amount of segmentation required.

Data Quality Dimensions

Data quality dimension is a characteristic of information that can be used to effectively organize and measure the information and properly address its data quality needs. Furthermore, data quality dimensions should be aligned with business processes to be measured.

In essence, data quality dimensions are distinguishable characteristics of a data element, and the actual distinction should be business driven. Since it is possible to characterize a particular data element in so many ways, there are nearly 200 terms used to portray data quality dimensions. There is not a single comprehensive list agreed upon by experts, but most would say it would include the following:

- **Completeness.** Level of data missing or unusable.
- **Conformity.** Degree of data stored in a nonstandard format.
- **Consistency.** Level of conflicting information.
- **Accuracy.** Degree of agreement with an identified source of correct information.
- **Uniqueness.** Level of non-duplicates.
- **Integrity.** Degree of referenced data.
- **Timeliness.** Degree to which data is current and available for use in the expected time frame.

Entities and Attributes

As explained previously, business paralysis can be an impediment when looking for a clear definition of what needs to be included as part of the data quality baseline. It may be necessary to start a bottom-up approach by using a conceptual, logical, or physical model of the data repository to help identify the main entities and attributes that need to be assessed. Conceptual or logical models are usually easier to follow for nontechnical people, and are probably the preferred models among business users. Referring to the physical model will likely be necessary to obtain more details about what is not represented in the other two models. Metadata, when present, can also be very useful in this activity. But more often than not, metadata is not existent at the detail needed.

If the repository is relatively unknown, and there is no metadata information and no database models, it will be necessary to obtain table descriptions directly from the database. An extremely useful exploratory activity here would be data profiling to learn more about the data before deciding what needs to be included in the baseline. This is also fairly common when migrating an unknown system into the primary repository.

To illustrate, let's use a simplified conceptual model entity relationship diagram (ERD), which is shown in Figure 6.7 representing the most common entities on a customer data repository. Please note all database examples and representations will be given using relational database notation and nomenclature since that is the most dominant technology today for data management systems.

The model in Figure 6.7 only shows entities, but it can be used as a starting point to question the business for feedback. Chances are the model alone is not sufficient, and it is necessary to drill down into what attributes those entities carry to better come up with what needs to be included in the baseline. Some logical models do include attribute information, and so do physical models and data dictionaries. If neither of those is available, it might be necessary to resort to a direct description of the database tables, which can be easily provided by a database administrator (DBA).

Remember, however, that those descriptions will simply list the name of the attributes and their types—integer, character, and so on. A well-designed database will have some minimum standards that can facilitate the understanding of some of the attributes/columns. For example, an operational database will likely be in third normal form (3NF), and its primary and foreign keys will probably follow a standard nomenclature making it relatively easy to spot relationships between entities.

Whatever technique is used, either using models, data dictionaries, metadata repository, existing documentation, or direct table descriptions, it should be possible to compile a list of the most important entities and attributes to be further analyzed. Obviously, *importance* is subjective, but keep in mind it must

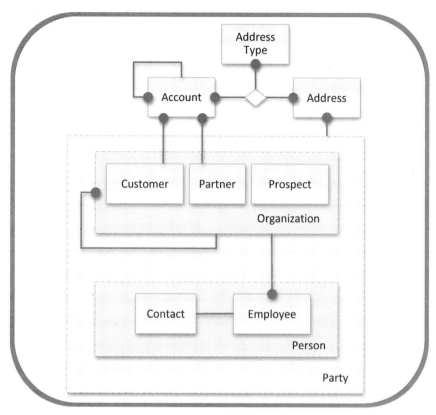

FIGURE 6.7 Simplified Conceptual Model ERD for Customer Information

serve a business purpose. When in doubt, the entity and attribute should be included until further clarification and review with the business.

One thing to keep in mind, though—the business doesn't know what they don't know. It is very common for LOBs to be reactive and not proactive with regard to data issues. A lot of times they don't specify a particular data constraint, because they *assume* there is no problem. Later, however, when they are presented with a given scenario, they come to the painful realization that there is a problem. This is why even though the main goal is to create a baseline that is representative of the actual business needs, it is vital to be forward thinking and proactive to identify what has potentially been overlooked. A bottom-up approach can assist with creating a more comprehensive list with elements that were unnoticed by the business.

Next are some sample entities, attributes, data quality dimensions, and contexts used to describe a method for compiling a data quality baseline that meets business needs and goals.

Putting It All Together

Chapter 2 makes the argument that a combination of top-down with bottom-up approach is critical to fully harvest the maximum benefits of data management. Creating a data quality baseline is a concrete application of this concept, where the proper combination is normally necessary to create a culminating list of entities and attributes to be included in a baseline for quality assessment. Context and data quality dimensions are added to the mix to help categorize the many elements and their many facets of data quality.

Figure 6.8 depicts a diagram combining a top-down with a bottom-up approach for compiling and classifying a list of elements to be measured when creating a data quality baseline.

A sample baseline report is depicted in Table 6.1.

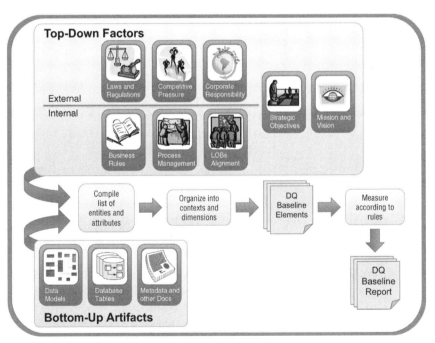

FIGURE 6.8 Creating a Data Quality (DQ) Baseline

Most of the columns in Table 6.1 were discussed previously, such as context, entity, attribute, and DQ dimension. But let's take a look at each of them:

- **Originator:** used to track where the requirement came from. For top-down requirements, originators are likely to be a particular LOB, or a combination of LOBs, data governance, or data stewardship. Bottom-up requirements were likely identified by the data quality team, or potentially by the data governance team, which is likely engaged in this activity, as well.
- **Context:** discussed in detail previously. It is not uncommon for originator and context to carry the same label. After all, a given requirement by finance, for example, could very well be applicable to that particular context. But they are not the same thing. Originator is simply who made the request, while context takes into account all the conditions affecting the assessment of the quality of the data.
- **Entity:** discussed in detail previously. Both top-down and bottom-up requirements can be traced to a given entity or combination of entities.
- **Attribute:** discussed in detail previously. Entities combined with attributes ultimately identify what needs to be measured.
- **Data quality dimension:** discussed in detail previously. Used to distinguish the characteristic of a data element. Can be further used to roll up the quality of the data into different views, which will be explained in more detail in Chapter 8.
- **Data quality rule:** a detailed description of the rule defining what is being measured. It is very important to be precise in the description to avoid incorrect interpretations. For example, when measuring *completeness* of a name, what does that really mean? Is it any combination of characters, with the exception of nulls and blanks? Is there a minimum length acceptable?
- **Score:** a measure of quality. It is important to be consistent with the score. Use the same approach for all elements. Don't use a high number for one element to identify high quality, while using a low number for another element to also identify high quality. For example, a high number for *completeness* is normally a good indication, while a high number for *duplicates* is not. Therefore, use *uniqueness* instead of *duplicates*. A high number for *uniqueness* is good. A common practice is to have a score between 0 to 100, which represents a percentage of *good* data. This means a score of 80, which indicates 80 percent of the data follows the specified rule.
- **Threshold** (not in Table 6.1): can be used to define acceptable tolerances. When creating an initial baseline, this particular characteristic may

TABLE 6.1 Sample Baseline Report

Originator	Context	Entity(ies)	Attribute(s)	DQ Dimension	Rule	Score
Data governance	Global	Customer	Name	Completeness	• Not null/not blank • More than 1 character	98
Finance	Finance/Marketing	Customer	DUNS	Completeness	• Not null/not blank	60
Finance	Finance/Marketing	Customer	DUNS	Conformity	• Nine digits	70
Finance	Finance/US	Address (US)	Postal Code	Conformity	• Must follow format: 5 digits, one dash, 4 digits	68
Data governance	Global	Customer	Name/ Country	Uniqueness	• Unique customer name per country	80
Data governance	Post Office/US	Address	Address lines City County State Postal Code Country	Accuracy	• Valid address according to US postal code reference	75
	Post Office/FR	Address	Address lines City County State Postal Code Country	Accuracy	• Valid address according to FR postal code reference	65

TABLE 6.1 (*Continued*)

Originator	Context	Entity(ies)	Attribute(s)	DQ Dimension	Rule	Score
Marketing	Marketing/US	Customer address	Customer name Address lines City County State Postal Code Country	Accuracy	• Valid address for given customer according to D&B	60
Finance	Finance/Global	Account	Account type	Uniqueness	• No duplicate accounts of the same type for a given customer	90
Sales	Sales/Global	Account customer	Account number Customer type	Integrity	• Every customer (not prospects) must have at least one account	85

135

not be of ultimate importance. However, as the understanding of the data increases, this attribution becomes critical. More about thresholds will be presented in Chapter 8.

Obviously, more columns can be added to the sample assessment on Table 6.1 according to a particular situation. It is easy to envision how the report can become very lengthy and the elements can potentially be very difficult to compile, let alone measure every single one of them. Measuring the data according to the predefined rule can be a very daunting task. The good news is that there are automated technologies to support this effort. It will require an excellent data-profiling tool combined with a very skilled group of professionals. It is very possible that not all rules can be fully measured; therefore, sampling techniques and other statistical data analysis must be considered as part of the profiling exercise.

One may argue a bottom-up approach can lead to a set of difficult rules to be measured and is consequently a wasted effort since it doesn't necessarily meet a particular business need. Implementing a phased baseline can mitigate this possible scenario. Keep in mind that the purpose of using the bottom-up approach is to show the business what they are potentially missing (remember, *the business doesn't know what they don't know!*). That means one can start a baseline of bottom-up elements with a simple set of rules. As the results uncover discrepancies, the baseline can be refined further as needed.

The step *creating a baseline* and the one described in the next section, *data alignment and fitness assessment*, may require a few interactions before the actual baseline can be fully completed.

 ## DATA ALIGNMENT AND FITNESS ASSESSMENT

It is widely accepted that data quality is about fitness for use. Therefore, the data quality baseline needs to be analyzed with that perspective in mind. It is not about achieving the score of 100 for every single element in the baseline. It *is* about achieving the proper score necessary to keep the business operating efficiently and confidently. Moreover, it is about identifying areas for data quality improvements.

Even though the initial assessment has a potentially non–business oriented component attained by the bottom-up approach, this step takes care of aligning the results to a specific business purpose. Simply speaking, the baseline is a superset, which can now be properly aligned.

It is expected the business will look at some of the results and say: "We had no idea!" Another expected outcome is the need to look further into a given element. For example, when the business finds out only 60 percent of the U.S. postal codes follows the proper pattern of five digits, a dash, plus four digits, they might want to know what other patterns exist.

Several interactions to create, analyze, and refine the baseline will most likely be required. But a fully finalized baseline is not necessarily required before actions can be taken. The baseline will have areas more clearly defined than others. If those areas require corrections, the proper data quality initiative should start as soon as possible. It obviously needs to be properly prioritized according to other ongoing activities and proper resource availability, but they don't necessarily all need to be part of a single data quality project. As a matter of fact, data quality projects can be very resource intensive and will need to be prioritized properly in consideration of other organizational activities.

It is important to decide what problem to tackle and how much of the data needs to be fixed. Use commonly known tactics such as *low-hanging fruit* and the *Pareto principle*, aka the *80-20 rule*, when prioritizing tasks and deciding what, when, and how much to fix. Data issues will always exist; consequently, focus the effort where it is most needed and where there will be the most impact on the business.

 ## DATA CORRECTION INITIATIVES

The ultimate goal for measuring the quality of the data is to identify what needs to be fixed. The data quality baseline will, in essence, lead to a series of data quality projects. Data correction could come down to two main activities:

1. Cleanup of existing bad data
2. Correction of offending system, process, or business practice causing the data problem

If the data quality baseline score is low for a given element, it will obviously require a data cleanup effort to improve the score. However, it's not always the source of the offending data that will be an ongoing issue. It is possible the bad data was caused by a one-time data migration effort, neglecting the need for correcting the migration code, for example. It is also possible an already corrected software bug or bad business process introduced the offending data, again negating the need for readdressing the origin of the problem.

Nonetheless, a detailed root cause analysis must be completed. No assumptions should be made regarding the reason why bad data was introduced in the first place. As discussed earlier in this chapter, proactive data quality measures are essential to increase the maturity and effectiveness of a strong data management program.

Assuming the data problem is ongoing, it will normally fall into one of the two following categories:

1. **A rule exists, but it is not being followed or implemented properly.** A particular rule can either be enforced at the application level or via business processes. A system bug would prevent an application level rule from working properly, while an incorrect business practice would prevent a business process rule from being followed properly. IT will most likely work on fixing the system bug, while data stewards and data governance will work with the offending LOB(s) to correct the bad business practice(s).

2. **A rule does not exist, but it is now required.** The design team should propose where it is best for the rule to be enforced. If it is through an application level constraint, IT will again likely be the best option. If it is through business process enforcement, data stewards will work with data governance and impacted LOB(s) to modify and/or create rules, policies, and procedures around the new requirement. Adding a new rule can be tricky since it is necessary to consider if it impacts or violates existing ones.

Normally, the data quality team will need to work with the business to decide if cleaning up the existing bad data has a higher priority than preventing more errors from being introduced. Needless to say, both activities will have to be prioritized along with other ongoing projects throughout the company competing for the same resources.

There are many ways to perform a data cleansing activity depending on the volume of data, level of access to the system, technical capabilities, system interface features, and existing rules, policies, and procedures.

Practically all Customer MDM repositories will offer some type of front-end interface allowing business users to modify master data records individually. For low volume data correction, that is usually the no-brainer option selected. As the volume increases, however, other considerations need to be made. If the interface allows for bulk updates, that could be a viable option. If not, some type of automation could be sought. The tool itself may provide some type of custom automation. Another possibility is utilizing data entry automation software tools to expedite and avoid errors when performing hundreds or thousands of similar changes through the front end. Lastly, it is possible to execute automated back-end scripts to make the proper changes directly into the database and bypass the front-end interface.

Clearly, the last option has implications. One is the coordinated efforts of a business member and a technical professional. Normally, a business user does not have the skills or the proper access to write and execute the database scripts. Meanwhile, the IT professional will have to rely on the business partner for proper understanding, testing, and validation. It was stressed earlier in this chapter how a professional with business/technical competency can go a long way by narrowing the gap between business and IT and achieving faster and more precise results. Keep this important option in mind.

Another implication regarding using back-end scripts is related to compliance to existing processes and other potential rules governing the company. Sometimes, the execution of back-end procedures is not approved because it could violate certain rules. For example, SOX requirements regulate what kind of information can be updated without close validation, sufficient testing, and appropriate tracking. Furthermore, some Customer MDM applications include data integrity constraints at the data entry point level and not at the database level. This means bulk updates done on the back-end would bypass those validations and consequently jeopardize the integrity of the data. Because of all these possibilities, it is critical to look for business- and data-governance-approved processes before starting a data cleansing effort.

Not uncommon either is to have to do the same type of data cleansing on a regular basis. This usually happens when it is not possible to correct the root cause of the problem immediately. Therefore, it is necessary to perform scheduled cleanups to maintain the business operating properly until there is time to fix the problem for good. Scheduled cleanups are subject to the same aspects just described regarding manual versus automated fix, front-end versus back-end correction, bulk updates, and so on. Obviously, the repetitive nature of these scheduled cleanups just exacerbates the potential need for automation.

Recall the data quality process described earlier in this chapter. Once a problematic issue is identified through the data quality baseline, it should be submitted to the data quality process team for proper evaluation, prioritization, feasibility analysis, risk assessment, solution design, and final corrective actions. The actual data correction itself is embedded within the data quality process and subject to the observations presented previously.

SUMMARY

Establishing a culture of quality throughout the enterprise is mandatory for maximum benefits. Data quality is everyone's responsibility, but requires the company to establish the proper foundation through continuous training, proper communication channels, effective collaboration, and an efficiently adaptive model that in spite of constant changes can continue to deliver results quickly.

As companies mature, their data quality focus moves from reactive to proactive. Anticipating issues is critical to minimizing risks and maximizing opportunities. But data quality is not a single project. It must be an ongoing and self-feeding effort focused on continuous improvement of data and the process itself.

The first step to a successful data quality program is to understand the data well and how it fits the business. Good quality does not necessarily indicate 100-percent compliance. Good quality is compliance sufficient to attend the business properly, which could be 60 or 80 percent, for example. It is not data quality for the sake of data quality, but it is about serving a business purpose.

Creating a data quality baseline helps companies to understand their data as well as to identify and prioritize areas for improvement. The first requirement to correct business decision is accurate information, which can only be achieved with measurement, business alignment, and fitness assessment.

Data quality management is likely the most pervasive MDM component and the one that requires the highest IT and business collaboration. There is a fine line separating technical and business aspects of data, which challenges the traditional separation of duties. A team of people with suitable skills to bridge the cross-functional gap is a coveted asset that can further advance the discipline inside the company.

NOTE

1. Tony Fisher, *The Data Asset: How Smart Companies Govern Their Data for Business Success* (Hoboken, NJ: John Wiley & Sons, 2009).

CHAPTER SEVEN

Data Access Management

Anything that can go wrong, will go wrong.

—*Murphy's Law*

 ## CREATING THE BUSINESS DISCIPLINE

Data access management—the control and monitoring of access to data—is largely overlooked as a business side discipline. Typically, it exists as part of an IT-managed process using an access provisioning model where a user can request certain access privileges that can be approved or denied by IT based on predefined types of access rights associated with job role authority and governed by policies and rules related to system security, privacy, regulatory compliance, and Sarbanes-Oxley (SOX) requirements in the form of Segregation of Duties (SoD) rules.

Many companies today require employees to complete internal training related to information protection and business conduct. In these training courses there are usually various examples cited where fraud, theft, insider trading, information privacy issues, and other types of accidents or misconduct have occurred in relation to company data and proprietary information. Many of these cases involve employees in business roles who are knowingly or unknowingly participants in the incident. These cases are used in training courses to help illustrate what not to do and how damaging a lack of information protection can be.

Yet, other than with these types of generalized training courses and use of access provisioning criteria to govern whether an employee can be granted data access, there is usually little if any responsibility for ongoing access control and monitoring of behavior assigned to the business organizations where much of the risk associated with corporate data exists. In fact, business users often are assigned default sets of access privileges as part of a generic job role setup that provides more access capability than they really need or should have. And, if their job responsibilities only focus on a specific set of tasks within the job role area, as is often the case, the user may have only been properly trained on the functionality and data associated with just those tasks, and as a result, be unfamiliar with the policies and rules associated with other data to which they have access.

This type of scenario is an example of how the overall practice and discipline around data access management is often inadequate and leaves the door open to risk. If managers and users were more intimately aware of the policies, rules, and the potential risks associated with all access privileges they have, and they were aware of ongoing monitoring and auditing processes related to this, at least the cases where employees have been unknowingly involved in data access issues could be greatly reduced. So let's look at how to become better engaged in the business operations to enable a more self-disciplined approach that will help minimize this type of corporate risk.

Beyond the System Administrator

In disparate system environments where business functions and application data is separated and contained to specific systems, it has been common practice to just use standard access control methodologies and provisioning solutions. These are based on an IT system administrator managed model to determine if and how business users are granted access to the system and data.

But as MDM moves forward, we are seeing applications and users being migrated to more integrated platforms and shared environments where common use of tools, interfaces, and master data exists. Suddenly, what have been independently controlled applications and groups of users now collectively become a much larger pool of users interacting with a common environment. The user, application, and data separation that physically existed before no longer exists.

Maintaining user and functional distinction now requires more specific user identification, classification, SoD management, and monitoring of business process interaction to the extent that a simple system administrator approach for managing access control is no longer adequate. In their book *Master Data Management and Customer Integration for a Global Enterprise*,[1] Alex Berson and Larry Dubov nicely explain the methodologies, technologies, and challenges associated with Enterprise Rights Management (ERM) and access control in relation to MDM and data hub implementations. They also point out the shortcomings and scalability issues involved in various authorization approaches that are commonly implemented within these environments.

In a shared customer master environment, there can be a complex variety of process interactions and data access needs from various user groups involving different combinations of create, update, delete (or deactivate), and read-only type requirements. Because of this, the access management methodology and control practices for this type of environment need to be more rigorous and should involve a business gatekeeper function associated with the MDM core team. The primary purpose of this gatekeeper function is to define and manage a more business process oriented set of checks, controls, and monitoring focus that is needed to augment existing access management and authorization processes in order to more precisely recognize and control who has and receives authority to access the customer master data. As we'll be explaining, this gatekeeper process can be an additional function and process layer integrated with an existing access control model.

While use of a gatekeeper role is not a new or unique concept within authority granting processes, in the MDM and data governance areas there seems to be very little content, models, or best practices related to implementing a business gatekeeper function for data access management. This would seem to suggest that companies launching MDM initiatives address this in unique or customized ways, or that the management of this continues to be largely an IT-driven process without much business engagement. If the former is true, then we hope the rest of this chapter will offer a more generic perspective and helpful approach to implementing the business gatekeeper layer and role. If the latter is true, then the risk is that access to master data is not being managed tightly enough, which can result in significant quality control or compliance issues and can place the MDM project and governance teams into a continually reactive position.

In an August 2010 Information Difference research study[2] involving 257 respondents worldwide and representing a variety of medium-size and large companies, 19 percent of the respondents indicated that either compliance and legislative requirements or reducing corporate risk was the key driver for the company to implement data governance. This indicates that there is sufficient concern related to compliance and corporate risk factors and that additional management focus is needed. Whether or not this is a main driver, data access control is a significant enough factor that it should be one of the key focuses in MDM and data governance planning.

Vendors of Identity and Access Management (IAM) solutions and MDM products are increasingly recognizing this need and continue to provide more profiling and reporting features in their identity management and access management solutions, but these solutions continue to be very IT administrator oriented and have yet to more broadly embrace or enable a data access gatekeeper function as a business side practice. With that gap in mind, let's take a look at how to enable this business side practice and the right gatekeeper model.

Creating the Right Gatekeeper Model

If within your company, you are fortunate enough to already have tight control over user access to your customer master data, you conduct frequent audits to verify and keep control of user access, you have real-time user and system access information to assist with gatekeeper decision making, and you can quickly spot and address any user access violations or unexpected variation, then give yourself a high-five and skip to Chapter 8. But we think this will not typically be the case and that what we present in this chapter will help drive more focus on the management practice and business control of data access.

Creating the gatekeeper layer will enable a more proactive data access management practice. Planning and implementing this type of gatekeeper function will actually be like conducting a mini business intelligence exercise involving getting access to specific data, profiling, tagging, and organizing the data, and then creating views or reports that will provide timely and accurate information that is needed for decision making and auditing. Figure 7.1 provides a high-level view of the gatekeeper model, which we'll be describing in more detail.

Figure 7.1 illustrates how IT and the business gatekeeper role need to work closely to coordinate and design the overall process, identify what data is needed, and organize this into a consolidated set of user access information that the gatekeeper can utilize as needed for decision making and auditing. In the next sections of this chapter, we will discuss how to prepare and execute this type of model. Keep in mind that this represents a generic approach and we

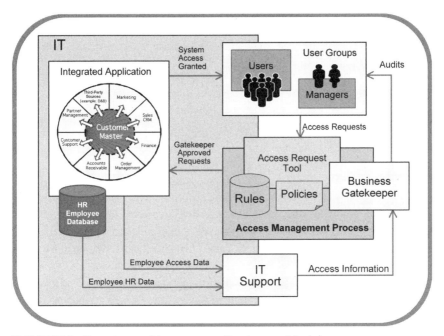

FIGURE 7.1 Data Access Management Gatekeeper Model

assume that in any company there is likely to be variation with how this type of model and gatekeeper process can be implemented within an existing infrastructure. As long as the end result is that business and IT are working effectively together to improve focus and control over user access to the master data, how you execute this is less important.

PREPARING

The gatekeeper will need to work with a person with good data profiling skills who, ideally, should already be part of the MDM core team or a member of the IT group who is supporting the MDM initiative. This person will be needed to help compile user access data and produce the end reports or views in the formats we'll be describing here. This person should also be aware of, or should inquire about, any data profiling, IAM-oriented, or MDM-oriented tools that may be available in the company and able to be utilized for any of the preparation, profiling, and reporting tasks involved in this process. Any technology that can greatly assist with the extensibility, repeatability, and automation of this process should not be overlooked.

With or without technology assistance, there are basic ingredients needed in the data access management process for preparation of the gatekeeper role. This includes employee data, user access management requirements, user group names, and the mapping of this information.

Employee Data

This comes in two flavors:

1. **Employee access data.** This data should cover all users with any assigned privileges (the privileges may also be referred to as responsibilities or rights) that allow any form of create, update, delete, or read-only capability with the customer master data. This data should include at least the employee name, employee ID, and the assigned privileges.
2. **Employee HR data.** This data will provide additional internal information about the employee. This should include data such as employee name, employee ID, company e-mail address, department number, manager name, and job title. This data will be combined with the employee access data to create the information needed to enable the gatekeeper to create the user access profiles needed for the access review, audits, and monitoring processes.

The MDM core team or the data governance council may need to work with IT and HR to ensure that this data will remain confidential and secure with the business gatekeeper role. The MDM team or governance council requesting this type of data should not come as a surprise to either IT or HR. In the planning stages for MDM initiative and in preparing the data governance charter, these needs should have already been discussed and expectations set.

Access Management Requirements

Having an integrated application with various functional groups sharing a common customer master means that there will be many user roles with various data access requirements that will need to be identified and managed. The gatekeeper will need to build a matrix that aligns user roles with the type of access requirements they have for the customer master data. Table 7.1 provides an example of this.

In a case where the customer master environment and user access assignments have existed prior to the MDM or data governance initiatives, check to see if this type of requirement information may already exist with the

TABLE 7.1 User Access Requirements

User Roles	Access Requirements					
	Limited Read	Full Read	Create	Update	Limited Maintenance	Full Maintenance
Sales Representative	X					
Account Manager	X					
Marketing Data Analyst	X					
Contract Specialist		X				
Telemarketing Agent		X		X		
Sales Quoter		X	X	X		
Customer Care Agent		X	X	X		
CRM Lead		X	X	X		
Order Administrator	X			X		
Accounts Receivable Lead	X			X		
Finance Credit Manager	X			X		
Data Manager		X	X	X	X	
Customer Data Steward		X		X	X	
IT Business Analyst		X				
IT Application Engineer		X				X

planning and implementation of that system. If this information doesn't exist, it will be necessary to create the matrix shown in Table 7.1 from scratch. Depending on a company's operational model, how job roles are defined, and how the system and data access privileges are defined, the matrix that you create could look very different than the example we have provided. What's important in any scenario is that this matrix will provide a high-level mapping between the user roles and their access requirements, which can serve as general guidance for what type of privileges should or should not be assigned to users.

Keep in mind that the privileges in combination with the associated user interface will dictate the specific views and functionality that the user will have. Default privileges that an application offers often do not fully align with the access requirements and restrictions needed, which is why the matrix will help provide a basis for evaluating this. For example, in an integrated application suite the default access privilege for an account manager or a telemarketing agent may be too broad and allow them to have create and update privileges when, per the company's business processes and job role guidelines, they should only be able to read and update specific customer data. In this case, the data access gatekeeper should work with IT to modify the privilege to be aligned to the business practice and associated guidelines.

As previously mentioned, access requirements may also be bound by SoD rules that limit ability to access or change customer data. For example, SoD rules may allow a contracts administrator role the ability to create and update the contract data but restricts this user to read-only access to the customer data. Depending on how a company handles their SOX compliance process, it may be necessary for the data access gatekeeper to be involved in management of the SoD rules. We'll touch more on this subject later in the chapter.

Add User Group Names

From the HR information, the job title or department name won't usually reflect the commonly used name for a user's functional group. A functional group name may include a geographic or regional element and may be more specific to a particular type of role. For example, a person with a Customer Care Agent job title may be in a functional group called North America Sales and Services, or a person with a Data Steward job title may be in a group called Asia Pacific Customer Operations, and so on.

This user group name is what will most often be referred to in internal meetings, presentations, planning, issues management, or other types of general interaction with users and teams. As the common identity for the

TABLE 7.2 User Group Names

Employee	Employee ID	Dept #	Job Title	User Group Name
Employee Name	#	#	Account Manager	North American Sales and Services
Employee Name	#	#	Marketing Data Analyst	Global Marketing & Business Reporting
Employee Name	#	#	Contract Specialist	Northern Europe Contract Management
Employee Name	#	#	Sales Quoter	Asia Pacific Sales Operations
Employee Name	#	#	Customer Care Agent	Central Europe Customer Operations
Employee Name	#	#	CRM Lead	Opportunity Management, U.S. Sales
Employee Name	#	#	Order Administrator	Order Management Support, Japan
Employee Name	#	#	Accounts Receivable Lead	Finance Administration, Germany
Employee Name	#	#	Finance Credit Manager	Latin America Credit Management
Employee Name	#	#	Data Manager	Global Customer Administration
Employee Name	#	#	Customer Data Steward	Asia Pacific Customer Operations

user group, it is important for the gatekeeper to recognize this group name and map it in with the other employee information. Table 7.2 provides an example of mapping the user group name to the other employee information.

Depending on the size of the company and number of users that have requirements for access to the customer master data, this mapping exercise could be quite time-consuming. If a large task is anticipated, this is a perfect example of when to engage the functional area data stewards to help size the effort and assist as needed.

Map Privileges to Requirement Categories

There are usually default user access privileges that come with the application. These privileges provide the capabilities for a user to read, create, update, delete, or maintain the data. For access to the customer master data there could be only a few default privileges or, with an integrated business suite, there may be privileges specific to the customer master module itself as well as privileges for other modules such as quoting, order management, customer support, or finance functions. These functions also include capability to create, update, or delete customer master data. All privileges that can access the customer master data need to be identified and provided in the user access data that IT supplies. Recall that in Chapter 4 we discussed the need for a data entry point matrix (Table 4.1). This matrix can serve as a baseline and cross-reference point to determine if the access data IT provided includes these entry points.

These default privileges can have rather cryptic names, which may not provide much indication of the specific type of access being granted; therefore, there will probably be a need to map these privileges to the capability categories (i.e., read, create, update, delete, maintain) in order to better relate these privileges to the gatekeeping process. Doing this can also greatly simplify the displayed results from the profiling activity. Table 7.3 provides an example of this type of mapping.

Once this preparation and mapping is completed, you are ready to start profiling the data.

 PROFILING THE DATA

With this user access data assembled and mapped properly, the gatekeeper should work with the data profiler to discuss the criteria and any specific validation logic needed for the profiling activity. Creating mock-up examples of the type of reports or views the gatekeeper would like to see will be very helpful for the profiler. Expect that the gatekeeper and the profiler may run through a few iterations before getting the logic and views to the desired end result. From the profiling, you are looking to produce a relatively simple output that can provide the following types of user access insight:

- Validate the type of privileges the users and groups actually have.
- Are these privileges correctly aligned to their access requirements and allowed capabilities? Are there any unexpected privileges?
- Are there any broader access issues or trends with certain individuals or groups that need to be addressed? It may be that an individual or group was initially assigned the incorrect privileges, or that someone changed roles and their prior privileges are still active, or perhaps that another

TABLE 7.3 Privileges Mapped to Capabilities

Privilege	Customer Data Access Capability					
	Limited Read	Full Read	Create	Update	Limited Maintenance	Full Maintenance
Customer Master Read Only		X				
Customer Master Data Maintenance		X	X	X		X
Customer Master Data Update		X		X		
Customer Master Data Librarian		X			X	
CRM User	X					
CRM Super User		X		X		
CRM Data Maintenance		X			X	
Quoting—Create Accounts		X	X	X		
Accounts Receivable Maintenance		X		X		
Credit Profile Maintenance	X		X	X	X	
Service Request Create	X		X	X		
Service Request Update	X			X		
Order Management Entry	X		X	X		
Partner—Create Account		X				
Partner—Read Only		X				

gatekeeper who controls, for example, the order management privileges, is broadly approving those requests without realizing this also allows access to customer master data.

There could also be other scenarios that can cause inappropriate access assignments, but the point here is to create a process that allows user access assignments to be regularly monitored and audited. These types of views also allow the gatekeeper to fully understand who the users and groups are, where they exist, with what business functions they are associated, and ultimately, to provide the insight needed to make decisions that are necessary to tightly control access to the customer master data.

Table 7.4 provides an example of the type of user access report that can be produced from the profiled data. This type of report can be used to regularly monitor individual and group access capabilities in alignment with their access requirements and allowed capabilities, or can reveal where inappropriate capabilities exist that will need corrective action. In Table 7.4, the darker highlighted cells are used to indicate cases where an individual or group has an access capability that is unexpected or inappropriate. Upon seeing this, the gatekeeper can review the case with the user, manager, or process area data steward to decide what actions to take.

The underlying logic and scripts used to generate this type of report should be reusable and should require only minor ongoing maintenance. Make sure that this type of report provides sufficient detail to act on but is still simple enough that the information can be easily shared as needed with the user groups, data stewards, or the governance council.

IMPLEMENTING AND MANAGING THE PROCESS

With the data access information compiled, profiled, and the results available, the gatekeeper should do some final validation checking and process testing before going live with the new process. Don't overlook the need to do sufficient data validation and testing with the functional area data stewards. They should be your first line of support where any local communications or data access issues need to be addressed. You certainly don't want these data stewards or the local managers and users to be surprised when new data access management processes and audits are implemented. Like any broad business process, a good validation and test plan is necessary. And because the user group mapping that has been compiled can also be nicely leveraged in other monitoring and quality

TABLE 7.4 User Access Report

Employee	ID	User Group	User Role	Access Capabilities					
				Limited Read	Full Read	Create	Update	Limited Maintenance	Full Maintenance
Employee Name	ID	North American Sales and Services	Account Manager	X					
Employee Name	ID	North American Sales and Services	Account Manager	X					
Employee Name	ID	North American Sales and Services	Account Manager	X	X				
Employee Name	ID	Global Marketing & Business Reporting	Marketing Data Analyst	X					
Employee Name	ID	Global Marketing & Business Reporting	Marketing Data Analyst	X					
Employee Name	ID	Global Marketing & Business Reporting	Marketing Data Analyst	X					
Employee Name	ID	Northern Europe Contract Management	Contract Specialist		X	X	X	X	
Employee Name	ID	Northern Europe Contract Management	Contract Specialist		X	X	X	X	
Employee Name	ID	Northern Europe Contract Management	Contract Specialist		X			X	
Employee Name	ID	Asia Pacific Sales Operations	Sales Quoter		X	X	X		

(continued)

TABLE 7.4 (Continued)

Employee	ID	User Group	User Role	Access Capabilities					
				Limited Read	Full Read	Create	Update	Limited Maintenance	Full Maintenance
Employee Name	ID	Asia Pacific Sales Operations	Sales Quoter		X	X	X		
Employee Name	ID	Asia Pacific Sales Operations	Sales Quoter		X	X	X		
Employee Name	ID	Central Europe Customer Operations	Customer Care Agent		X	X	X		
Employee Name	ID	Central Europe Customer Operations	Customer Care Agent		X	X	X		
Employee Name	ID	Central Europe Customer Operations	Customer Care Agent		X	X	X		
Employee Name	ID	Opportunity Management, U.S. Sales	CRM Lead		X	X	X		
Employee Name	ID	Opportunity Management, U.S. Sales	CRM Lead		X	X	X		
Employee Name	ID	Opportunity Management, U.S. Sales	CRM Lead		X	X	X		
Employee Name	ID	Order Management Support, Japan	Order Administrator	X			X		
Employee Name	ID	Order Management Support, Japan	Order Administrator	X			X		

TABLE 7.4 (Continued)

Employee	ID	User Group	User Role	Access Capabilities					
				Limited Read	Full Read	Create	Update	Limited Maintenance	Full Maintenance
Employee Name	ID	Order Management Support, Japan	Order Administrator	X			X		
Employee Name	ID	Finance Administration, Germany	Accounts Receivable Lead	X			X		
Employee Name	ID	Finance Administration, Germany	Accounts Receivable Lead	X		X	X		
Employee Name	ID	Finance Administration, Germany	Accounts Receivable Lead	X			X		
Employee Name	ID	Latin America Credit Management	Finance Credit Manager	X			X		
Employee Name	ID	Latin America Credit Management	Finance Credit Manager	X			X		
Employee Name	ID	Latin America Credit Management	Finance Credit Manager	X			X		
Employee Name	ID	Global Customer Administration	Data Manager		X		X	X	
Employee Name	ID	Global Customer Administration	Data Manager		X		X	X	

(continued)

TABLE 7.4 (Continued)

Employee Name	ID	User Group	User Role	Access Capabilities					
				Limited Read	Full Read	Create	Update	Limited Maintenance	Full Maintenance
Employee Name	ID	Global Customer Administration	Data Manager		X		X	X	X
Employee Name	ID	Asia Pacific Customer Operations	Customer Data Steward		X		X	X	
Employee Name	ID	Asia Pacific Customer Operations	Customer Data Steward		X		X	X	
Employee Name	ID	Asia Pacific Customer Operations	Customer Data Steward		X		X	X	
Employee Name	ID	Global IT Application Support	IT Application Engineer		X				X
Employee Name	ID	Global IT Application Support	IT Application Engineer		X				X
Employee Name	ID	Global IT Application Support	IT Application Engineer		X		X		X

management processes, you want to be sure this profile information is accurate and can become a familiar point of reference with the data stewards.

Testing and Launching the Process

The data validation process should essentially consist of reviewing the various data points and results from the profiling process. With a good cross section of managers and data stewards, explain and verify the type of data and results as shown in our examples in Tables 7.1 through 7.4. From this there may likely be some new insights gained and corrections needed with the underlying access requirements, profiling logic, or group mapping. Gaining the feedback and support from the managers and data stewards is critical to the execution, adoption, and effectiveness of this process.

Once the data has been validated and the user groups have sufficiently acknowledged the process expectations, you should conduct a few test runs to validate the actual execution and run time of the process. The frequency with which the underlying employee access data can be refreshed, the turn-around time for the data profiling tasks, and the ability for the gatekeeper to review and initiate actions will all play into the timing and repeatability of the process. Repeatability on a weekly or monthly cycle would be optimal to ensure that any changes in employee status, user group dynamics, or assignment of privileges are accounted for in a timely manner with the monitoring and audit steps. Inconsistency or too much latency with the underlying reference information can negatively impact the accuracy and effectiveness and diminish the stakeholder perception of the process. As a control process, it's important to maintain a regular pulse of monitoring and corrective action so that the user groups are continually aware of the process and its purpose.

Once testing has concluded, complete all necessary process and administrative documentation and begin communicating the process go-live date. Any general information about this process should be posted with other governance process information.

Resolve Issues Immediately

From the profiling and testing, you may have already noticed some privilege assignment or alignment issues, such as those illustrated in Table 7.4. If you haven't already corrected this, immediately begin resolving these issues with the appropriate data stewards or user groups. Whether lingering or newly identified, issues should be addressed as quickly as possible.

In a shared customer master environment, a user or group can, without realizing it, change data that can negatively impact another group or process. For example, multiple groups may have the ability to enter or update customer addresses. One of these addresses is likely to be considered the customer's primary address, billing or shipping address, or possibly all of these. These types of addresses should be highly controlled by a central customer data management team. If there are not sufficient rules, awareness, and constraints in place, it is very possible that other teams such as customer service, marketing, or sales, who also may have access privileges that allow changes or updates to the address, will cause problems for invoicing, shipping, or other account management functions that are not expecting the change. Unmanaged, these types of issues can reflect underlying risk and compliance issues that can turn into severe and costly problems further down the line.

Auditing and Monitoring

Key to the effectiveness of this gatekeeper process is the ability to regularly monitor and address the user access requests and changes in relation to current policies, rules, requirements, and access assumptions. Periodic audits are needed to continue to ensure that the user requirements, job expectations, user status, group names, and so on, are still valid, or that any lingering violation issues and expected actions have been formally addressed. Monitoring and auditing activities may also be necessary to meet SOX or ISO requirements.

A well-implemented gatekeeping process with the type of data and insights we have covered in this chapter can make the auditing process very straightforward and easy to manage, because much of what is audited is part of the ongoing monitoring and corrective actions on which the gatekeeper is already focused. In other words, with a robust gatekeeper process in place and good housekeeping already occurring on a regular basis, auditing can be a simple and well-aligned process without any major surprises for the gatekeeper or users.

We briefly mentioned already that the user group mapping, as shown in Table 7.2, can also be nicely leveraged in other monitoring and quality management processes involved in the customer data governance process. For example, a data quality monitor that is tracking customer name changes could also leverage this user group mapping to indicate what functional groups are performing customer name changes. This can enable the ability to easily check what authority and data access privileges the group has—such as a cross-check with the data shown as with Tables 7.1 and 7.4—to determine if the name change activity is appropriate or not. Similarly, the data touch-point matrix we discussed in Chapter 4 (Table 4.1) could be augmented to also include the names of the groups who are responsible for entering or updating these specific master data attributes.

Expanding the use of this user group mapping will help increase the ability of the governance process to uniformly recognize who is interacting with the data along with how and where this interaction is occurring. Doing this is also a sign of a maturing governance model, something we will cover more in Chapter 9.

Segregation of Duty (SoD) Management

Complying with SOX rules and regulations requires users who have various types of authority with certain data, such as ability to access and create customer accounts, to be restricted from having similar authority with other types of data, such as contract or financial data. In an integrated environment with shared master data, segregation of duties must be very carefully managed and can involve fairly complex sets of rules and violation combinations that need to be clearly understood.

Violations can often stem from user groups or support functions that are engaged in cross-functional activity, or simply because more specific user access monitoring is now occurring. Similar to what we mentioned regarding the names used for access privileges, SoD definition and violation messages can be rather cryptic. In such cases, it may be necessary to map the unique violation messages to a simple code that will be much easier to utilize in the monitoring and reporting of the violations.

Table 7.5 shows an example of a simple codification approach for the SoD violation messages. Table 7.6 shows how this is used in a violation report that a

TABLE 7.5 Codification of Segregation of Duties (SoD) Violations

Segregation of Duties Rule Violation	Violation Code
Contracts Author with Customer Setup	A
Contracts Maintenance with Customer Setup	B
Contracts Maintenance with Customer Maintenance	C
Create Service Requests with Customer Setup	D
Create Service Requests with Customer Maintenance	E
Create Sales Account with Create Finance Account	F
Create Sales Account with Update Finance Account	G
IT Application Management with Customer Setup	H
IT Application Management with Customer Maintenance	I

TABLE 7.6 Segregation of Duties (SoD) Violation Report

SoD Violations By Manager

Manager Name	Dept #	Group Name	# Employees with Violations	Violation Types (Codes)
Manager Name	#	Northern Europe Contract Management	4	A,B,C
Manager Name	#	North American Sales and Services	3	D,E
Manager Name	#	Global Customer Administration	2	F,G
Manager Name	#	Global IT Application Support	2	H,I

SoD Violations By Employee

Employee Name	Dept #	Group Name	Violation Count	Violation Types (Codes)
Employee Name	#	Northern Europe Contract Management	3	A,B,C
Employee Name	#	Northern Europe Contract Management	3	A,B,C
Employee Name	#	Northern Europe Contract Management	2	B,C
Employee Name	#	Northern Europe Contract Management	1	B

gatekeeper can use to quickly zero in on the types of violations and where they are concentrated.

Again note how these examples use the common user group name to maintain consistency and alignment with the other user access report examples we have previously shown. Doing this enables the ability to consistently evaluate how these groups are doing across all the monitoring and reports involved in this data access management process.

SUMMARY

The key takeaway from this chapter is that information protection, and the ability to more tightly manage compliance and other risk factors associated with uncontrolled events or any misconduct involving customer master data, can be greatly enhanced if the concept and practice of data access management process also recognizes the need to enable more business involvement and discipline.

In this chapter, we have laid out an approach using a business-oriented gatekeeper model with examples of how to implement the process using what should be existing internal data and fundamental support provided by IT, data governance, and the functional area data stewards. None of this requires any particular vendor product or solution to implement.

However, it is even better if you are able to leverage vendor products that can make this a more automated job flow and actually result in what could, in effect, be presented as a gatekeeper job console. Not only would a console of this nature greatly help to enable the gatekeeper function, but it can also serve as a consistent and repeatable process foundation to meet ISO standards. As vendor products continue to evolve in the MDM and IAM space, keep an eye on new solutions that begin to more fully support this type of gatekeeper function and the concept of a data access gatekeeper console.

NOTES

1. Alex Berson and Larry Dubov, *Master Data Management and Customer Data Integration for a Global Enterprise* (New York: McGraw-Hill, 2007), Chapters 9 and 10.
2. The Information Difference Company Ltd., "How Data Governance Links MDM and Data Quality," August 2010.

PART THREE

Achieving a Steady State

8

Data Maintenance and Metrics

We are what we repeatedly do. Excellence, then, is not an act, but a habit.

—*Aristotle*

 ## DATA MAINTENANCE

Chapter 6 focused on establishing a data quality model and process to baseline the current quality of the data, handle requests for data quality improvements, and self-feed through metrics for continuous improvement. It briefly covered aspects of data correction and data quality metrics, which will be expanded further in this chapter.

Figure 6.1 in Chapter 6 depicts the interaction of the many roles within the company needed on a data quality process. In essence, the underlying method within that process is represented in Figure 8.1.

Here is how the process and the method overlap:

- The *specify* task is achieved by the many drivers within the company, including the data governance council and the data quality forum.

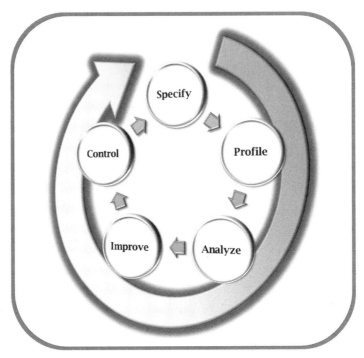

FIGURE 8.1 Data Quality Maintenance Method

- The *profile* task is performed by the data analysts to uncover many aspects of the data.
- The *analyze* task is executed by the design team and the data quality forum with feedback from the data governance council and applicable drivers and stakeholders.
- The *improve* task is carried on by IT support and/or data stewards upon proper approvals.
- The *control* task is implemented by the data quality team through monitors and scorecards, and reported to proper teams and data governance for proper tracking and future improvements.

Understanding how the method is embedded within the process helps envision the continuous data quality improvement behind it. Chapter 6 focused on the roles while this chapter will get deeper into the data quality activities themselves, more specifically in the areas of *improvement* and *control*.

Specify, Profile, and Analyze

These three areas are grouped together in one section because they have been mostly covered already. The *specify* activity is the problem statement or requirement submitted by a driver stating the issue to be addressed.

The *profile* activity is typically executed by data analysts. Data profiling was covered in detail in Chapter 3 since it is a critical activity during data integration. But it is also extremely important in data quality improvement efforts.

Finally, the *analyze* activity is done in tandem with profiling with the combined effort from data analysts, the data quality forum, and the data governance council.

Improve

In Chapter 6, data correction was described as an overarching data quality activity, performed either reactively or proactively to clean up existing bad data as well as to fix the root cause of a problem.

But data quality activities within data correction vary, and understanding its particular nature can help to identify the most effective techniques to use. Figure 8.2 depicts the many specific data quality activities. Data cleansing and scrubbing are not on the diagram, but they are terms used to describe data quality activities more generically.

Let's take a more detailed look at these activities.

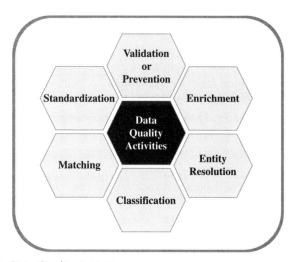

FIGURE 8.2 Data Quality Activities

Data Validation or Error Prevention

Preventing bad data from entering the system is certainly the most effective way to avoid data issues. Unfortunately, this is not always possible. Technological limitations, time constraints, and ever-changing business rules are some of the factors preventing real-time validation at the data entry point level.

The technology behind MDM varies from vendor to vendor, but will typically encompass software applications, middleware, and databases. Therefore, data validation can be accomplished by a combination of client and server side techniques. Both client and server side validations have advantages and disadvantages.

Thin or *fat* clients will dictate the type of tools available for client side validation, but will include varying levels of built-in code along with GUI elements such as drop-down lists, checkboxes, list boxes, radio buttons, and lookup tables.

The *pros* of client side validation include:

■ Some GUI elements prevent users from entering incorrect values because they have to select from a predefined list.
■ Performance is improved since there is no need to process a request/ response message exchange with a remote server for further validation.
■ When presented with a predefined list of options for a given attribute, users have the opportunity to choose the best one.

The *cons* of client side validation include:

■ Any operation not done using the front-end interface will miss on the client side validation logic, and potentially corrupt the data.
■ Most GUI elements used for client side validation are impractical when dealing with large amounts of data, adversely impacting user experience and productivity.
■ Client side validation can be maliciously bypassed and is subject to security concerns.
■ Validation done via application code on the client side can be difficult to update and distribute depending on the architecture in use.

Server side validation can also be accomplished in multiple ways, with the most common being database referential integrity rules and software code embedded in the middleware layer or in the database layer via stored procedures and batch scripts. Some products will offer database independent solutions with most of the server side validation accomplished in a middleware layer, while others will be heavily database driven.

The *pros* of server side validation include:

- Technology on the server side typically allows for higher sophistication of validation rules.
- Validation rules developed directly into the database via referential integrity rules or triggers and stored procedures cannot be bypassed providing the highest level of corruption prevention.
- Changes to existing rules are typically easier to make because they are centralized.

The *cons* of server side validation include:

- User response time is impacted because of the additional request/response message exchange with a remote server.
- Valid options are not immediately obvious to the user.
- Software validation code embedded in the middleware or database batch scripts can still be bypassed with direct access to the database, risking data corruption.

The best approach is to combine client and server side validations to achieve optimal results. It is also important to minimize validation code duplication to prevent discrepancies or redundant work when rules change.

Companies also try to prevent data corruption through business process rules. However, this approach can be very ineffective depending on the size of the company, quantity and skills of users, level of training, and emphasis on quality. Business processes will always exist, but for data quality error prevention to be effective using this method, it is necessary to have constant communication and ongoing training and monitoring, coupled with incentives and rewards for high-quality data entry and maintenance.

Business rules, policies, and procedures can be very dynamic. As they change, software upgrades may be required to incorporate additional data entry or maintenance validations. Those software changes can take a long time to occur due to IT resources and constraints. The business will typically opt to amend business processes to convey the new rules until the actual software change is complete. In this case, it is also critical to plan for a comprehensive data cleanup of previous data that no longer comply with the new rules. In summary, two projects may potentially come out of a business rule change:

1. One project to make any necessary software changes to support the new rules and associated validations.
2. A second project to clean up data that is no longer compliant, or data that is temporarily entered or changed incorrectly until the change goes into effect.

The two projects will need to be planned, prioritized, and executed independently according to business needs, also taking into consideration their mutual dependencies.

Unfortunately, it is not always possible to prevent bad data from entering the system. Many data elements can be very difficult to validate in real-time, either because reference data does not exist at the level needed or because it can take a long time to search when you consider a customer could be on the phone while data is being entered. Mistakes do happen when users are entering information into free-form fields due to incorrect interpretation of business processes, typos, or miscommunication with customers, partners, and vendors. In the end, it is necessary to constantly monitor and measure the quality of the data and the process to improve both the data and the level of data validation and error prevention.

Data Standardization

Data standardization is about conforming data elements of the same type into a pre-established set of rules and policies. Format compliance, although not necessarily easy to achieve, is probably the simplest form of data standardization. For example:

- U.S. telephone numbers must conform to a format such as 1-AAA-BBB-BBBB, where 1 is the long-distance access code, AAA is the area code, and BBB-BBBB is the subscriber number.
- U.S. postal codes must follow either a basic format of five decimal numerical digits, or an extended format, which includes five digits, a hyphen, and four more digits that determine a more precise location.

Another type of standardization encompasses *parsing* or *tokenization*, which is the analysis of a string and its separation into a sequence of tokens. For example:

- Breaking down a contact name into First Name, Middle Initial, and Last Name.
- Properly identifying the correct elements of an address, such as street number, street name, building number, suite number, floor number, city,

county, state, P.O. Box, and postal code, and correctly assigning them into their suitable fields.

Standardization can include multiple types of reconciliation, such as abbreviations for extensions (e.g., *Corp.* for *Corporation* or *Ave.* for *Avenue*), values (e.g., *U.S.* for *United States*), and semantics (e.g., treating *Centre* and *Center* as equals).

Finally, data standardization is the backbone supporting the standardization of processes. The proper execution of a given process, either through automation or not, is dependent upon the correct attribution of data into proper elements to support the correct decision making. For example, clients meeting a certain criteria need to be flagged properly to receive future benefits and offerings according to a given customer rewards program.

The following are some of the benefits of data standardization:

- Data validation or error prevention becomes a lot easier to implement if a testable set of rules exists for a given data value.
- Data comparison is much easier to accomplish when data is in conformance, facilitating the identification of duplicates.
- Standardization facilitates audit trails, helping to identify the root cause of data errors.
- Proper parsing and formatting is a critical step when validating accuracy against data reference sources.

Although there is little contention about the benefits of data standardization inside the company, its actual implementation can be quite challenging. First, there can be technical limitations, such as not having the proper reference sources, or not having tools mature enough to meet desired requirements. Second, there can be business limitations, such as consumers of the data not agreeing on a common standard. Third, there can be resource limitations to collect, implement, and test standards. Finally, as with any other data quality initiative, enforcement through business process workflows can be very ineffective due to a lack of an automated verification.

Data governance becomes an important catalyst in the process of proposing and collecting standardization requirements. One of the roles of data governance is to arbitrate rules, policies, and procedures within the company. Oftentimes, this activity will lead to data standardization. The data governance council can facilitate the understanding and approval of standards, and engage the data quality forum for proper execution as described in the data quality process proposed in Chapter 6.

The business has to be realistic regarding standards. Lack of them is clearly detrimental to the company, but trying to enforce certain ones can be short-sighted, leading to too many exception requests or to a weak form of compliance. Managing exception to standards can be as difficult as managing no standards at all in some cases. Here are some examples of standards that may make sense at first, but should be carefully analyzed before implemented:

- Using only uppercase characters for the company name and no punctuation or special symbols. At first, this could facilitate the identification of duplicates and simplify data entry. On the other hand, non-English characters may not convert properly to uppercase. Another potential issue is not being able to represent a company's true legal name if it carries lowercase or special characters, such as eBay, CiCi's Pizza, Yahoo!, or E*TRADE.
- Forcing the use of the company's legal name only. This standard may make sense for LOBs concerned with legal aspects of the transaction, and could be accomplished by using a reference source, such as Dun & Bradstreet. However, the customer may request the name to represent a particular subdivision of the company, or to include a given department name or location, or some other variation not legally recognized. To fulfill the customer's request, it is necessary to break the standard.
- Usage of "DO NOT USE" next to a company name to prevent a record from being used in future transactions. This is a common approach to preserve a record in active status to support existing transactions, while signaling it should no longer be associated with new transactions. This is a very weak standard, difficult to enforce, and likely hard to process within existing automated business rules provided by the software application. Generally, using an existing field for additional information other than its original purpose leads to confusion and quality issues that are hard to reconcile.

When analyzing a requirement for a particular standard, it is important to take into account its viability and ramifications. It needs to have a business reason, fulfill the requirements of every data consumer, and not cause any unforeseen long-term data quality damages. Look for alternatives. For example, if it is important to have both a standardized company name and a name the customer wants to see, consider using an *also known as* (*AKA*) field or equivalent. This could also be viable for local language representation of company names if both an English and a non-English version are required for legal reasons.

Data standardization usually implies updating the data. It is certainly an important first step to support the identification of duplicates. However, standardizing the data for the purpose of attending a business need should not be confused with standardizing the data for the purpose of identifying duplicates. For the purpose of finding duplicates, the amount of data cleansing and scrubbing can be much higher than what is required to fulfill a given standard. For example, the standard for company name may be a combination of lowercase, uppercase, some label abbreviation, and punctuation. However, to normalize the data for duplicate evaluation, a company name may have to be transformed to all uppercase, no punctuation, and so on. This transformation usually happens in memory or some other alternate repository without impacting what the user sees. We like to distinguish this purpose from the data matching concept, which is explained in more detail later in this chapter.

Global companies face additional challenges because they have to adhere to a multitude of localized rules, policies, and procedures. Do *not* overlook this aspect during a data standardization effort. For an outstanding reference on international address formats, please refer to Graham Rhind's book.[1]

Data Enrichment

Data enrichment or augmentation is the process of enhancing existing information by supplementing missing or incomplete data. Typically, data enrichment is achieved by using external data sources, but that is not always the case. In large companies with multiple disparate systems and fragmented information, it is not unusual to enrich the information provided by one source with data from another. This is particularly common during data migration where customer information is fragmented among multiple systems, and the data from one system is used to complement the other and form a more complete data record in the MDM repository.

As with any other data quality effort, data enrichment must serve a business purpose. New requirements come along that may require data to be augmented. Here are some examples:

- A new marketing campaign requires non-existing detail information about a set of customers, such as Standard Industry Code (SIC), annual sales information, company family information, and so on.
- A new tax calculation process requires *county* information for all U.S. address records, or an extended format for U.S. postal code, which includes ZIP+4.

■ A new legal requirement requires *province* information to be populated for Italian addresses.

Much of this additional information will need to come from an external reference source, such as Dun & Bradstreet (D&B) or OneSource for customer data enrichment, or postal code reference for address augmentation, and so on.

It can be quite a challenge to enrich data. It all starts with the quality of the existing data. If the existing information is incorrect or too sparse, it may be impossible to match with a reference source to supplement what is missing. It can be quite expensive, as well, since the majority of the reference sources will either require a subscription fee, or will charge by volume or specific regional data sets.

When matching data with another source, there is always the risk of accuracy of the match. Most of the companies providing customer matching services with their sources will include an automated score representing their confidence level on the match. For example, a score of 90 means a confidence level of 90 percent that the match is good. Companies will need to work with their data vendors to determine what is acceptable for their business. Typically, it will be possible to define three ranges:

1. Higher range, for example, 80 percent and above, where matches are automatically accepted.
2. Lower range, for example, 60 percent and below, where matches are automatically refused.
3. Middle range, for example, between 60 and 80 percent, where matches have to be manually analyzed to determine if they are good or not.

Once a match is deemed *correct*, the additional information provided by the reference source can be used to enrich the existing data.

Address enrichment is very common, where the combination of some address elements is used to find what is missing. For example, using postal code to figure out city and state, or using address line, city, and state to determine postal code. The challenge comes when there is conflicting information. For example, let's say city, state, and postal code are all populated. However, when trying to enrich county information, postal code suggests one county, while city and state suggest another. It comes down to the confidence level of the original information. If the intent is to automate the matching process, it may be necessary to evaluate what information is usually populated more accurately according to that given system and associated business practice. If it is not possible to make that determination, a manual inspection is likely to be required for conflicting situations.

Data Matching

Data matching is about comparing records and finding matches according to a given criteria for a given purpose. The three most common applications of data matching are:

1. **Entity resolution or record linkage.** This encompasses two steps. The first step is finding similar records according to a set of rules. The second step includes deciding if the similar records are indeed duplicates or not, and linking or consolidating them properly. Data matching helps with the first step. Entity resolution is discussed in more detail later in this chapter.
2. **Reference source matching.** Data quality initiatives may require matching existing data with a reference source for further validation or enhancement of existing data.
3. **Data classification.** Records are matched together according to established criteria for the purpose of proper organization, such as the creation of groups or hierarchies. Classification is discussed in more detail later in this chapter.

The most primitive type of data matching is achieved through an *exact match* comparison. As the name implies, records are considered the same only if they match exactly. This type of matching is typically insufficient to find duplicates, because many variances exist on the data that will cause them to be different, such as misspellings, different abbreviations for company name extensions and addresses, punctuations, extra spaces, use of nicknames, and so on. Even when strong data standards are defined and highly enforced, variations still do occur. Therefore, data will need to be transformed before they can be compared. Transformation for matching purposes happens behind the scenes and does not change the data seen by users. It is done in memory or using an alternate repository.

A very common transformation for comparison purposes is achieved through fuzzy logic. Fuzzy logic is the foundation for *fuzzy matching*, which is a generic term used to describe a technique used to help in finding similar records, or records that are not exactly alike. Similar records are identified by alleviating common typos and transposed characters; normalizing company name extensions, nicknames, and address complements; phonetic similarity; and so on.

Many data quality tools include some form of fuzzy matching capability with one or both of the following methods:

- **Deterministic matching.** Uses rules and patterns to determine two records are the same. For example, manipulating vowels for phonetic comparison, ignoring extensions in company names (e.g., Corporation, Incorporated), defining rules for initials (e.g., IBM matches International Business Machines), and so on.
- **Probabilistic matching.** Uses statistical techniques to determine the probability that two records are the same. For example, calculating distance between string segments, measuring number of transpositions necessary to make two strings alike, measuring number of substitutions required to change one string into another, and so on. Some of the algorithms utilized are Hamming distance, Bigram, Jaro-Winkler distance, Levenshtein distance, and Damerau-Levenshtein distance.

Out-of-the-box fuzzy matching has improved considerably in the last few years. Many of them are entity specific to account for the different rules required when matching company names instead of addresses, or contacts, for example. Some data quality tools provide means for customizing built-in fuzzy matching with complementary rules for certain specific cases. However, before spending a lot of resources customizing your own fuzzy algorithms, discuss your needs and problems with your vendor. Your vendor may be willing to incorporate your needs into their product. Many matching algorithms are rule-based, and can be expanded to include new rules without breaking existing ones. Fuzzy matching can be very complex, and data quality vendors have spent a lot of time and money on research. They are better equipped than most companies to enhance fuzzy matching algorithms.

No matter how good a data matching tool is, it will invariably have two undesirable outcomes. Obviously, the better the tool, the lower the likelihood of these results, but it is practically impossible to avoid them with the technology we have today. They are:

- **False positives.** These are distinct records, incorrectly identified as similar. Compared to false negatives, false positives are typically easier to detect through manual inspection of the data batch qualified as similar prior to consolidation.
- **False negatives.** These are similar records, but not identified as such. Compared to false positives, false negatives are harder to detect, because

they require an additional search to find what was not included in the data batch originally qualified as similar.

Another characteristic of some fuzzy matching tools is the capability to adjust their matching sensitivity. A tighter sensitivity will yield more false negatives while a lower sensitivity will yield more false positives. Since false positives are relatively easier to spot with manual inspection, a lower sensitivity is desired if the process includes a thorough manual inspection step. However, if the process is mostly automated, it is likely better to have a high sensitivity to avoid false positives. It also depends on the objective of the matching. False positives will lead to incorrect records merged together, while false negatives will lead to duplicates. If the objective is a marketing campaign, for example, false negatives will cause prospects to be contacted multiple times, but if the objective is consolidating online accounts, false positives will drastically cause two distinct real-life entities to share information that does not belong to both.

To minimize false positives, it is recommended to perform a match in more than a single attribute. For example, finding duplicate companies by matching company name only will lead to a lot more false positives than using both company name and an address element, such as city or state.

When performing data matching, it is important to take into account the characteristics of the data, the purpose of finding potential duplicates (business need), and the tools and processes needed to support the activity. Exact and fuzzy matching—probabilistic or deterministic—should be combined to achieve maximum accuracy, efficiency, and throughput.

Entity Resolution

Entity resolution, also known as Record Linkage (RL), is about finding records that reference the same entity. Examples of entities in the context of Customer MDM include company, people, contact, address, account, and so on. The result of an entity resolution activity is typically data consolidation/ de-duplication, or mapping. When the same entity is identified across multiple systems, a mapping is created to signal the relationship. When the same entity is identified within the same system, records are consolidated or de-duplicated into a surviving or golden record.

The tricky part is agreeing on the meaning of *same entity*. For instance, in one company, two customers with the same name might be considered the same entity, while in another company, both customer name and address have to match for them to be considered the same entity. The definition can get a lot more complex, because it encompasses a multitude of attributes related to that entity and their many uses across the multiple LOBs. There is also the issue about consolidation versus segmentation discussed in Chapter 3. Finally, data model constraints may also prevent certain operations, transactional or not, from being executed properly if records are merged together, further limiting what entities are actually the same.

Entity resolution is both a business and a technical challenge. From a business perspective, it is about creating the proper definition of what constitutes a duplicate, taking into account business needs and technical limitations. From a technical perspective, it is about applying the right techniques to find the duplicates and merge them, when appropriate.

Many companies fail to clearly define what rules to follow to identify a duplicate. Furthermore, even though this is clearly a business task, it shouldn't be done without understanding the data first. A lot of emphasis has been put on data profiling throughout this book, and it is a very important first step here, as well. For example, as much as the business may like to establish that two or more companies are the same if they have the same tax ID number, this is likely not viable if only a small percentage of them carry that information.

The main steps for entity resolution are:

1. Entity definition.
2. Duplication discovery.
3. Survivorship determination and final disposition.

Entity Definition   Figure 8.3 depicts the *entity definition* step. Many companies incorrectly assume the definition of a duplicate is obvious and skip this step. It is important to define and agree on what a duplicate really is, and state this clearly. The *computer* and *people* icons indicate automated and manual activities respectively.

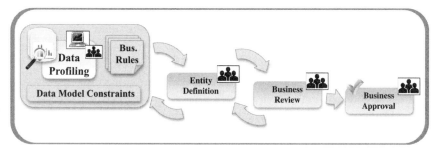

FIGURE 8.3 Entity Definition

Notice the input to this step includes data profiling, business rules, and constraints that may be imposed by the data model itself. Data profiling is typically achieved with a combination of heavy business analysis and the employment of data profiling tools, which is indicated by both *people* and *computer* icons.

Good Customer MDM repositories will usually offer a clear distinction between customer identity and their transaction relationships, minimizing constraints when defining an entity. However, certain repositories combined with some business practices may tightly couple those distinct concepts.

Let's take a look at a couple examples of things to be considered during the definition step:

- Assume there are two records with the exact same customer name and address; however, one is flagged with *credit hold*, while the other is not. Merging the two records could prevent the record without the hold from being used in certain operations, or vice versa, depending on how the surviving record is flagged. Therefore, a possible definition of a duplicate has to take into account the *credit hold* flag. Granted, the actual flagging could be incorrect, because shouldn't both records be flagged the same if they represent the same customer in the same address? This is a good side effect of the entity resolution as a whole: uncover other potential quality issues with the data.
- Assume your company has both an end-user and a partner relationship with another company. Even though the end-user/partner is the same physical entity, the model may require two records to exist independently because of how they are used throughout the company. A good model and appropriate process should support a single customer with multiple relationships, but this may not always be the case.

The process in Figure 8.3 suggests an iterative method. The definition of an entity is refined until a final agreement and approval is reached.

Lastly, a huge challenge of Customer MDM is to deal with the ever-changing business environment. Mergers and acquisitions are happening constantly. Marketing, for example, may want to immediately merge records from the acquired company into the acquiring one so they can market the new company properly. On the other hand, for legal reasons, finance may need records to remain separate for proper accounting processing. This should also be taken into consideration when working on the definition of an entity. Agreeing on a solution can be a struggle.

Duplication Discovery   Once an entity is clearly defined, it is time to look for duplicates according to that definition. There are a few situations where it may be necessary to identify a duplicate. It could be during a special project to clean up the data by eliminating duplicates, or it could be during data entry to detect if a new customer or contact already exists on the system. Nonetheless, the ultimate goal is typically the same: group similar records together for proper determination of whether records are indeed duplicates.

Figure 8.4 depicts a high-level approach that can be employed in this particular step.

Target entity is the record or records to match. On a data entry activity, for example, it would be the new data coming in. On a particular project, a company may want to prioritize a list of customers, contacts, and/or addresses that need to be evaluated and eventually consolidated. Target entity could also be optional, as indicated by the dashed lines. A given project may take only the entity definition as criteria for finding duplicates, and thereby use it to find redundancy in the repository.

Entity definition was discussed previously. It works as rules and constraints to the overall design and execution of the discovery process as a whole.

Data matching was mostly discussed in the previous section. A company can apply deterministic and/or probabilistic techniques to match a target entity

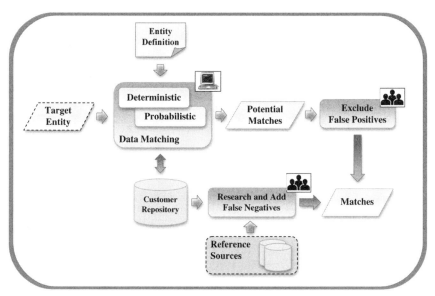

FIGURE 8.4 Duplication Discovery

to the existing ones in the customer repository, or simply collect the entire existing list of records already in the repository and identify which ones are similar. Notice the *computer* icon suggests this can be mostly automated with a good data quality tool.

The output of the data matching routine is a list of potential matches. As discussed previously, false positives and false negatives will typically exist.

False positives are usually easy to spot though manual inspection of the results. It can be a tedious activity depending on the volume of data, quality of the tool used, and complexity of the entity definition. If some type of scoring was applied during the matching step, it is likely some records were put into a *sure match* category, others were already discarded, and others were placed in a final bucket with records that need manual confirmation. Look for opportunities to automate this classification to minimize the amount of manual work necessary to flag false positives.

Researching and adding false negatives can be trickier since it is hard to know what was missed. They are not presented on a list like the false positive records. As indicated by the *people* icon, this is mostly manual and can usually be accomplished by queries to the repository combined with research to *reference sources*—if they exist at all for a particular situation. Examples of reference sources when looking for duplicate company records would include D&B, OneSource, and so on. You would use reference sources in some cases to find out about mergers and acquisitions, company family tree, and mostly other things that couldn't be automated.

Once false positives are excluded from the list of similar records, and false negatives are added to it, a list of true *matches* is completed and ready for the next step.

Survivorship Determination and Final Disposition Figure 8.5 depicts a process to determine which record or records should remain active in the system after duplicates are identified.

The same way it is important to define what an entity is, it is necessary to establish the rules for deciding which record(s) should remain active in the system. The attributes used to solve for entity definition and survivorship determination are typically different. For entity definition, they are mostly identity attributes, while for survivorship determination they are both identity and transactional attributes. For example, when two records are identified as matches based on company name and address, one company might want to retain the one with most service contracts or install base attributes associated to minimize the time it takes to move the transactions of the merged record into

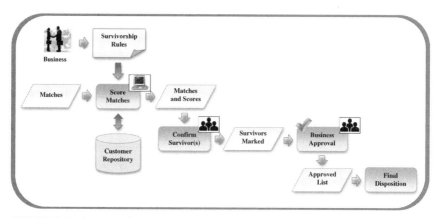

FIGURE 8.5 Survivorship Determination

the surviving record. *Survivorship rules* specify those conditions, and must be defined and agreed on by the business.

The *matches* input is the result of the previous step. It is a list of similar records organized into groups. The list could be manually evaluated for proper disposition; however, that could be a very time-consuming effort depending on volume and number of attributes to be considered. A typical approach is to have a scoring mechanism to facilitate the decision-making process.

The *score matches* step can be the automated activity, which takes into consideration the survivorship rules, reads any additional attributes necessary for the decision from the repository, analyzes the input file, and outputs the results organized by scores. A scoring mechanism can be established where the higher the number, the higher the probability the record needs to be maintained, and the lower the number, the higher the probability the record should be either inactivated or merged into another one.

The scores alone are not sufficient to make a final determination. As usual, thresholds can be established for automatic acceptance or automatic rejection. But there is always that intermediate layer that requires a manual inspection and disposition. *Confirm survivor(s)* is this manual evaluation to validate the scores, and mark which records should survive or not. Ideally, only one survivor would remain for each group of similar records, but that is not always the case. Depending on the amount of data segmentation, transactional dependencies, sequence of events, and other business needs, it is very likely many records initially indicated as duplicates will have to remain active on the system.

Once the *survivors marked* list is validated by the business, an *approved list* is created and ready for proper disposition, which could include a simple inactivation, a merge into a surviving record, or a combination of activities required by a particular system design and/or configuration.

Data Classification

Data classification is about categorizing and/or organizing data for better analysis and decision making. There are many ways to classify data. For example, categorizing data based on criticality to the business and frequency of use can be important to business process definitions. Classifying data based on compliance and regulations can be part of a risk management program. Data profiling is highly driven by data types, and collections of data with similar content.

A particular type of data classification highly sought in a Customer MDM program is customer hierarchy. Customer hierarchy management entails managing customer data relationships to represent company organizational structures, for example.

From a BI perspective, hierarchical organization of data is essential. It allows for a vastly superior understanding of market and industry segmentation. The volume of master data can be quite overwhelming. Classifying this data hierarchically is a critical first step to make the most sense of the information. The results can be applied to market campaigns, cross-sells, and up-sells.

From an operational perspective, hierarchy management is also critical in improving efforts to maintain master data. Some LOBs, such as sales, may have a vested interest in hierarchical organization for means of territory segmentation and sales commissions.

It is doubtful that a single hierarchical representation for each data entity will meet the needs of all LOBs within any large company. Multiple representations are not uncommon but add to the project's cost. Maintaining a single hierarchy can be very challenging already. As the different perspectives grow, companies risk compromising the main reason that they engaged in an MDM project in the first place: an agreed-upon view of master data across the entire company. Finding the right balance is key.

Most likely, the MDM repository will have relational relationships (e.g., a customer has multiple addresses or accounts). These types of relationships are inherent to the structure of the repository, and are conceptually different from hierarchy management. What's more, your MDM repository may not support hierarchy management.

Hierarchy management is discussed in more detail in Chapter 10 as part of creating the customer 360° view.

  DATA QUALITY METRICS

In Chapter 6, we briefly described the purpose of data quality metrics as part of a self-feeding process for continuous improvement. We also discussed establishing and creating a data quality baseline for better understanding the current state of the data and its proper business alignment and fitness for use.

This chapter expands that concept by defining means for creating a scalable and sustainable process in which data quality metrics become the central point for data quality assessment and consequently a critical source for data quality proactive initiatives.

Data quality metrics falls into two main categories: (1) monitoring and (2) scorecards or dashboards. Monitors are used to detect violations that usually require immediate corrective actions. Scorecards or dashboards allow for numbers to be associated with the quality of the data and are more snapshot-in-time reports as opposed to real-time triggers. Notice that results of monitor reports can be included in the overall calculation of scorecards and dashboards, as well.

Data quality metrics need to be aligned with business key performance indicators (KPI) throughout the company. Each LOB will have a list of KPIs for its particular needs, which need to be collected by the data quality forum and properly implemented into a set of monitors and/or scorecards.

Associating KPIs to metrics is critical for two reasons:

1. As discussed earlier, all data quality activities need to serve a business purpose, and data quality metrics are no different.
2. KPIs are directly related to ROI. Metrics provide the underlying mechanism for associating numbers to KPIs and consequently ROI. They become a powerful instrument for assessing the improvement achieved through a comprehensive data quality ongoing effort, which is key to an overall MDM program.

The actual techniques for measuring the quality of the data for both monitors and scorecards are virtually the same. The difference is primarily related to the time necessary for the business to react. If a critical KPI is associated with a given metric, a monitor should be in place to quickly alert the business about any out-of-spec measurements.

Data quality level agreements (DQLAs) are an effective method to capture business requirements and establish proper expectations related to needed metrics. Well-documented requirements and well-communicated expectations can avoid undesirable situations and a stressed relationship between the data quality team and the business and/or IT, which can be devastating to an overall company-wide data quality program.

The next two sections describe typical DQLA and report components for monitors and scorecards.

Monitors

Bad data exists in the system and is constantly being introduced by apparently inoffensive business operations that are theoretically following proper processes. Furthermore, system bugs and limitations can contribute to data quality degradation, as well.

But not all data quality issues are made equal. Some will impact the business more than others. Certain issues can have a very direct business implication and need to be avoided at all costs. Monitors should be established against these sensitive attributes to alert the business regarding their occurrence so proper action can be taken.

A typical DQLA between the business and the data quality team will include the following information regarding each monitor to be implemented:

- **ID.** Data quality monitor identification.
- **Title.** A unique title for the monitor.
- **Description.** A detailed description that expresses what needs to be measured.
- **KPI.** Key performance indicator associated with what is measured.
- **Data quality dimension.** Helps organize and qualify the report into dimensions, such as completeness, accuracy, consistency, uniqueness, validity, timeliness, and so on.
- **LOB(s) impacted.** List of business area(s) impacted by violations being monitored.
- **Measurement unit.** Specifies expected unit of measurement, such as number of occurrences, or percentage.
- **Target value.** Quality level expected.
- **Threshold.** Specifications for lowest quality acceptable, potentially separated into ranges such as acceptable (green), warning (yellow), or critical (red).
- **Measurement frequency.** How often the monitor runs (e.g., daily or weekly).

- **Point of contact.** Primary person or group responsible for receiving the monitor report and taking any appropriate actions based on the results.
- **Root cause of the problem.** When a monitor is requested for an out-of-spec condition, it is important to understand what is causing the incident to occur.
- **Has the root cause been addressed?** Prevention is always the best solution for data quality problems. If a data issue can be avoided at reasonable costs, it should be pursued.

Table 8.1 describes a potential scenario where a monitor is applicable. Notice the explanation of the root cause of the problem, and the measures that

TABLE 8.1 Sample Monitor DQLA

ID	DQ001
Title	Number of duplicate accounts per customer
Description	Business rule requires a single account to exist for a given customer. When duplicate accounts exist, users receive an error when trying to create or update a service contract transaction associated with one of the duplicated accounts.
	The probability of users running into duplicate accounts is linearly proportional to the percentage of duplicates. A 1% increase in duplicates translates into a 1% probability increase of running into an account error. Each account error delays the completion of the transaction by 4 hours, which increases the cost by 200% per transaction. Keeping the number of duplicates at 5% helps lower the overall cost by 2%.
KPI	Lower the overall cost of completing service contract bookings by 5% this quarter.
Dimension	Uniqueness
Impacted LOB(s)	Services
Unit of meas.	Percentage of duplicates
Target value	5%
Threshold	$\leq$ 10% is Green, between 10% and 20% is Yellow, >20% is Red
Frequency	Weekly
Contact	services_alias@company.com
Root cause	Duplicate accounts are a result of incorrect business practices, which are being addressed through proper training, communication, and appropriate business process update.
Fix in progress?	___Yes ___No _x_Mitigation ___N/A

are being taken to minimize the issue. Sometimes it is possible to address the root cause of the problem, and over time, eliminate the need of a monitor altogether. In these cases, monitors should be retired when no longer needed.

The monitor report result is best when presented graphically. The graph type should be picked according to the metric measured, but almost always it is relevant to include a trend analysis report to signal if the violation is getting better or worse with time.

Scorecards

Scorecards are typically useful to measure the aggregate quality of a given data set and classify it in data quality dimensions.

Recall the data quality baseline in Chapter 6, and the sample shown in Table 6.1. In essence, the numbers for a scorecard can be obtained from regularly executed *baseline* assessments. The individual scores can be organized in many ways needed by the business, and presented in a dashboard format.

Table 8.2 shows a subset of Table 6.1, but it also adds *threshold*, which will be discussed shortly. The objective is to obtain a score for a particular combination of context, entity(ies), attribute(s), and data quality dimension. Once the score is available, the scorecard report or dashboard can be organized in many different ways, such as:

- The aggregate score for a given context and entity in a certain dimension, such as *accuracy* for *address* in the *U.S.* is 74 percent.
- The aggregate score for a given entity in a certain dimension, such as *completeness* for *all customer attributes* is 62 percent.
- An overall score for a given data quality dimension, such as *consistency* is 64 percent.
- An overall score for all data quality dimensions, which represents the overall score of the entire data set being measured. This associates a single number to the quality of all data measured, which becomes a great thermometer regarding the data quality efforts within the company.

The threshold should be set according to business needs. Data quality issues represented by scores in the *red* or the *yellow* categories should be the targets of specific data quality projects. Furthermore, the scorecard itself will become an indicator of the improvements achieved.

The scorecard becomes a powerful tool for the following reasons:

- It assigns a number to the quality of the data, which is critical to determining if the data is getting better or suffering degradation.

TABLE 8.2 Foundation Scores for the Data Quality Scorecard

Entity(ies)	Attribute(s)	DQ Dimension	Score	Threshold		
				Red	Yellow	Green
Customer	Name	Completeness	98	≤ 95	> 95 and < 98	≥ 98
Customer	DUNS	Completeness	60	≤ 55	> 55 and < 70	≥ 70
Customer	DUNS	Conformity	70	≤ 80	> 80 and < 95	≥ 95
Address (US)	Postal Code	Conformity	68	≤ 75	> 75 and < 90	≥ 90
Customer	Name/Country	Uniqueness	80	≤ 70	> 70 and < 90	≥ 90
Address	Address lines 1–4 City County State Postal Code Country	Accuracy	75	≤ 70	> 70 and < 85	≥ 85
Account	Account type	Uniqueness	90	≤ 85	> 85 and < 95	≥ 95
Account	Account number	Integrity	85	≤ 85	> 85 and < 95	≥ 95
Customer	Customer type					

- It can be used to assess the impact a newly migrated source has on the overall quality of the existing data.
- It clearly identifies areas that need improvement.

Notice the scorecard alone may not be sufficient to determine the root cause of the problem or to plan a data quality project in detail. The scorecard will highlight the area that needs improvement as well as measure enhancement and deterioration, but it might still be necessary to profile the data and perform root cause analysis to clearly state the best way to solve the problem.

The DQLA for scorecards between the business and the data quality team can follow a format similar to Table 8.2.

SUMMARY

Improving the quality of the data is a constant battle. The challenges range from the definition of good quality to the actual data correction. Disputes will exist when creating standards, which can be followed by technical difficulties when automating their conformance verification and rectification.

Error prevention is certainly the ideal scenario, but cannot always be achieved. Companies are constantly dealing with existing data, which is suddenly susceptible to new rules, new structures, and new referential integrity constraints. Furthermore, there is the typical lag between requirements and implementation, leading to a transitional period of adaptation to new business processes and system changes. All these disruptions can cause further corruption of the data in addition to the necessary correction of previous problems and preparation for eventual new practices.

Adding to the mix is the incorporation and assimilation of data quality tools. An effective data quality management program requires powerful and flexible technology. Still, as much as data quality tools have improved lately, a large amount of human intervention is still necessary in some areas.

The good news is there is hope for this perceived chaos. As companies mature from a data quality perspective, it is possible to better deal with the constant maintenance struggles. People, process, and technology maturity will certainly minimize the bumps on the road and create an environment supported by a metrics based framework fostering constant improvement.

However, even in a mature state, companies will still be required to react to issues. Maintenance will always be both proactive and reactive, and as much as companies strive to be proactive, they have to be prepared to deal with unforeseen situations. That's why it is important to combine a strong data maintenance program with practices of data governance and stewardship safeguarding the administration of overarching rules, policies, procedures, and standards.

 NOTE

1. Graham Rhind, *Global Sourcebook of Address Data Management* (Amsterdam: GRC Database Information, 2010).

CHAPTER NINE

Maturing Your MDM Model

The first sign of maturity is the discovery that the volume knob also turns to the left.

—*Jerry M. Wright*

 HOW TO RECOGNIZE AND GAUGE MATURITY?

Up to this point, we have covered the planning and implementation of a Customer MDM model with particular emphasis on the business practices needed to drive the disciplines of data governance, data stewardship, data quality, and data access management. All of which are about moving from an unfocused state of data management to the highly managed and controlled state necessary to achieve true Customer MDM.

As much focus needs to go into institutionalizing and maturing these practices as is needed to initiate them. But it is necessary to first consider what constitutes a mature MDM model and how this can be gauged. This needs to be put into perspective because until a mature state has been reached, it's unlikely that you will be able to fully realize the true potential and extended benefits of MDM, such as improving the value of your data and creating an accurate and trusted customer 360° view.

Let's examine what constitutes a mature Customer MDM model and how to gauge where you are in this continuum. Evaluating maturity should start with your definition of MDM. You'll recall that in the Introduction we offered a definition of MDM. Whether you embrace the one given or another definition, achieving what has been defined and envisioned for MDM requires progress, adjustment, and control across the four disciplines on which we have been focusing. These disciplines also represent the areas where the maturity of the MDM practice can be assessed. Being able to gauge maturity across Data Governance, Data Stewardship, Data Quality Management, and Data Access Management will not only help differentiate where the focus, progress, and issues exist within the MDM model, but can also serve as an excellent overall program dashboard to use with the data governance council and for executive-level updates.

In the area of data governance, there already exist a significant number of definition and maturity models that have been defined and presented by a number of firms in the data management and MDM space. And not wanting to reinvent the wheel here, we can examine these governance maturity models to formulate a similar approach for measuring the overall MDM maturity.

Figure 9.1 is a simple example of this and indicates the dimensions we'll use for gauging maturity across the four discipline areas. As with data governance maturity models or with various types of data quality dashboards, the actual dimensions chosen for use in the model can be different than what we have

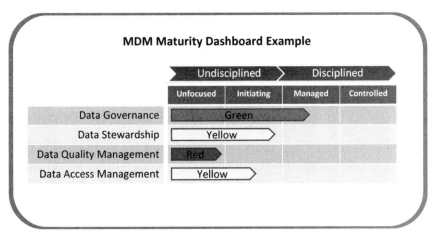

FIGURE 9.1 MDM Maturity Dashboard Example

chosen. No matter which are chosen, they should reflect dimensions that are clear, consistent, and meaningful to the audience and executive teams.

The dashboard in Figure 9.1 reflects the following scenario:

■ Data governance council has been initiated now for a number of months. The governance process is being well managed and progressing with increasing influence and effectiveness, but has a ways to go yet before it is able to establish the broader span of control and data management consistency it expects to achieve.

■ Data stewardship discipline is lagging behind the maturity level of governance. Full global implementation of the data steward model has been delayed due to budget issues preventing some functional area data steward roles from being filled right away, but these roles are expected to be filled in the next two quarters.

■ The intended focus and improvement projects around data quality management have yet to get started. Starting these efforts is dependent on getting the additional data steward resources in place.

■ The data access management plan is moving forward with some adjustments to the schedule. Additional auditing and control processes are on target to be ready beginning next quarter; however, due to the delay in getting the additional data steward resources in place, in some areas the auditing and control processes will need to phase in later than had been planned.

When presenting a dashboard of this nature, be sure that for each measured area there is accompanying explanation to support the status and sufficiently highlight the positives or negatives. We'll dive further into each of these maturity areas to more fully distinguish the various aspects of maturity.

Data Governance Maturity

As previously mentioned, data governance maturity has been well studied and there exist a number of excellent perspectives on this topic. For additional reference on this, we recommend the NASCIO Governance Services publication titled "Data Governance Part II—Maturity Models—A Path to Progress"[1] and Tony Fisher's book *The Data Asset: How Smart Companies Govern Their Data for Business Success.*[2]

In Chapter 4, we discussed how the success of an MDM initiative will rest largely on an early and effective implementation of data governance. Therefore, it would be logical to assert further that the maturity of Customer MDM is highly dependent on the ability of the data governance to first reach a mature enough state so that it can influence and drive the maturity of the other MDM disciplines we have been discussing. When and how data governance reaches a mature state will basically come down to gauging a few things:

- When ownership, partnership, and cross-functional collaboration are established and continually work well.
- When the governance council can repeatedly make timely, actionable decisions.
- When it is clear that control is being maintained from both a reactive and proactive perspective. This refers to how effective the governance process is with turning the dials left or right to control its data domain.

Although a clear sign of maturing is moving from a more reactive state to a more proactive state (as many of the governance maturity models point out), becoming more proactive doesn't fully eliminate the reactive state. In a complex customer data domain, there can be many moving parts and process or people variables; therefore, there is always opportunity for surprises or unexpected events. Often, there are known uncontrolled areas or events in an environment that by design or decision are left that way due to the situation being considered a nonissue, low impact, or low priority. These cases, as well as unforeseen situations, can suddenly become significant or blow up unexpectedly due to any number of reasons, shift in events, or change in priorities.

So, whether a proactive or reactive scenario, the most important factor in approaching a disciplined state is to be able to recognize and effectively manage the scenario so as to avoid or minimize the potential for business risk and operational issues. This can be accomplished by having established a responsive and pervasive management dynamic where awareness, review, and decision making are well orchestrated in a timely and fluid process.

With achieving a well-managed state of governance, a controlled state can be achieved when people, process, and technology are well positioned and can be fine-tuned as needed to maintain a steady state and to successfully drive progressive initiatives that support the ongoing MDM goals, objectives, and priorities.

Data Stewardship Maturity

In Chapter 5, we stated that once the concept of data stewardship is fully recognized and a model is defined, it boils down to the combination of the people, processes, and a data caretaking focus that will establish the practice of data stewardship. We also stated that for data stewardship to be effective, the concept and practice of data stewardship needs to be clearly embedded in the key junction points between the entry and management of the master data. It's at these junction points where governance control, quality control, and control of data access management can best be influenced through use of committed and well-focused data stewards.

Probably the most difficult challenge with data stewardship is getting a broad enough and consistent enough commitment for the data steward roles. If this challenge isn't well recognized and addressed early in the MDM and data governance planning stages, this is likely to pause momentum of the MDM initiative due to forcing unplanned budget and resourcing issues to emerge or because the functional or geographic areas may open debate about the data steward model and plan. Late emergence of these types of underlying issues can be very disruptive. The concept and expectations for data stewardship must be agreed upon early and consistently applied in order for MDM practices to be well executed because the *actionability* of MDM largely rests in the hands of the data stewards.

The ability for data stewardship to reach a mature state will require that the data steward model is fully executed and functioning cohesively in alignment with the data governance process. It's this dynamic that lays the foundation for data stewardship to reach a controlled state whereupon the reactive and proactive needs we discussed in the data governance maturity section can be executed through responsibilities and action plans and assigned to the data stewards.

Similar to data governance, maturity of data stewardship will be gauged by how well this discipline can be orchestrated in a timely and fluid manner, but also by how successfully and consistently actions are addressed by the data stewards. A mature data stewardship model should have a visible closed-loop process tracking the major action items and mitigation plans that involve the data stewards. Not having clear or consistent closure from data stewards regarding global and local initiatives usually suggests a problem with accountability or priority, and signals that the MDM practice may be stuck too much in meeting mode and not enough in action mode.

Data Quality Maturity

In prior chapters, we have covered the planning, implementation, process, and execution of data quality management. We indicated that data quality is likely the single most important reason that organizations tackle MDM, and that trusted data delivered in a timely manner is any organization's ultimate objective. We also stated that establishing a culture of quality throughout the enterprise is mandatory for maximum benefits. Data quality is everyone's responsibility, but requires the organization to establish the proper foundation through continuous training, proper communication channels, effective collaboration, and an efficiently adaptive model that in spite of constant changes can continue to deliver results quickly.

To achieve a quality culture and quality improvement, there are many programs, mechanisms, roles, and relationships that need to work in harmony. Using our dashboard example in Figure 9.1, data quality management can't reach a mature state unless the data governance, data stewardship, and data access management practices are all enabled, functioning well, and have progressed to a managed state. That shouldn't be a surprise, though, because a quality culture depends on people, process, and technology to be in sync with the recognition, management, and mitigation of quality issues.

Determining the level of cross-functional collaboration and quality management effectiveness is the first factor in gauging data quality maturity. That collaboration is first established through the maturation of data governance, and should then translate into creating a foundation to drive and mature data quality management. Recall that in Chapter 6 (see Figure 6.4), we stated that reaching maturity in data governance should mean less effort is needed with regard to data quality management, since better-governed data needs less correction.

The second factor in gauging this is how well the quality of the data is serving the business intelligence process. We have previously indicated that data quality and integrity issues are the primary cause of the conflict and divide between operational and BI practices. Solving for this gap starts by creating more awareness and connection between the front-end and back-end processes, but ultimately it is about improving the quality, consistency, and context of the master data to increase the *value* of the data in terms of driving more top-line and bottom-line benefit through improving operational efficiency and sales opportunity. Value of the data needs to be measured by how well it is servicing both the operational and BI process. How valuable the master data is or needs to become should be a well-recognized factor and a key driver in a highly functioning and mature Customer MDM model.

Data quality maturity essentially equates to having reached a state where an acceptable level of quality management and control *and* a shared view about data value exists between operations and BI. Reaching this state of acceptability and harmony is, of course, a very tall order, but recall that in previous chapters we have stated that making significant strides with quality improvement will require time and stems from well-coordinated efforts, which are orchestrated from the data governance council and data quality forums. This is exactly why MDM and data governance need to be approached as long-term commitments and become well entrenched as priorities in both the operating and analytical models of a company.

Data Access Management Maturity

As important as this discipline is, and as it is probably the easiest of the four disciplines to gain tighter management and control over, it is often the most overlooked and undermanaged area of MDM focus. In Chapter 7, we pointed out how compliance and legislative requirements or the need to reduce corporate risk were the key drivers for a company to implement data governance. We also pointed out that the process and control used to manage data access is typically an IT-driven solution with very little management and monitoring responsibility assigned to the business side.

As we stated that data quality is everyone's responsibility, so too is data access management. IT needs to play a key role, but until you can more fully engage business users and managers through more awareness and participation, risk and opportunity for misconduct will have an open door. Gauging maturity of data access management is largely a matter of determining the control zones a company needs to have, and how much of these areas are being managed well. In Chapter 7, we provided a process and approach that enables the ability to identify and gauge data access control via a business-oriented gatekeeper. Whether using this type of model or another model, it's the ability to specifically pinpoint, monitor, analyze, and manage data access that will register on the maturity scale.

Data security, privacy, compliance, and regulatory control are broad concerns with any major company, but when you take a deeper dive into these subjects and ask very pointed questions or try to get specific reports to help qualify and quantify the management of this, there seem to be a lot of black holes and gray areas in the process, measurement models, and available data. Not being able to get really specific about the level of monitoring and control is a sign that focus and maturity are still lacking.

It should be expected and acceptable for the data governance team to examine this discipline area and begin to ask probing questions to at least get a baseline read on how well data access is being managed and controlled.

By simply initiating more analysis and seeking more quantitative information, it shouldn't take long to get a realistic perspective on what, if any, gaps exist.

Organizations that can produce very specific user access detail and can demonstrate rigor with monitoring and auditing their processes are organizations that clearly recognize the need to manage and control their data. This also goes hand-in-hand with recognizing and protecting the value of the data. A maturity state of data access management can be recognized when both IT and the business organizations have implemented effective auditing and control practices that help augment, support, and substantiate corporate policy and employee training related to information protection and regulatory compliance.

 ## SUMMARY

Although reaching a mature state of Customer MDM may not be stated explicitly as a goal or objective in the strategy and planning, it certainly is implied in the concept of Master Data Management. In other words, reaching maturity is a requirement for achieving a successful end state result from MDM. We stated that as much focus needs to go into institutionalizing and maturing these practices as is needed to initiate them, but it is necessary to first consider what constitutes a mature MDM model and how this can be gauged.

We have presented a methodology for measuring the overall maturity of the MDM model by gauging maturity more discreetly across the four key disciplines. Each discipline area needs to develop in relationship to and in coordination with the other areas, with data governance and data stewardship being the most influential areas.

A mature Customer MDM model is reliant on having a mature state of data governance where, within that process, dials (figuratively speaking) can be adjusted to the left or right to control the data domain. This means having control from both a reactive and proactive perspective.

There are certainly other perspectives and details on MDM maturity that we also encourage you to examine such as the DataFlux white paper prepared by David Loshin titled "MDM Components and the Maturity Model."[3]

Lastly—and again we emphasize—that getting to a mature state of MDM can be a slow, deliberate process that will require some adjustments and out-of-the-box thinking. Do take the time to consider what constitutes a mature MDM model and how this can be gauged. This will enable an effective tracking approach that will provide valuable guidance about your investment in MDM.

NOTES

1. "Data Governance Part II: Maturity Models—A Path to Progress," NASCIO Governance Series, 2009.
2. Tony Fisher, *The Data Asset: How Smart Companies Govern Their Data for Business Success* (Hoboken, NJ: John Wiley & Sons, 2009).
3. David Loshin, "MDM Components and the Maturity Model," A DataFlux White Paper, 2010.

PART FOUR

IV

Advanced Practices

CHAPTER TEN

Creating the Customer 360° View

Knowledge is power.

—*Sir Francis Bacon*

 INTRODUCTION

The customer 360° view is not an MDM-originated concept. Its origin is from CRM systems that were specifically designed with a focus on customer management. The ultimate goal is to be able to understand the history, preferences, and buying patterns of a customer to better service them in the future, thereby increasing the probability they will be loyal and generate more revenue, directly or indirectly.

But a true 360° view can only be achieved if the data behind it is conducive for that purpose. CRM systems have remained siloed, which becomes a huge limitation when trying to clearly understand what is important to the customer and convey the proper message at every contact point throughout all stages of the purchase cycle.

Abstractly speaking, an effective 360° view requires data fitness for use as well as timely distribution and availability.

Fitness for use in this case comprises data integration, data quality, and data organization. If data is not integrated, it is practically impossible to have a complete and accurate view. That is the primary problem when data is fragmented among the multiple LOBs across the enterprise. If data is of bad quality, the resulting view will be untrustworthy. Finally, data has to be properly organized otherwise its understanding is blurry.

But it is not sufficient to have data that is well organized, highly integrated, and with great quality. It must also be available where and when it is needed. A services support person on the phone with a customer must be able to have at their fingertips all the information necessary to provide the utmost experience to that customer. At the other end of the spectrum, a marketing team must be able to have the proper business intelligence to decide on marketing campaigns and advance cross-sell and up-sell opportunities.

CRM systems continue to be important for means to distribute data to the many users interacting with customers. But the integration, quality, and organization of customer master data are better when performed at a centralized hub. Furthermore, the centralized information can be leveraged for business intelligence.

For proper decision making, a 360° view requires the association of master data to transactional data. Chapter 8 covered entity resolution, which is an important first step to uniquely recognize a person or company. Moreover, by linking the distinct entities to transactional information, it is possible to get a clear picture of the many relationships established by each single real entity and ultimately reach a complete view for each one.

Figure 10.1 depicts a partial view of a customer life cycle. As a prospect, the hypothetical company "On The Edge Corporation—OTE" shows interest in two products and two services. Eventually, that company decides to purchase a product and a service. Notice how the information can potentially get fragmented across the many LOBs, with possible inconsistencies. In this particular configuration, it is difficult to have a clear view of OTE.

Notice in Figure 10.2 how a proper entity management function is critical to resolve the many instances of OTE and provide a complete view of that company. It is possible to identify all transactions performed by OTE as well as detect its prior interest in other products and services, and potentially pursue additional selling to them. Furthermore, if there is enough intelligence about OTE, it is viable to find other companies in the same industry and/or with the same buying patterns and pursue cross-sell and up-sell opportunities.

As powerful as this complete view is when available at the many points of contact with the customer during the life cycle, it is typically beneficial to

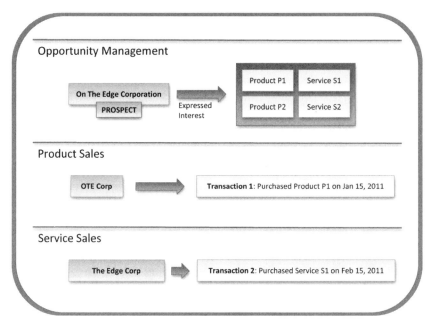

FIGURE 10.1   Partial Customer Life Cycle

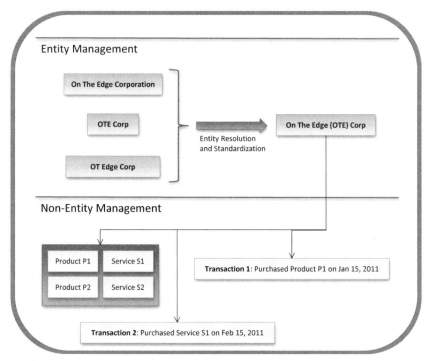

FIGURE 10.2   Entity Management Performed at the Customer Data Hub

organize customer information even further for additional business intelligence. The creation of a customer hierarchy is the standard approach in Customer MDM. Hierarchy management is discussed in the following section.

HIERARCHY MANAGEMENT (HM)

There are many reasons why it is advantageous to arrange customer data into some type of classified grouping. Sales teams may be interested in grouping customers by region for proper field rep assignments. Services may be interested in grouping customers by level to give proper discounts. Marketing may be interested in grouping customers by industry to define effective campaigns.

Sometimes these needs can be met by creating reports on existing attributes associated with customers. But quite often, it is necessary to create a more permanent structure with attributes and relationships that are not readily available, or it could take too long to determine on the fly. Customer hierarchy falls into this last category.

A customer hierarchy adds a vertical dimension to the horizontal 360° view, as depicted in Figure 10.3. It is possible to uncover relationships not readily available on the hub, especially when doing business with large companies with many subsidiaries and/or departments. The hub will normally carry the

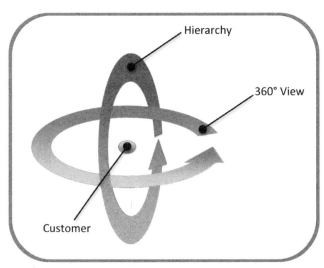

FIGURE 10.3 Customer Hierarchy as a Vertical Dimension to the 360° View

atomic set of information about a given customer, located at a particular address, with a certain account type, and through a specific contact, has engaged in a selling relationship. But a lot of these atomic records can be associated with distinct departments and/or subsidiaries; have separate bill-to, ship-to, and installed-at addresses; and/or were carried on by a specific sales channel. A customer hierarchy enables the proper connections and abstractions, especially because the volume of data can be quite overwhelming.

But some considerations should be made when deciding on a customer hierarchy structure, usage, and maintenance. Let's take a look at these next.

Operational versus Analytical Hierarchies

Hierarchies can be maintained either at the operational level or at the analytical level depending on your MDM implementation. In analytical or operational MDM implementations, there is obviously a single option for each of them. But in enterprise MDM implementations, there is a choice.

Recall from Chapter 1 that enterprise MDM is a combination of operational and analytical MDMs. Therefore, a customer hierarchy may reside in either environment. There are advantages and disadvantages in both cases.

Customer hierarchies are traditionally more utilized at the business intelligence level. Since business intelligence is intrinsically an analytical task, HM in the analytical world has matured more quickly from a technology perspective. But some operational customer data hubs do support hierarchy associations, and many HM tools are quite independent from the underlying data repository and with means for proper integration at either level.

Knowledgeable staff is a necessity no matter where HM occurs. It is easy to underestimate the amount of experience necessary to manage customer information. Furthermore, it is a very time-consuming activity that requires a lot of data analysis and research. Research on company and contact information is mostly accomplished through two main mechanisms:

1. Internet resources, including company web sites and search engines and other information sites such as Google, Bing, Yahoo, and Wikipedia.
2. Third-party data providers, for example, D&B, Acxiom, OneSource/ Infogroup, Experian, Equifax, and IXI.

Generally speaking, HM at the operational level is preferred over the analytical level for the following reasons:

- Analytical MDM is downstream from operational MDM; therefore, the hierarchy information can be more easily transferred.

- When HM is done at the analytical level, but is needed by operational teams, it must either be transferred regularly to the operational hub, or be made available through other applications and/or reports. This alternative obviously complicates maintenance.

But that is not necessarily a clear-cut decision. Other factors may drive the decision, such as:

- **Technology.** As stated previously, HM is a very time-consuming activity. A tool that provides a friendly graphical user interface comes a long way to facilitate and expedite hierarchy updates. Therefore, if technology is much better at the analytical level than at the operational level, this can drive the final determination.
- **Access capability.** The HM team obviously needs access to the data to perform their functions. But sometimes this is an issue as certain LOBs are very sensitive to operational data access and on-the-fly changes. Furthermore, hierarchies do change quite often. If a company is very sensitive to constant changes in the operational environment, it may be more appropriate to perform HM at the analytical level, and make scheduled updates in the operational environment.
- **Where the information is needed.** Hierarchy information is always needed for business intelligence, but depending on each LOB strategy, it can also be required at the operational level. Where the hierarchy information is needed may drive where it is best maintained.

When considering hierarchy management, take into account the overall strategy for your company as well as the adopted Customer MDM solution as a whole. Remember, MDM is about people, process, and technology, and to base a decision on just one of those elements is usually not recommended.

Single versus Multiple Hierarchies

Different LOBs may have different classification needs. Sales may have a vested interest in hierarchical organization for means of territory segmentation and sales commissions. Services may want to organize customer information to better structure service-level delivery and pricing. Finance may be interested in a legal hierarchy disposition for regulatory compliance. Marketing may want to create a hierarchy that better represents buying patterns and demographics to improve marketing campaigns.

It is doubtful that a single hierarchical representation will meet the needs of all LOBs within any large company. Multiple representations are not uncommon but add to the project's cost. Maintaining a single hierarchy can be very challenging already. As the different perspectives grow, companies risk compromising the main reason that they engaged in an MDM project in the first place: an agreed-upon view of master data across the entire company. Finding the right balance is key.

Number of Levels in the Customer Hierarchy

Most HM tools will support many levels of parent-child relationships, but more levels typically add to the complexity and the maintenance effort. On the other hand, more levels will provide a more segmented view, potentially leading to better intelligence.

Figure 10.4 depicts a hierarchy structure for a fictional Global Company with three levels shown.

But it is important to realize a given hierarchy does not necessarily need to include a level for each required segmentation, otherwise management of the hierarchy can get very convoluted. Remember that attributes are associated with the records in the hierarchy, making it possible to combine hierarchy information with data attribution to obtain desired reports. Let's take a look at an example.

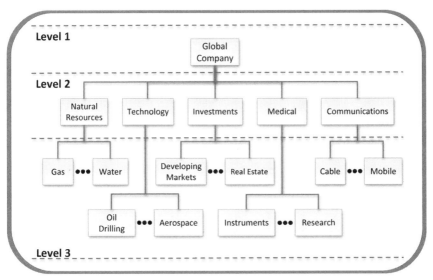

FIGURE 10.4 Fictional Global Company Three-Level Hierarchy

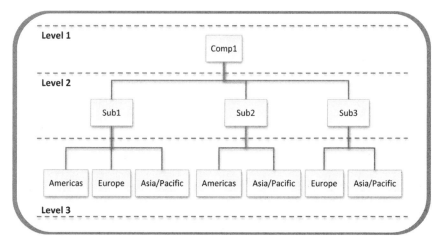

FIGURE 10.5 One Possible Hierarchy Structure for a Company (Comp1)

Let's say a company, Comp1, has three subsidiaries: Sub1, Sub2, and Sub3. Sub1 does business in the Americas, Europe, and Asia/Pacific; Sub2 does business in the Americas and Asia/Pacific; and Sub3 does business in Europe and Asia/Pacific. Two possible hierarchy arrangements for this scenario are depicted in Figures 10.5 and 10.6.

Both structures are valid; however, they may be more complex than necessary. For instance, both structures have children with multiple parents.

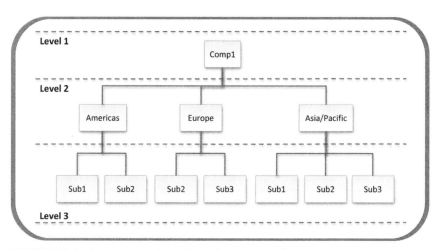

FIGURE 10.6 Another Possible Hierarchy Structure for a Company (Comp1)

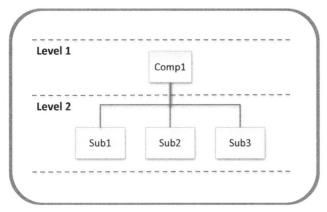

FIGURE 10.7 Yet Another Hierarchy Structure for a Company (Comp1)

It is important not to confuse reporting needs with hierarchy structure. If it is necessary to report on Comp1 either by subsidiary or by region, it is possible to do so with a structure such as the one in Figure 10.7. It is obvious to see how a report can be generated by a subsidiary. As far as a report by region, remember that records associated with the hierarchy do have attached attributes. Country is likely one of them, making it possible to generate a report by region even though this is not explicitly maintained in the structure.

The bottom line is: Do not complicate company hierarchy structure any more than necessary. Hierarchy maintenance is already a daunting task when the number of levels is kept low and only single parents exist. Weight your requirements carefully.

Virtual versus Physical Customer Records

A *virtual record* is a record that is created for the purpose of organizing other records only, like a label. It does not represent a customer engaged in a transaction as a *physical record* would. In essence, virtual records are entries created for the purpose of forming a skeleton for the hierarchy, to which physical records are then attached.

Some HM tools do not support the concept of virtual records; therefore, the hierarchy structure has to be created by associating physical records with each other. It can be a challenge sometimes to decide which physical record best represents a customer and/or one of its subsidiaries and set it as the *parent* in the tree or in a branch.

Even when a tool does not support virtual records, it is usually possible to fake it by creating a *pseudo-physical record* that is not really referenced by any transaction, and can be used for the purpose of labeling. But be aware that this can be dangerous, as it may be difficult to control how the pseudo-physical record is used outside of the HM scope. Before you know it, users will be consuming the pseudo-record as a real customer.

The advantage of virtual records is the capability to create a structure that is independent from the existing customer records. For example, the fictional Global Company structure on Figure 10.4 can be created with virtual records even if you don't do business with every single subsidiary. But as you increase your reach, the structure is ready.

On the other hand, virtual records add to the volume of data and consequently increase maintenance effort. If entity resolution is performed at efficient levels, it may be beneficial to stick with physical records only, since the definition of a parent will be facilitated by a higher level of data de-duplication. But if not, the use of virtual records may be more advantageous. Be realistic about the quality level of your data when making a decision as to which is best for your company.

Legal versus Non-Legal Hierarchies

Companies are formed as legal structures. The factors driving the legal establishment of a company are typically tax liability, ability to borrow money or attract investors, and legal liability protection and jurisdiction. These motivators are not necessarily the same as the ones driving the selling relationships developed by that company. Therefore, mimicking your customer hierarchy on a legal model may not always be the best approach.

Ultimately, a legal structure is determined by outside forces while a customer hierarchy may be more effective when it takes into consideration internal strategies and a very specific and unique ongoing relationship with that company. A non-legal hierarchy is also known as account hierarchy if it represents mostly a selling view of the association.

Some third-party data providers, such as D&B, sell company legal structure information and some HM tools will include integration with those data providers, making it easier to create an internal customer hierarchy based on a legal model. But as stated previously, that is not necessarily the best for your company.

A typical approach is to maintain both a legal and a non-legal hierarchy. The non-legal hierarchy sometimes has gaps because of sparse business endeavors. In these cases, it may be desirable to use the legal hierarchy as a complement.

As we discussed previously in this chapter, the classification needs of each LOB can be quite different, but maintaining multiple hierarchies is very resource intensive. Adopting a legal hierarchy and a single non-legal hierarchy may be the happy medium desired, but evaluate your needs carefully.

 ## THE ELUSIVE, YET ACHIEVABLE, 360° CUSTOMER VIEW

Globalization and a multitude of sales channels, including the Internet, contribute to increasing competition and decreasing product differentiation. Customers are constantly looking for cheaper and better products and services. Companies have come to the realization they need to be customer-centric to remain abreast of all these challenges and find the differentiating factor that will allow them to retain their existing customers and gain new ones.

Companies have gone through many transformations in the last three decades with process re-engineering, lower manufacturing defects, better inventory control, more efficient supply channel management, and other efforts to decrease production costs and increase product quality. While there is always the possibility for technology advancements and other types of improvements in these areas, the knowhow is mostly widespread, lowering the opportunity for differentiation.

Customer information becomes that unique asset that smart companies can use to gain a competitive edge. While some companies have agreed with this logic and have tried to foster a customer-centric view in the last few years, the actual execution has been mostly flawed. Companies have engaged in a widespread effort to collect as much information as possible from their customers, but they have retained all that information fragmented across their multiple silos.

MDM disciplines can finally help overcome that barrier, and bring management of customer data to an enterprise level and ultimately enable a true 360° view, which had been intangible until then. Moreover, as companies adopt additional MDM disciplines for other data entities such as product, supplier, partner, and so on, they will be able to create a multidimensional web of information that can be arranged and extrapolated to provide any desired intelligence and unlimited benefits.

 ## SUMMARY

It is a tenuous road to reach a 360° view of the customer. Probably the most important lesson to learn is that a lot of information does not necessarily translate into intelligent information. Obviously, data needs to be collected, but it doesn't end there.

It requires a solid customer data integration effort to bring disparate and fragmented data together. Once data is integrated, it enables the application of data quality disciplines to correct disparities, resolve entities, and finally achieve a single view of the customer.

The single view of the customer is utilized to connect the many relationships a given customer has established across all stages of the purchase cycle, and finally reach the elusive 360° view. Hierarchy management adds another dimension to the maintenance and intelligence aspect of the customer relationship, enabling the organization and segmentation of information for increased benefits.

Finally, all these activities require proper coordination and proper establishment of roles, responsibilities, and ownership. Therefore, the disciplines of data governance and stewardship become essential components to successfully achieve the holy grail in the Customer MDM discipline, which is the customer 360° view.

CHAPTER ELEVEN

Surviving Organizational Change

It is not the strongest of the species that survives, nor the most intelligent that survives. It is the one that is the most adaptable to change.

—*Charles Darwin*

HOW ADAPTABLE IS YOUR CUSTOMER MASTER DATA?

Whether it is due to a market shift, merger, acquisition, restructuring, departmental change, or infrastructure transition, in the corporate world we know that change is a regular occurrence.

Although companies go to great lengths to build data warehouse models to retain corporate data, it's the business operations, business intelligence teams, and strategic decisions that dictate what data is actually most important and useful. Because of this, the data that is stored often becomes optimized to best serve the operational and BI needs. However, when a large organizational or operational change occurs in a company, it's not unusual for the value, context, or even the need for that data to quickly diminish in light of new priorities, new applications, change of ownership, or simply a loss of ability to maintain what may now be considered legacy data.

Changes in business practices and data requirements are a constant challenge for IT. This is particularly true with operational processes and data, but can also be the case for master data where internal system transitions or mergers and acquisitions occur.

The good news is that customer master data can be much more adaptable, transferable, and able to retain its context and value if good MDM practices have existed with it. The ability to quickly integrate the customer master data into new models and environments can equate to not only a large cost savings compared to the cost of a much larger effort usually needed to align and integrate data of poor quality and integrity, but it also enables the new environment or acquiring company to minimize disruption and maintain business continuity.

Let's talk about some good MDM practices to keep in mind that can help the customer master data and the MDM model best adapt to and survive organizational change. We'll look at this topic both from a data quality perspective in terms of how quality factors such as data completeness, consistency, and integrity can inhibit or enable the transformational ability of the master data and its context, and from a change management perspective in terms of how the data governance council and the data steward process can greatly assist with managing change.

DATA QUALITY FACTORS

So much has been said in previous chapters about establishing a culture focused on data quality. In an ever-changing business environment, applications come and go, and even though data is more permanent, the surrounding business practices and data requirements are also changing. Therefore, you can't expect sporadic data quality projects to properly address persistent issues and changing conditions. Good data is needed all the time, but data quality management projects can be very resource intensive and time-consuming if not orchestrated on a more regular basis. Therefore, the best approach is to foster the disciplines of data quality on an ongoing basis and throughout the entire enterprise. Data quality is everybody's responsibility, but it is a company's duty to create a favorable environment and an ongoing focus with appropriate technology, effective processes, proper skills, and a mechanism to recognize and reward quality efforts.

Chapters 6 and 8 articulate the many dimensions of data quality and how they can be used to qualify data quality issues, as well as structure a strong data metric program. But the actual enforcement of quality of information according to a given set of dimensions can render data more adaptable. Let's take a look at some of the basic data quality dimensions and explore this concept further.

Data Completeness

Completeness of information typically serves two primary purposes:

1. **Better knowledge.** More attributes populated translate into more information provided about their respective entities.
2. **Easier entity resolution.** The better characterized an entity is, the easier it is to identify duplicates. Missing information does not translate into matching information. Therefore, when performing entity resolution, completeness of information becomes a differentiating factor.

But there is another aspect of data completeness that makes it more adaptable to constant changes. Evolving application systems will typically become more restrictive and require more information to define or characterize a given entity. Therefore, as companies progress through technology changes, records that do not comply with the new required standards will fall out or require work before the transition is completed.

Maintaining the highest level of data completeness can lessen the burden. Obviously, if non-existing information is required as systems evolve, it may be impossible to prepare. However, upholding existing information as completely as possible can definitely help absorb the impact of changes.

Fragmentation of key information, particularly in a customer data domain, is a common problem that also needs to be addressed in order to maintain consolidated and complete information. Good customer data integration (CDI) processes along with regular data merge and alignment routines will greatly help with the consolidation of fragmented data into a complete master record.

Data Consistency

Keeping information consistent is probably the single most important factor in a smooth transition. It is an extremely time-consuming activity to manipulate inconsistent data because multiple rules have to be created for the same set of data elements.

Consistent data is much easier to migrate, augment, cleanse, standardize, and consolidate. One of the challenges during a data migration effort is to intelligently combine multiple disparate sources of data. Adding to that problem is that many of those sources will have inconsistent information. Therefore, it is necessary to perform both inter-system and intra-system reconciliations. Expanding data quality analysis and metrics across that master data environment and the source systems will drive more end-to-end consistency and can reduce issues later if and when both the master data and transactional data needs to be migrated and realigned.

Adding to the challenge is that consistency of information at the data entry point is very difficult to validate. Users have a very creative imagination, and are capable of entering the very same information in many different ways, especially when utilizing free-form entry fields. Most of the consistency is left to business process instructions, which are usually weakly enforced. Training and creative ways to recognize and reward good practices become critical tools to minimize these issues.

Implementing a Customer MDM program in your company will help solve many prior discrepancies, but the work doesn't end there to withstand ongoing changes. Quality of information, at all dimensions, is not a single project; therefore, its significance must be constantly reiterated.

Data Integrity

Data integrity is multifaceted and reached by multiple means, such as data accuracy, validity, and referential integrity. In the end, data that is validated against or maintains a link to a given trusted source or reference is better positioned to withstand data conversions, migrations, and newly added operational and BI requirements.

Referential integrity is two-fold:

1. It guarantees entered information meets predefined values, which is one of the most effective mechanisms to assure healthy data.
2. It aids in the expansion of concepts. When support of new functionality is added to the system, it is easier if the new functionality is based on reference information that can be easily modified and made available automatically to entities and attributes that are mapped to it. For example, today, a given system may only support a set of five account types. If account type information is normalized, it can more easily be expanded in the future to support newly required types.

External and even internal data references can also be great resources for expandable knowledge and functionality. If the source of information can be delegated to specialized systems, there is a better chance for enhancement. Naturally, specialized systems will be more prepared to evolve their own disciplines and associated information. Consequently, it makes it easier to tap in to newly developed insights through existing mapping. For example, a DUNS number associated with a customer record allows for retrieval of whatever information is provided today by D&B. As D&B expands its reach, additional insight can become readily available.

Internal references are also subject to the same concept. A given LOB may be more apt to control a given set of information and associated rules and algorithms. Other LOBs dependent on that resource are better off making references to it, instead of creating their own version. For example, a customer-pricing structure may be very complex and rigid. Replicating much of this can further hamper upgrades.

Accurate and valid data also indicate better preparation. Data validated for accuracy against a given reference source typically signals an acceptable level of completeness and consistency, which, as discussed previously, are key factors in an evolving data program.

 ## THE CHANGE MANAGEMENT CHALLENGE

Because change can often be very disruptive and is usually expected to be completed under a specific plan with a fixed time frame, the quality and execution of a data migration effort can suffer due to the time constraints. Customer data that has been poorly translated and mapped into new models can cause significant issues down the road with operational processes and customer transactions. In many cases, this could have been avoided with early engagement of an existing data governance or data steward team in the change management plans and expectations.

During organizational and operational change, subject matter experts on the business side who have been intimate with the business processes and context of the data, are often transitioned quickly into new organizational structures and environments, or possibly even let go, while IT has the responsibility to transition the systems and data without much context to the data and prior usage. This often results in poorly migrated and mapped data that can degrade overall data quality and create many operational issues until this can be corrected at a later time.

Data Governance Can Greatly Assist a Transitioning State

In Chapter 4, we mentioned that when positioned correctly, a data governance function can nicely fill a data management authority void and serve a very valuable role with an existing IT decision-making process and design methodology (see Figure 4.2). This also holds true with other forms of change. Mergers, acquisitions, and internal operational or organizational changes will usually involve various combinations of system, process, data, and resource changes, usually as part of integration or migration activities. A well-established Customer MDM and data governance model can greatly assist in these processes.

Existing policies and standards, metadata, work instructions, user information, and of course, knowing how clean and consistent the master data is, are all extremely important factors in a successful transition or transformation of customer data. A lack of accurate or complete information and poor data quality will present time-consuming and costly problems that can significantly impede a transition process. For example, in Chapter 6 we indicated that the usage and perceived quality of customer data is very context dependent, and this can vary across the business functions. A good data governance team should be well aware of this and able to recognize where any internal change or transition of this data can have widespread operational impact or other risk. In the case of a merger or acquisition, the mapping and realignment of this data needs to be carefully planned and executed so that the value of the data from the acquired company can be fully leveraged.

Where a data governance team has a good handle on the usage, quality, and context of its data, this will inherently create a more proactive and conducive state for change management. And because there are more common industry standards, tools, practices, reference data, and universal identifiers associated with customer data than with other data domains, a mature MDM model and data governance process will typically already be leveraging many of these common factors and solutions. Therefore, it makes perfect sense to engage an existing data governance team in a transition process so that these tools and common factors can still be leveraged and help enable the transition. Losing too much of the governance team's knowledge and data steward expertise too early in the transition process can be a critical mistake that can create unnecessary challenges with the execution of the transition plan.

Leveraging the Data Stewards and Analysts

We just mentioned that to assist change there is the benefit of and opportunity to leverage existing knowledge and resources within an existing MDM model and data governance team. Here are some specific examples of how data stewards and analysts can be leveraged for various scenarios:

- **Migration to a new environment.** Often enough, knowledge about data and processes surrounding existing systems is spread among multiple individuals and/or organizations. The new environment also presents its challenges, with still quite a bit of unanswered questions and how it will be possible to move into a new structure and accompanying processes and practices. Data stewards and analysts become critical pieces to understand existing and new structures, profile existing data, uncover potential issues, and assure a smooth migration.

- **Business process automation or reengineering.** Where there is transition to new environments, such as the result of a merger or acquisition or because of internal system changes, the reorientation of data and associated processes may require or provide a great opportunity for process automation or reengineering. Or, it's not unusual for an acquired company to have better processes and practices in some areas than the acquiring company. In either case, existing data stewards and analysts are usually well versed on these data and process areas—often just waiting for an opportunity to further improve a process—and can be an invaluable asset with opportunities for process automation or with repositioning a best practice.

- **Organizational change.** Internal organizational changes can often result in rather cursory chops at who and what goes where. Cross-functional teams and processes, such as a Customer MDM team and the data governance process, don't always fit well into a new structure and reorganization plan. In some cases, a new organization may not be very interested in supporting the MDM function, its budget, and the facilitation of cross-functional issues. A new organization may even let a Customer MDM function die on the vine if the transition and acceptance of the function has not been well orchestrated. To avoid this scenario, the data governance council should be engaged early in the plan for organizational change to ensure that an MDM practice and its merits are well recognized and will continue to receive proper commitment and support after the reorganization.

- **Outsourcing.** Similar to what we have just mentioned about organizational change, outsourcing of IT or business functions such as a call center can suddenly cause disconnection between the Customer MDM practice and that function. The negotiated contract terms with the outsource vendor may not have considered and covered certain MDM-related support expectations or services that had existed previously. Support or services related to data entry, management, standards, analysis, cleanup, monitoring, and so on, can significantly change. Again, there should be a strong data governance presence when considering an outsourcing plan and how to mitigate potential disruption to the MDM practice.

The overarching message here is that it's very hard to recover discipline of your master data once it has been lost, so be mindful of the impact organizational change can have on an MDM practice, and be prudent in handling this to minimize negative impact on the data integrity and management.

Adopting Best Practices

MDM needs to build on itself. Organizational or operational changes that cause regression to MDM practices will only be a data management ticket to nowhere. MDM and quality control can quickly lose its grip and momentum where best practices and tools associated with data governance, stewardship, and quality management are left behind in the transition to a new environment.

At the risk of being overly repetitive, MDM practices must be ongoing. A lot has been said about *not* approaching it as a one-time project. Moreover, it requires maturity combined with a constant effort to remain current to be able to sustain it at an optimal level. It is still very much an evolving discipline, and the best way to remain efficient is to continuously adopt existing best practices and be on the lookout for new ones.

The encompassing nature of MDM impacts people, process, and technology; plus, it requires an even stronger collaboration between IT and business than ever before. A strong MDM program in itself can trigger some organizational and operational changes. Once the initial impact is resolved and solid MDM practices take root, staying atop of the best practices will help the management, orchestration, and synchronization of the many changes affecting pre-established dynamics.

 SUMMARY

Some will say change is one of the guarantees in life along with death and taxes, and that is very likely true. Organizational change is a constant, and preparation is key. Stiff competition and shrinking product differentiation is forcing companies to constantly search for creative new solutions.

Coupled with this is the new generation of young adults who will be joining the workforce in the upcoming years. They have been exposed to an ever-increasing complexity of technology and information. Social media, smart phones, video games, and the ecosystem surrounding these technologies are overwhelming. For better or for worse, young adults today multitask at an alarming rate. Studies still don't show clear results on how all this behavioral change will shape the human brain and how it will impact society as a whole.

As an enterprise practice, MDM is obviously susceptible to organizational changes, as well, due to its encompassing nature. Customer MDM has tentacles reaching many levels of the organization, potentially increasing its exposure to risks and impacts. But because MDM is essentially a bridging and unifying function, change management plans should consider where those break points are and how this can be repaired and readapted in the new environment so that MDM practices can continue to provide value.

Change and the associated challenges can also bring increased opportunity. Organizations better prepared to adapt to new driving forces will be able to survive and even thrive amid the constant pressure. Customer MDM as a core competency can help companies to be more nimble and clever with regard to their strategic decisions.

CHAPTER TWELVE

Beyond Customer MDM

What lies behind us and what lies before us are tiny
matters compared to what lies within us.

—*Ralph Waldo Emerson*

THE LEADING AND LAGGING ENDS

In this last chapter, we will examine how emerging technology and the need to solve for existing business constraints are likely to influence Customer MDM and the direction of MDM in general.

By looking at both the leading and lagging ends of the Customer MDM spectrum, we can best see the potential for it to evolve. This will also reflect some of the strengths and weaknesses of MDM as a whole, and how MDM will influence what emerges as the next generation of data management needs and solutions. Consider that CRM's failure to deliver a broader enterprise-wide approach for customer data management contributed to the emergence of more general CDI solutions, and use of CDI solutions exposed data management needs that contributed to the emergence of Customer MDM solutions, which were designed to bring more end-to-end focus on data governance, quality management, and stewardship. So just as CDI and Customer MDM solutions emerged to fill gaps, it's reasonable to suggest that new gaps and next generation solution needs will emerge from a maturing MDM market.

To better understand what will influence the direction of MDM and what will emerge next as a result, following are some key questions we need to examine:

- Will new technology actually enable more MDM efficiency and accelerate ROI, or just be a lot of similar technology that can quickly oversaturate the market as more and more vendors jump in with offerings?
- Will the rate of organizational change be a constantly disruptive factor that precludes many MDM initiatives from reaching maturity and realizing the expected end state benefits?
- Can traditional IT models sufficiently adjust to provide more flexibility and collaborative support with business-driven MDM initiatives? And how much capacity will IT organizations have to support demands from multi-domain MDM initiatives?

Let's take a closer look at these.

TECHNOLOGY'S INFLUENCE ON MDM

Although many who have written about MDM, including ourselves, have emphasized that MDM is not just about technology, we do recognize that there is continual opportunity for MDM-focused technology to significantly influence MDM implementations and practices.

This is especially true with Customer MDM because much of its data, context, and governance are largely associated with industry-common standards, rules, logic, definition, and reference data—all of which are conducive to business process automation opportunities. These opportunities will drive continued development of technology that improves MDM value and effectiveness in the following ways:

- More integration of MDM components at the platform level
- More independent plug-and-play type product offerings that can deliver more modularized functionality as needed within an existing MDM environment
- More open source code and configurability options to better adapt solutions to existing platforms or multi-vendor environments

MDM customers essentially need all the above for their MDM implementations to continue to mature and ROI to more rapidly occur. Most technology-driven markets hit a wall due to product saturation and/or diminishing value and demand. There is still a large market for good MDM technology, but the value and demand for this will be determined by factors such as these:

- Ability to accelerate MDM ROI
- A company's ability to overcome internal constraints to better leverage technology and their internal resource pool
- Multi-data domain MDM growth and the ability for technology to provide extensible and scalable solutions that minimize cost and redundancy

The technology spectrum for MDM is very wide. In fundamental terms, MDM requires data storage, data collection and distribution, data presentation, data integration, business process work-flow implementation and orchestration, data quality, metadata management, hierarchy management, metrics, and reporting. This is in addition to foundational corporate technologies, which help organizations communicate better, provide more effective training, and better disseminate information internally and externally.

Adding to the mix is the fact that most companies are not starting from scratch when it comes to establishing their overall MDM technological solution. They likely have existing storage systems, distributed infrastructure, and/or applications they want to leverage and integrate. It becomes a technological challenge to evaluate all pieces and decide on the best combination.

Understanding new technological trends alone can be overwhelming. Phil Simon collaborated with a team of experts in many technological fields and compiled an outstanding book that offers great insight into the latest trends, such as cloud computing, software as a service (SaaS), service-oriented architecture (SOA), open source, mobile computing, social networking, and more.[1] We highly recommend his book to increase awareness on technological trends. Not that everything shared will have a direct impact on your MDM implementation, but with the pervasive nature of MDM, it is important to stay aware of the many possibilities.

Some open source MDM solutions are slowly emerging, but they are still lagging behind leading MDM products in both functionality and capability. Most notable open source solutions include the Mural community started by Sun Microsystems, Inc.—acquired by Oracle Corp.—and Talend open MDM community. Neither one has had any significant commercial success to date.

One of the big challenges regarding technology for MDM is related to its wide range of applicability and use. Some tools are used by IT, some by the business, and others by both. Creating powerful tools that are easy enough for business users to utilize can be quite an ordeal. On the other hand, IT users may be able to understand the concepts behind complex tools more easily, but don't quite know how to best apply them to solve a business issue. Because MDM and data governance are primarily business-driven efforts that need to be supported by well-positioned data stewards, there is still quite a bit of room for technology to evolve in the coming years in support of MDM practices and to better enable and optimize the data steward roles.

OVERCOMING THE IT AND BUSINESS CONSTRAINTS

In prior chapters, we have talked about how a successful MDM practice will often require cultural and political change across the IT and business functions to enable the cross-functional collaboration and investment required for a robust MDM model. We have mentioned that an MDM initiative should not be launched as an IT project bound by fixed time and delivery expectations, and that IT needs to break out of its traditional box in terms of how IT can help enable MDM. We have also emphasized how the business team needs to commit to the support of data steward resources and a quality culture.

It's actually to an IT organization's advantage to stimulate and support more responsibility and accountability in the business with regard to data management, data access, and governance because most of the data context and data quality issues are tied to business practices. Supporting more business-driven governance and front-end data management is an opportunity to enable more support and control where many of the root problems exist. It's also to the advantage of the business organizations to have more responsibility and accountability so that they can become more connected to the fitness and governance of their data, have more influence on quality control, and drive a more direct link between their operational and analytical data needs.

The difficulty is getting IT and the business to fully appreciate these advantages and develop a more collaborative relationship. Getting organizations to commit budget and resources to cross-functional projects can be a difficult task. The most critical point for addressing this is during the MDM proposal and ROI stage. The proposal and ROI need to call out specific benefits associated with developing a collaborative and flexible model. This continues to be relevant after an MDM initiative has been approved because, over time, the MDM initiative will continue to be subject to strategic review or stress related to resources and budget. In these situations, it will be important to circle back to the original ROI and what was expected so that IT or business teams don't selectively pull back and jeopardize the investments already made.

Another critical factor in overcoming traditional constraints and avoiding pullback is the ability to monitor and communicate MDM progress and successes. No one generally wants to get in the way of a successful initiative. Even during challenging budget times, if there is good involvement and a general perception of value, the program will likely stay sufficiently funded so that the value proposition can continue. Make sure there is a broad and consistent communication plan to demonstrate value, progress, and future plans.

One less conventional aspect companies need to consider is to review their required job roles and the personnel skills they currently have. People will develop their careers based on market demand. Traditionally, specialization requirements have led people to choose between technical and nontechnical work, with very little demand for cross-functional expertise. A hybrid role that can speak both business and IT languages can greatly reduce the gap and advance effectiveness.

Outsourcing has also contributed to the segregation between IT and the business. We're not advocating against outsourcing at all. There are obviously advantages and economies of scales that would be impossible to achieve without it. As a matter of fact, it has more to do with how outsourcing is done than with outsourcing in itself. Companies usually choose to outsource their non-core competencies, and IT is typically one of the first ones to go. But with this intense collaboration required for MDM, shouldn't outsourcing competencies be reassessed for increased benefits?

Usually, the bigger the company, the larger the gap is between IT and the business. In smaller companies, fewer resources force employees to expand their responsibilities and consequently their skills. But large companies are the ones that need data management the most since they have a larger volume of data, are likely to go through more mergers and acquisitions, are subject to more regulatory controls, and so on. The bright side is they should have more financial resources as well, and as such, should be looking to transform themselves for the better.

MDM is a transformational discipline. Companies can't continue to do the same thing and expect different results. Creativity and innovation have continuously transformed the business world in search for better ways of doing things. IT and business collaboration may be on tap for big changes, and individuals that can bridge the gap between both may become highly coveted assets.

ACHIEVING AN EFFECTIVE ENTERPRISE-WIDE MDM MODEL

As companies look to implement MDM across multiple data domains, this naturally creates the need to examine how to best coordinate and prioritize multi-domain activity and focus, particularly in regards to technology needs, quality improvement priorities, and demand for budget and IT resources. As with Customer MDM, the other data domains will typically start their MDM initiative by creating a charter and data governance team to establish the foundation needed to move forward. Although much of the MDM context and needs will be unique within each MDM domain, there are many common elements of MDM that can begin to compete and cause unnecessary redundancy across multiple domains if they are not effectively coordinated.

Coordination of these common elements may initially fall to an executive steering committee expected to oversee multiple MDM initiatives, but over time this responsibility is likely to shift to an enterprise MDM or Enterprise Data Governance type program office where a more specific team and set of resources are responsible to help facilitate and support cross-domain MDM needs by providing various tools and services. Figure 12.1 provides a simple example of an enterprise MDM model.

The concept and charter for an enterprise MDM program office makes sense from a coordination and efficiency standpoint, but—a word of caution here—if the program office charter is too broad and overly controlling it can start overshooting its value if it takes away authority and empowerment from the domain specific MDM teams by attempting to create too much of a homogeneous enterprise MDM. Because many aspects of quality management, governance, and stewardship are unique within each domain, they should not be impeded with excessive central program office control. A well-conceived enterprise MDM program office should always be cognizant of how to continually coordinate and enable MDM programs and avoid over-managing where control and conformance is unnecessary. Otherwise this can become a path back to a stiff, stifling model that, as we have stated frequently, is not conducive to MDM growth and maturity.

If an MDM program is already successfully underway, a program office should continue to keep that runway open and as clear as possible. A program

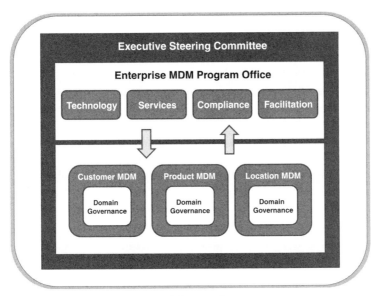

FIGURE 12.1 Enterprise MDM Model Example

office needs to cultivate an environment where a maturing MDM team can lead by example with developing best practices, which other MDM teams can leverage to accelerate their domain implementations. Because Customer MDM is often the first MDM implementation, the foundation it creates for data governance, data stewardship, data quality management, and data access management practices create very repeatable models that can provide extensible technology to help prime the start-up or sustainability of other MDM implementations. Techniques and examples we have provided throughout this book can easily be adapted to other data domains, and it makes perfect sense to leverage the knowledge and experience from an existing MDM practice to help launch more MDM initiatives.

There are also many IT-oriented services needed in MDM such as metadata management, data analysis, data integration, data cleanup, or development of reports where competing demand is likely to occur across multiple MDM programs. An MDM program office needs to ensure that these services are as extensible and scalable as possible in order to manage the demand as economically and efficiently as possible. Launching too many MDM initiatives side by side with common dependencies and demand on IT can quickly lead to overload and bottleneck scenarios causing deliverables to be delayed, which can negatively impact the progress and expected deliverables across all the MDM initiatives. For example, consider these hypothetical scenarios:

- An aggressive enterprise MDM plan has launched MDM programs across multiple master data domains. In support of the MDM master plan, IT is implementing a third-party product that will provide the platform, methodology, and functionality for data quality analysis, metrics, scorecards, and quality monitoring across multi-domains. Use of this solution for completing the initial data analysis and quality scorecard is a required step before the MDM core teams can complete and submit their quality improvement proposals for the executive steering committee to review. However, IT has just indicated there will be a delay in the product implementation due to some recently determined technical complications and the need to work out some contract support issues with the vendor. Availability and use of the product will be more limited than expected until these issues are fully resolved. The MDM program office and MDM core teams are considering the impact of this and what options exist in the interim to still move forward with the data analysis and quality assessment needs.

- Internal development and deployment of a common metadata management repository is expected to enable the MDM teams to formally capture, organize, and support their metadata, business policies, standards, and work instruction material. However, the initial plan and conceptual design of this seems to be getting overrun with more requirements and functionally complicated elements that apparently will be needed to support the multi-domain and multi-entity levels of segmentation that are expected in this solution. There is growing concern that this may not be a feasible solution due to the growing complexity. The enterprise MDM steering committee is reevaluating the metadata management plan and approach.

These scenarios are examples of where overdependence or overkill may exist with technology plans. Where technology implementations are a key part of the plan for launching MDM programs, a program office should be prepared with alternate or interim plans to help mitigate technology delays or if the technology needs to phase in more slowly than had been expected. An MDM master plan and program office needs to carefully weigh out how and where technology can potentially create major dependencies, timing issues, and program implementation impacts.

WHERE DOES MDM LEAD?

New data management technologies and disciplines emerge to solve existing problems, address new demands, bridge gaps between existing technologies, or to drive innovation and change in the marketplace. Whether that is CRM attempting to better address and manage the notion of customer relationships, or CDI practices driving better integration of customer data, or Customer MDM initiatives bringing together more front-end and back-end synchronization of the customer master data, the overall concept and capability of data management becomes more rounded out as these technologies and disciplines bring more technique and data management practices into play. Regardless of the initial data domain or functional context, good technologies and practices usually find their way into more generalized usage over time.

For example, although CRM initially raised the focus and technique for distinguishing and managing customer relationships, this is not a practice limited to sales and opportunity management functions, nor just CRM technology. Identifying and managing customer relationships now also plays heavily into ERP, customer service, marketing, partner management, or a business intelligence model, and has become a broad underlying factor in Customer MDM in order to drive a customer 360° view. Similarly, CDI technology and practices have evolved from being more BI-centric to use in broader data migration efforts such as in transitioning from legacy applications to a new integrated platform or to assist in M&A-driven data integration efforts.

As MDM brings more technology and discipline to the table and as these mature and become more imbedded in the business model, we can expect that MDM's underlying techniques and disciplines such as data governance, data quality management, data stewardship, and data access management become further exploited beyond just the master data management context. These type disciplines can and already are being applied to other types of data.

To better understand where MDM is going and what it will influence, we need to look at the current drivers and consider what are likely to be the future drivers. Currently, MDM initiatives are focused primarily on improving data quality and operational efficiencies that, in turn, are expected to help yield better business intelligence and sales opportunity. Just how much yield can be expected is an ongoing debate and a constant sticking point when trying to project a hard ROI. The ability for MDM to improve operational efficiency is the more predictable part of the ROI equation because there are usually many tangible opportunities to improve data and the associated processes, which can immediately start improving operational efficiency and provide more accurate and consistent data to the BI processes. But how much this can translate to new sales opportunity is the intangible part because this is influenced by many other analytical, business, and market factors beyond MDM's scope.

We believe that MDM's ability to drive more operational efficiency through continued maturity of its core disciplines and with the influence of new technology will certainly continue and contribute to improvement in a company's bottom-line performance. But how much MDM can contribute to BI improvement and a company's top-line growth is still a very open question and an indirect proposition. As MDM practices continue to mature, this will go a long way toward improving the foundation and data integrity issues from which the analytical models and business intelligence processes have long suffered. But even as the underlying data gets better and becomes more trusted, the emphasis will be primarily on the shoulders of the BI teams to clearly demonstrate how better data transforms into more dynamic and real-time information, insight, and services that can drive strategic decisions and better business opportunity.

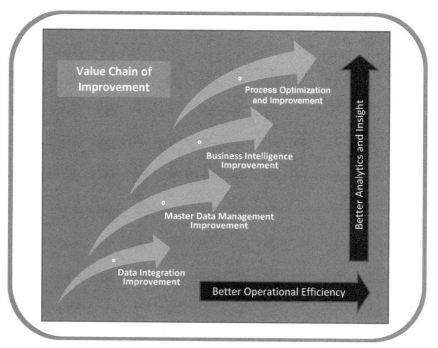

FIGURE 12.2 Value Chain of Improvement

Therefore, we believe that more technology and business focus will shift toward understanding, improving, and optimizing the value chain between the operational and the analytical processes. As Figure 12.2 shows, this shift will expose where more improvement and synergy is needed across a value chain of data integration, MDM, BI, and business process areas to create a more integrated and optimized relationship between the operational and analytical functions.

In general, there is still enormous opportunity to create more closed loop value streams between the operational and the analytical processes. As we discussed in Chapter 1, operational-based or analytical-based MDM approaches can each bear fruit in their own right, but eventually either approach is likely to reveal the need to address both operational and analytical data management under a common enterprise MDM model. Enterprise MDM focused solutions and the shift toward SOA-based technologies will greatly help solidify the foundation needed to create a more beneficial relationship and more end-to-end synchronization between the operational and analytical dynamics in order to help drive more top-line growth.

SUMMARY

This chapter concludes our book. The journey through MDM is a constantly learning, churning, and maturing experience. Hopefully, we have contributed with enough insight to make your job easier.

A Customer MDM program cannot be taken lightly. It is *not* another IT or business only project. It starts with a strong executive buy-in that can truly mobilize the many needed resources and sponsor the sure-to-be required radical changes.

The pervasive nature of Customer MDM can potentially impact everyone in the company. It has been repeated over and over that MDM is about people, process, and technology, but it also simply boils down to enabling the ability to take good care of your data by creating a quality culture through cross-functional collaboration. Customer MDM spreads both vertically and horizontally across the organization. It is its ubiquitous nature that makes Customer MDM a powerful capability to have. Its holistic set of techniques and approaches span business-specific orientation, and therefore enable more enterprise-wide practices and governance.

And finally, it is important to *not* lose sight of the business case for the MDM solution. After all, it is about solving a business problem and aligning data management practices with better decision making and improved strategic planning. Data integrity and fitness is a critical component for accurate business assessment.

Achieving true Customer MDM is:

- To properly establish data ownership, governance, and stewardship practices that effectively enable and focus data management practices to create true company-wide cohesion.
- To aptly integrate customer information from disparate sources and effectively employ data quality techniques to reach a 360° view of the customer.
- To suitably create a more integrated and optimized relationship between the operational and the analytical functions to maximize competitive advantage.

Due diligence will pay off, but it can be a long and bumpy journey. Fasten your seatbelts!

 NOTE

1. Phil Simon, *The Next Wave of Technologies: Opportunity in Chaos* (Hoboken, NJ: John Wiley and Sons, 2010).

Recommended Reading

Adelman, Sid, Larissa T. Moss, and Majid Abai. *Data Strategy*. Upper Saddle River, NJ: Pearson Education, Inc., 2005.

Berson, Alex, and Larry Dubov. *Master Data Management and Customer Data Integration for a Global Enterprise*. New York: McGraw-Hill, 2007.

Berson, Alex, and Larry Dubov. *Master Data Management and Data Governance*. New York: McGraw-Hill, 2011.

Dreibelbis, Allen, Ivan Milman, Paul van Run, Eberhard Hechler, Martin Oberhofer, and Dan Wolfson. *Enterprise Master Data Management: An SOA Approach to Managing Core Information*. Boston: Pearson plc/IBM, 2008.

Dyché, Jill, and Evan Levy. *Customer Data Integration: Reaching a Single Version of the Truth*. Hoboken, NJ: John Wiley & Sons, 2006.

Fisher, Tony. *The Data Asset: How Smart Companies Govern Their Data for Business Success*. Hoboken, NJ: John Wiley & Sons, 2009.

Maydanchik, Arkady. *Data Quality Assessment*. Bradley Beach, NJ: Technics Publications, LLC, 2007.

Loshin, David. *Master Data Management*. Burlington, MA: Morgan Kaufmann Publishers/Elsevier, 2009.

Loshin, David. *The Practitioner's Guide to Data Quality Improvement*. Burlington, MA: Morgan Kaufmann Publishers/Elsevier, 2011.

McGilvray, Danette. *Executing Data Quality Projects: Ten Steps to Quality Data and Trusted Information*. Burlington, MA: Morgan Kaufmann Publishers/Elsevier, 2008.

Sarsfield, Steve. *The Data Governance Imperative*. Cambridgeshire, United Kingdom: IT Governance Publishing, 2009.

Simon, Phil. *The Next Wave of Technologies: Opportunity in Chaos*. Hoboken, NJ: John Wiley and Sons, 2010.

About the Authors

Dalton Cervo has over 20 years experience in software development, project management, and data management areas, including architecture design and implementation of an analytical MDM, and management of a data quality program for an enterprise MDM implementation. Dalton is a senior solutions consultant at DataFlux, helping organizations in the areas of data governance, data quality, data integration, and MDM. Prior to DataFlux, Dalton served as the data quality lead for the customer data domain throughout the planning and implementation of Sun Microsystems' enterprise customer data hub. Dalton has extensive hands-on experience in designing and implementing data integration, data quality, and hierarchy management solutions to migrate disparate information; performing data cleansing, standardization, enrichment, and consolidation; and hierarchically organizing customer data. Dalton contributed a chapter on MDM to Phil Simon's book, *The Next Wave of Technologies—Opportunity in Chaos.* Dalton is a member of the Data Quality Pro expert panel, has served on customer advisory boards, and is an active contributor to the MDM community through conferences and social media vehicles. Dalton has BSCS and MBA degrees, and is PM certified.

Mark Allen has over 20 years of data management and project management experience including extensive planning and deployment experience with customer master initiatives, customer data integration projects, and leading data quality management practices. Mark is a senior consultant and enterprise data governance lead at WellPoint, Inc. Prior to joining WellPoint, Mark was a senior program manager in customer operations groups at both Sun Microsystems and Oracle Corporation. At Sun Microsystems, Mark served as the lead data steward for the customer data domain throughout the planning and implementation of Sun's enterprise customer data hub. Mark has led implementation of various Customer MDM–oriented programs including customer data governance, data quality management, data stewardship, and change management. Mark has championed many efforts to improve customer data integration practices, improve quality measurement techniques, reduce data duplication and fragmentation problems, and has created hierarchy management practices that have effectively managed customer entity structure and corporate linkage. Mark has served on various customer advisory boards and user groups focused on sharing and enhancing MDM and data governance practices.

Please also visit their web site at www.mdm-in-practice.com.

Index